Fired-Up Fundraising

Fired-Up Fundraising

Turning Board Passion into Action

GAIL PERRY

John Wiley & Sons, Inc.

For general information on our other products and services, or technical support,
please contact our Customer Care Department within the United States at 800-762-2974,
outside the United States at 317-572-3993 or fax 317-572-4002.

Wiley also publishes its books in a variety of electronic formats. Some content that
appears in print may not be available in electronic books.

For more information about Wiley products, visit our Web site at http://www.wiley.com.

Library of Congress Cataloging-in-Publication Data:

  ISBN: 978-0-470-11663-0 (cloth)

Printed in the United States of America

10 9 8 7 6 5 4 3 2 1

The AFP Fund Development Series

The AFP Fund Development Series is intended to provide fund development professionals and volunteers, including board members (and others interested in the nonprofit sector), with top-quality publications that help advance philanthropy as voluntary action for the public good. Our goal is to provide practical, timely guidance and information on fundraising, charitable giving, and related subjects. The Association of Fundraising Professionals (AFP) and Wiley each bring to this innovative collaboration unique and important resources that result in a whole greater than the sum of its parts. For information on other books in the series, please visit:

http://www.afpnet.org

THE ASSOCIATION OF FUNDRAISING PROFESSIONALS

The Association of Fundraising Professionals (AFP) represents 28,000 members in more than 185 chapters throughout the United States, Canada, Mexico, and China working to advance philanthropy through advocacy, research, education, and certification programs. The association fosters development and growth of fundraising professionals and promotes high ethical standards in the fundraising profession. For more information or to join the world's largest association of fundraising professionals, visit *www.afpnet.org.*

2006-2007 AFP PUBLISHING ADVISORY COMMITTEE

Samuel N. Gough, CFRE, Chair
Principal, The AFRAM Group

Nina P. Berkheiser, CFRE
Principal Consultant, Your Nonprofit Advisor

Linda L. Chew, CFRE
Associate Director, Alta Bates Summit Foundation

D. C. Dreger, ACFRE
Senior Campaign Director, Custom Development Solutions (CDS)

Audrey P. Kintzi, ACFRE
Chief Advancement Officer, Girl Scout Council St. Croix Valley

Robert Mueller, CFRE
Vice President, Hospice Foundation of Louisville

Maria Elena Noriega
Director, Noriega Malo & Associates

Leslie E. Weir, MA, ACFRE
Director of Gift Planning, Health Sciences Centre Foundation

Sharon R. Will, CFRE
Director of Development, South Wind Hospice

John Wiley & Sons:

Susan McDermott
Senior Editor (Professional/Trade Division), John Wiley & Sons

AFP Staff:

Jan Alfieri
Manager, New Product Development

Walter Sczudlo
Executive Vice President & General Counsel

You must be the change you want to see in the world.

—Mahatma Gandhi

This book is dedicated to all board members who are working hard for positive change in the world.

Contents

Preface

This book was written in response to a fundamental challenge in fundraising: how to help well-meaning but reluctant volunteers get up the nerve to raise money for causes they care deeply about. This also means that we tackle a deeper pervasive problem of nonprofit boards: how to overcome entrenched group culture that sees fundraising as "dirty work" to inspire new energy, passion and action.

As a staff fundraiser and consultant for over two decades, I have had too many experiences with anxious fundraising volunteers who needed to be coaxed every step of the way, just to talk to their friends about their favorite cause.

Many of these trustees knew many people with major financial resources, and they had the ability to open many doors. In fact it was amazing whom they knew! But I could not guide them past their nervousness, to take actual action and reach out to their connections.

Why did their excitement for the cause suddenly disappear when confronted by even the *idea* of fundraising? Why did they lose their energy and motivation? I found that the closer we got to solicitation the more my enthusiastic volunteers would turn cold and lose their passion. Resolve would melt when the board members thought about picking up the phone.

I also found my own fundraising success inextricably bound up with these nervous volunteers. How could I commit to fundraising results when our fragile volunteer fundraising team was losing steam and backing off? Urgent services to the needy, or to students, or to children might have to be cancelled.

I started thinking to myself, *what's going on here? There must be a better way! They say they want to help raise money for their cause, but they won't do it.*

I decided that I needed to explore alternative ways of introducing fundraising to volunteers and to learn more about motivating teams. I needed a new skill set in addition to the many fundraising skills I had built up over two decades in the business.

So I sought out additional training and explored new ideas on change management, leadership, organizational development, and human motivation. It has been a fascinating journey into a different world.

First I hired organizational development gurus to tutor me on how to create "team" in the largest sense, how to develop alignment within a group, how to establish communications and decision-making processes that will keep people happy and motivated, and how to design strategic planning processes that inspire involvement and result in committed action instead of a lot of talk.

I decided to add formal coaching skills to my consulting practice and began the process of certification as a business coach. I learned how to listen, support, and motivate, rather than just inform and give answers, as most consultants do. I had learned the hard way that just telling clients what they "should" do would often not work.

Workshops on personal transformation inspired me to bring new passion and focus into my own life. I learned about the power of visioning, of setting positive expectations and assuming responsibility for what I wanted in life. I saw how people can get extraordinarily fired up to tackle any obstacle when they go after their own vision for what they want to create in their lives and in the world.

High-level experts taught me facilitation skills: how to stage powerful meetings, facilitate focus groups, and bring groups to consensus quickly—again to create results-oriented outcomes. Of course, I studied the work of all the fundraising gurus—particularly pioneers Penelope Burk and Terry Axelrod—to see what they recommended to engage board members in fundraising.

I attended every fundraising or nonprofit seminar around to see who was talking about transforming boards to break through old ways of being, thinking, and acting. I talked to other fundraisers, consultants, and board members to understand their views on what was working or not working.

Then a master corporate trainer helped me develop a truly interactive training experience that would introduce board members to fundraising. We created a fast-paced, experiential seminar that would move board member participants to break through their preconceived notions and fears of fundraising, spark their passion for the change they wanted to make in the world, and set them up to take ownership for the results they wanted to create.

I even explored the new research in chaos theory, quantum physics, and new science, particularly how these provocative concepts apply to organizational change. I learned the scientific basis of the concepts that energy states are contagious among people (we fundraisers knew that all along!) and that our point of view on anything directly impacts the outcome.

Peter Senge and the for-profit change management gurus also provided cutting edge thinking that could be applied to nonprofits. Knowing that we nonprofits are in the "persuasive marketing" business, I incorporated the latest thinking from for-profit "idea marketing" experts such as Malcolm Gladwell's *The Tipping Point* and Seth Godin's edgy *Unleashing the Idea Virus*.

During this process, I began looking at my client volunteer groups and board members from a whole different perspective. I experimented with different ways to introduce nervous board members to fundraising, and break down their barriers by taking the emphasis away from soliciting and focusing instead on cultivation.

It occurred to me that we had been approaching fundraising from the wrong place with our board members. We had been letting them think it was all about the "ask" and not about long term relationships with friends/donors/investors in our cause.

I found a new role for reluctant board members in fundraising by setting up board members as dignified ambassadors. The board members assumed responsibility for managing the "customer" relationship (like an account manager in a for-profit concern) with an important donor or prospect, with great results. We were applying for-profit Customer Relationship Management (CRM) in the context of fundraising, and it was working nicely.

It turned out there were *many places* to use reluctant board members in all areas of the fundraising cycle—*ways that could directly impact the bottom line*. My clients proved the adage that if board members are involved in simply thanking donors, then gifts go up!

Over and over again, I saw board members shift into more active roles in the fundraising process. Once they learned how to do this and what it was all about, incredibly, their attitudes shifted from anxiety and fear to almost glee when discussing possible supporters.

A Place of Possibility and Potential

I began to approach my board committees from a new place of possibility, looking for ways to activate the power, passion, and creativity of the board members—not deaden them! I started working differently with my volunteers, and I started bringing people together in fundraising retreats from a new angle with great results.

My vocabulary changed drastically. I talked about potential, vision, possibilities, alignment, setting "stretch goals," and "going for it." I smiled more with my volunteers. And, since energy is contagious, I saw people smile back, instead of tensing up when we talked about fundraising.

The fundraising training seminar for board members kept being refined. We worked to create an experience that was more like a two-way conversation that could transform their point of view about the organization, about their roles, and about what they could do to support fundraising.

These seminars became retreats that people would always remember: retreats that resulted in a permanent, transformational shift in perspective about each board member's role on the board and as an agent of change for the organization; retreats that would conclude with personal commitments for action by each person present.

I found myself speaking around the country on how to fire up board members for fundraising. These talks seemed to touch a nerve and offer some good suggestions, because people were packing my presentations. Heads would nod as I offered my new perspective on board members and how to get them over their fears. My audiences' feedback told me I was on the right path.

When I presented these concepts to board members themselves, they seemed more open, eager, and happy to embrace a new point of view. They responded warmly when I began by telling them they could aid directly fundraising in many ways without having to solicit.

When board members learned more about how to stand squarely in their passion and vision for serving the community, they would come back and say, "maybe soliciting isn't so scary after all!" We had lots of fun and laughs at my fundraising retreats and seminars. It seemed that if people could see the humor, the bold outrageousness, and, especially, the possibilities contained in fundraising, then much of the battle might be won.

I put some of these ideas to work in the field with clients. Louise Coggins, Board Chair of VISIONS, an organization that works to eliminate racism, classism, and ageism around the world, found that within six months after we trained her board members as Ambassadors and set them to open doors to their friends and contacts, the gifts to her organization began to go up.

After a retreat with the Ronald McDonald House of the Rio Grande Valley in Texas that had lasted only a day, Board Chair Jeff Weller shared with me six months later that a permanent change among his board members had showed up quickly in higher fundraising totals:

> Now, when we discuss fundraising no one begins to make excuses or shies away. More importantly, they are stepping up to foster the relationships with donors, love to tell our story to anyone who will listen and certainly aren't shy or "ashamed" to ask for money/goods/services. Now they show confidence that we are a cause that offers something so critical and worthwhile. They know people will want to support us. They truly have been "transformed."

Passion-Driven Fundraising

After all this study, experimentation, and fine-tuning, I found I was working with a new approach: Passion-Driven Fundraising. It is far, far bigger than just Fundraising 101 for board members, because it grows out of treating board members as real people with real concerns. It is firmly based in the power of a vision to change the world.

In this book I attempted to lay out a clear series of steps that can guide any nonprofit executive to introduce this new perspective to fundraising for their board, an approach that is realistic, easy to implement, and will result in an enjoyable experience for all concerned—and the result will be improved fundraising results.

Passion-Driven Fundraising describes a new, different context to engage board members in fundraising and in their organizations. They will not run for the door when you mention the F-word: "fundraising."

Passion-Driven Fundraising pulls from the best thinking in all the areas I studied: organizational change, transformational training, coaching for results, for-profit marketing and leadership models, and the latest cutting edge fundraising practices. I worked hard to make it straightforward and simple to put into practice. Clearly the outcome could be measurable in dollars raised, and in board member engagement, excitement, and happiness.

A fundamental precept of the Passion-Driven Fundraising approach is that not all board members are very good at, much less willing to do, solicitation. There are plenty of board members that you do not want to be out there soliciting! However, those folks can and should play other, very important supportive roles—and we can put them cheerfully to work in these other areas.

This book is written for leaders and staff of nonprofit organizations. We are the ones who shoulder much of the ultimate responsibility for our boards—who they are, what they do, and what level of excitement and passion they offer our organizations. We can deaden their energy or bring it to life. If we assume responsibility for our board members' results, then we can change them.

If you create a Passion-Driven Fundraising experience for your board members, you can tackle the myths about fundraising and instill new, more positive approaches that will have them excited about the difference they can make. Your board members will embrace your mission so thoroughly that they can become agents for change.

You will have them not just willing—but also wanting—to participate in finding expanded resources for your organization. You will rekindle individual passion for your nonprofit's mission and harness that passion into shared fundraising success. You will be able to create a board that is passion-driven—not fearful—about fundraising. A board that will be on fire for the cause, working to make the world a better place, and actually being, as Gandhi said, the change they want to see in the world.

Acknowledgments

This book would never have been possible without the support and encouragement of many wonderful colleagues, friends, and clients.

I will always owe a debt to Jane Kendall and Trisha Lester of the NC Center for Nonprofit Organizations for believing in my early ideas and for giving me a speaking platform to introduce them to other nonprofit executives.

Deep thanks to my friends at Visions—Angela Bryant, Valerie Batts, and Board Chair Louise Coggins—for enthusiastically helping me test my first Ambassador program for board members.

I would like to personally thank Tom Ross of the Z. Smith Reynolds Foundation for his support and encouragement, and for the Foundation for funding several board development projects in which I developed many of the ideas in this book. My hat is off to my friends and board members at the Orange County Rape Crisis Center for enthusiastically tackling a challenging board training program with me and sticking with it all the way.

A warm personal thank you to Betsy Buford, former Deputy Director of the Department of Cultural Resources and former Director of the Division of State History Museums, for always believing in me, and for her ongoing kindness, support, and encouragement.

Thanks to my AFP colleagues and friends for their support and for offering me a podium to hone my ideas and training skills, notably George O'Neal, April Anthony, Tom Norwood, Rebecca Worters, and Michael Guillot.

A special thanks to a team of colleagues and friends who were always there for me: my long time friend Chic Dambach for his enthusiastic and consistent encouragement over the years; Joseph Wheeler for teaching me how to fill the room with energy; Diane Paces-Wiles for her creative branding and messaging skills; Dr. Thomas Griggs for teaching me about the deeper level of what goes on in a board room, and to my personal friends for pushing me along: Ellen Pizer, Joe Stallings, and Joyce Fitzpatrick.

Lastly, I could never have created this book within its tight timetable without the support and guidance of author Peggy Payne, who served as my local editor and writing coach.

She provided gentle and consistent coaching, help and editing at all hours and days. I'd like to thank John Wiley & Sons and the folks at the national Association of Fundraising Professionals for helping me bring this to print, and for their invaluable coaching.

And to my children, Cassie and Ellie Gilbert, for their love, pride, and patience.

Introduction

Well, it looks like we have a financial crisis on our hands.

The Board Chair looked glumly at the rest of the trustees. Everyone avoided making eye contact with her. This was a specially called board meeting of a nonprofit organization, one with a great track record and credibility in its community.

All the board members around the table stared at each other uneasily, in disbelief. They were community leaders who were pleased to serve but didn't anticipate this! *A financial crisis? Oh dear! What on earth to do?*

The organization had actually been struggling for some time to maintain its financial footing. The staff was working hard, at fundraising and everything else, but funding was a perennial problem.

The staff looked at the board members around the table with hope. They were thinking: *maybe now, since the need is so very urgent, the board will get to work. Each member will step up to the plate and finally assume some responsibility for bringing in resources. After all, isn't fundraising the board's job, not ours?*

The CEO fought back a sense of resentment as he thought of the daily struggle to provide services despite continued budget cutbacks. To make matters worse, he thought, board members were also trying to saddle the staff with all the responsibility for fundraising. He was worried about his employees: they were overworked and underappreciated as it was.

Board members shifted nervously in their seats. They knew they were ultimately responsible for the organization's financial stability. Still, you could see them thinking: *But isn't that what the staff is for? We focus on policy; the staff is supposed to run the organization. We set the fundraising goals, and the staff executes the fundraising plan.*

These board members were all well-meaning people, but they were jumpy about fundraising. Actually, to be frank, they didn't really like the idea of personally being involved in fundraising at all.

Some of them had even agreed to serve on the board with the stipulation that they wouldn't have to "ask for money." Most of them felt that running around the community "begging" for money was distasteful and demeaning. And why should they, as volunteers, have to expose themselves to that kind of rejection?

The invisible buck passed from board to staff and back to board, again and again, in a never ending circle. No one was willing to assume responsibility for raising the money needed to deal with the financial crisis.

Finally the Board Chair came up with a plan. It was quick and dirty, but she thought it would work. "If we can find 50 people who would give $1,000 each, we could raise the needed $50,000."

Staff members eyed each other uncertainly. They had heard this kind of thinking before, and suspected it was a naïve approach that would exhaust everyone, while ultimately failing.

The Chair asked the other trustees to identify potential donors they would be willing to approach on behalf of the organization. She passed a sheet of paper around the table, asking them to enter names of funding sources they would be willing to contact.

As the paper made its way silently around the table, the board went on to conduct other business. At the end of the meeting, the Executive Director reached for it eagerly, excited to see what it might offer, and hoping that his board members had finally been motivated to help with fundraising.

But there were only two names on the list! The paper was otherwise empty. Apparently no one was willing to reveal their relationships with possible funders—much less offer to approach anyone. The staff, expecting help at this moment of need, was devastated.

Why was the board so reluctant? Here's why: The trustees were anxious about fundraising. What would be asked of them if they named their contacts? They felt ill-trained, nervous, and awkward. They didn't know what to say. They feared failure. They were afraid of asking for money.

They were approached in the wrong way.

So the effort to get the board members to help with fundraising fell flat. The staff again shouldered the responsibility, and they grumbled more and more about their uninvolved and unresponsive board.

Tension continued to grow between the staff and the board, and morale and productivity both continued to decline.

A Familiar Experience

This scene is not unusual. Well-meaning and highly successful board members too often sidestep their fundraising responsibilities, even when they know they are expected to shoulder at least part of the fundraising burden.

Both the board and the staff expect the other to do the heavy lifting when fundraising is concerned. There is often a breakdown between the board and the staff regarding who's responsible for what. This kind of difficulty is so widespread you can almost say it's "across the board."

While I am acknowledging this unspoken conflict between staff and board where fundraising is concerned, please know that the last thing I want to do in this book is to polarize staff and trustees. We don't need more of that dynamic—we need more teamwork and cohesion. If we are going to tackle the huge social and environmental challenges of the 21st century, then we need a fusion of energy between staff and board rather than separation. It's going to take a lot of cooperation and teamwork to solve planet Earth's problems.

Besides, I've served on many boards myself and have had my own struggles honoring my commitments as a volunteer board member. The time and attention I give those boards typically comes after I take care of my professional and family commitments. Like many board members, I sometimes find there is not enough of me left over to fulfill my responsibilities as a board member.

I know well the generosity and good intentions that volunteer trustees bring. They are usually people who are highly successful in their own fields; it is easy for staff and consultants, as nonprofit professional fundraisers, to expect them to be experts in ours also.

However, no matter how talented our board members are in their own fields, too often they simply don't understand fundraising.

IT IS OUR RESPONSIBILITY TO SET BOARD MEMBERS UP TO WIN

We—and by "we," I mean nonprofit professionals, including staff, consultants, and all leaders of the organization—should assume full responsibility for the situation with our board members. "We" are the CEO, the Development Director, and the Board Chair. In fact, it is the Board Chair who must play the strongest leadership role in this whole effort.

"We" is our organization's leadership team and by extension everyone in the organization. It is our responsibility to think and work *together* to make major changes in the way we approach our boards.

Our boards' effectiveness and engagement is directly related to our input and guidance. We actually do we get the boards we deserve.

This is the stance that will create results. We *can* find ways to activate these groups of high-powered people who are often doing low-level work; these smart people really longing for something meaningful to do that could make a real difference for our cause. Yet they are wasting away in boring meetings and meaningless work.

We *can* offer a way for them to "find their passion and pursue it to improve the lives of others," as philanthropist Tom Darden says.

We *can* lead the whole process—from our board members' initial enlistment, to creating opportunities for them to connect deeply with our organization's work, to stimulating their passion and excitement for our cause, to appropriate training in raising money, to creating useful and enjoyable ways for them to support fundraising.

We are the professionals at work on this full time; they are the part-time volunteers trying to make an impact with limited time and energy. *It is up to us to introduce our board members to fundraising in the right way.*

We make plenty of mistakes with our good-hearted trustees. We let them operate on sketchy and often inaccurate views of how fundraising works. We do not show them easy ways they can support fundraising that do not involve soliciting. For example, they may not know that when board members simply thank donors personally, and gifts will go up. Everyone can do certain activities that can still make a *major impact on the bottom line.*

For one thing, most uneducated board members equate "fundraising" with the moment of "asking"—and therefore will take no part in the other 95% of the overall fundraising cycle.

But we all know that fundraising is a much more complex process than just asking. Focusing simply on soliciting will never bring in the results we want. Fundraising involves pulling in the right people and cultivating their interest in our cause. This is what generates the larger gifts. And thanking them properly personally leads to closer relationships and even greater gifts.

We need our talented and highly able board members to work with us on all aspects of fundraising—opening doors, cultivating prospects, and thanking donors. Some will eventually be willing, in fact, eager, to do the "ask." And we need them! Others will never be comfortable soliciting, but they can still be passionate and highly effective "friend raisers," providing important backup to the entire fundraising process.

The situation we have now is that many board members don't want to (and are simply not going to) get involved in fundraising as they currently understand it and as we present it to them.

However, staff members continue to hope—and expect—that their board members will come to understand their responsibility to help generate gifts and contributions. The literature of the fundraising world is full of books and articles laying out detailed directions on how to turn board members into dynamite fundraisers. Everybody talks about how to get the board to raise more money, especially how to get them to do the asking.

Staff thinks if the board is not successfully soliciting money, then they have a board that is not living up to its duties. Staff read the pundits' writings, hold up their board members to the accepted standard, expect more, receive less, and become more and more disappointed.

Guess what? We've been wishing for something that simply is not going to happen. Only a few board members will ever be comfortable with, much less good at, doing the asking. But the rest of our board members can still be put to work happily and effectively supporting the fundraising program.

It is time for fundraisers to acknowledge reality. It is time to create a broader approach to fundraising based on a clear-eyed appraisal of our board members as real people, highly successful in their careers, but who are also untrained volunteers when it comes to raising money. This is an approach to the process that is much broader than the moment of asking.

I don't mean that we should neglect the soliciting aspect of fundraising. Asking is always the fundamental moment of fundraising. The board chair and CEO have the responsibility to be sure that the right prospects are solicited for the right purpose at the right time by the right people.

But the soliciting will be tremendously more effective when "non-asking" board members are also doing their jobs. Their work can assure, for example, that the "asks" are set up properly. If prospects are cultivated by enthusiastic board members, they will be ready to give at higher levels.

Best practices in fundraising show that the more contacts you have with a donor prior to the gift, the higher the gift. And we all know that donors' investments follow their involvement with our organizations.

Also, we know that donors often respond better to cultivation by unpaid board member volunteers rather than by paid staff. The volunteer/staff relationship is the underpinning of all successful fundraising.

We just have to get our reluctant board members to the table and introduce them to a style of fundraising that they will find, not only comfortable, but satisfying and fulfilling.

WE NEED A FRESH, REALISTIC APPROACH: PASSION-DRIVEN FUNDRAISING

This book will show you how to create engaged, passionate board members who are actively involved in supporting fundraising and who are even enjoying it!

Most books about getting board members fired up to raise money focus on other issues. They talk about recruitment and setting high expectations early and then move right on to educating the reader on Fundraising 101: how to set up each type of fundraising program and the board members' appropriate role in each.

In this book, we will certainly discuss proper selection of board members and the establishment of clear, high expectations, *but* we add an important new piece to the process of creating a fundraising board. We do not think that just recruiting good board members and then plugging them into the right fundraising program will "get it."

Board members have other issues that must be dealt with before they are willing to give raising money anything more than lip service and before they take any part in the overall process at all.

Their attitudes have to be transformed: they have to be brought back to the mission of the organization and reconnected with their *passion for the cause*. Passion is what sustains us through thick and thin and is, more often than not, infectious. Wish more of our folks would catch it!

Our board members need to get re-energized about what our organization is trying to accomplish—its possibilities and its wonderful work. They also need deeper training in the philosophy of philanthropy: why it can be so powerful, what its ultimate purpose is, why volunteers matter so much.

Board members can easily learn a new way of looking at fundraising that focuses not on the moment of asking but on changing the world. Here's the essence of Passion-Driven Fundraising: *the conversation is not about money, it is about the cause.*

What they need to know to be effective is this new approach to fundraising. It's grounded in and driven by their own passion and commitment for the important work your organization is doing to make the world a better place.

Our system of clear and workable steps will fire up your board and make them into the Dream Team you want.

CHAPTER 1

An Understandable Problem

(Feel Free to Skip Ahead to the Solution)

Tell me what to do with my board!

—Executive Director's plea

WHAT IS KEEPING BOARD MEMBERS AWAY FROM FUNDRAISING?

Two major barriers stand between our board members and their willingness to venture out on the short and skinny branches of the fundraising world:

1. Board members equate fundraising with the awful experience of "asking for money."

2. Board members are not engaged in or passionate enough about their organizations.

Let us take a look at these two key issues.

Board Members Think Fundraising Is "Asking for Money"

Typically members of boards do not understand the full context of fundraising—not only how we do it, but what it is all about: the bigger picture of developing friends/donors/investors/partners who are on our organization's team and who will stick with our cause for the long run, providing both money and moral support for our mission.

Also, they do not understand the reasons we work so hard to raise money—reasons that are among the most noble and altruistic imaginable. We know that we are ultimately working to make the world a better place, *and* to improve or save lives, but our board members do not equate this with fundraising.

The real issue is that trustees just do not understand fundraising at all—they make up their own stories about it, and, unfortunately, they think that "fundraising is begging." So they are stuck, really stuck, in a very uncomfortable place, because the idea of "asking for money" strikes anxiety and fear into most nice, well-meaning board members' hearts.

Let's remember the most fundamental motivators for human behavior. We humans seek experiences that will bring pleasure and avoid anything associated with pain or discomfort. We are naturally drawn toward positive experiences that will yield some type of good-feeling payoff, and we try to stay away from anything that is negative or stressful.

It takes not courage alone but also tremendous commitment to tackle something really scary and stick with it. I have the utmost respect for the brave board members who are quite nervous about fundraising but courageously step up to the plate regardless of their fear, because they are so committed to the cause.

They are my heroes, because they are standing up for something that is deeply important to them personally. They are willing to challenge their deep inner discomfort, because they believe they can make a difference and help create change for the good.

However, most board members do not have enough passion and commitment to the cause to propel them through their fear. The mission is not for them a full-time commitment or career as it so often is with staff.

The board members are simply kind-hearted people wanting to help their communities and do good works in their spare time. And so for most, the motivation isn't high enough to get them to take on what they imagine fundraising to be: "asking for money."

Board Members Are Not Sufficiently Committed to or Involved in Their Organization's Good Work

The best way you can get most board members to engage in fundraising is to get them super-charged up and deeply committed to the change they want your organization to achieve out in the world. That is why, first of all, they have to be engaged, active, excited, and involved.

This book will describe ways to create this change. Many nonprofit board members are disconnected, in varying degrees, from the work and mission of their organizations. We have all seen too many boards with members who are not particularly knowledgeable about their organization or the results it is achieving.

These days there is a lot of talk in our sector about nonprofit boards, much of expressing deep disappointment. There is now an entire "board-improvement" field offering suggestions on how to create more effective boards

Nonprofit experts talk about a "crisis" of underperforming boards. Leadership and governance models spew forth assorted new ideas and approaches to address board inaction, misdirection, and dissatisfaction.

This is a very real problem that most organizations simply muddle through and do not know how to address. Where is the "constructive partnership" that we all seek with our board members?

The board members themselves are not to blame. Trustees are often dissatisfied with their own experience. Talented and high-achieving people, they are typically asked to do low-level, meaningless work that does not inspire action or create commitment, much less tap their real creative talent.

It is time for us to recognize this second reality about board members and their lack of involvement, a truth that is important to understand: If you have a situation in which your board is disconnected or not engaged, then its members will not—repeat, not—tackle fundraising enthusiastically. They may get dragged into it, but they will not do it with passion, care and heart. If they are not fired up enough about your organization, they will avoid you when you even mention fundraising.

To be sufficiently motivated to venture into fundraising, these talented men and women need to have the chance to "own" the organization's goals, its mission, its plans, and its challenges. They need to be able to participate in substantive discussions that will help chart the organization's future.

Are your board members really helping to determine where your nonprofit organization is heading and what you need to accomplish? Are they given the opportunity to provide what we might call "effective governance"?

They need an atmosphere of openness and trust with the staff, particularly the CEO and development director. They need to feel that they are active contributors to, and part of, your organization's success.

That commitment must come first and you, the nonprofit professional, are the one to make it happen. Remember, it is our responsibility to set the board up to win in fundraising.

So please do not ask consultants for a magic solution, hoping that a quick pep talk will get your disengaged board to bring in the big bucks. I cannot work miracles with a group of people who are not offered the opportunity to be co-partners with the staff—in appropriate roles, of course—to make the organization's work possible.

What I can do is show you here is how to stir passion in your board members and then steer them into action.

WHAT DO BOARD MEMBERS WANT, ANYWAY?

The role of a nonprofit trustee today is just as likely to be confusing and demoralizing as invigorating and rewarding. We are not paying the attention we need to our boards as a whole and to their individual members.

The care and feeding of our board members is an oft-neglected art. And I do not say that lightly—it really is an art. Drawing a board member into happy action on behalf of our cause is much like the delicate process of cultivating a potential major donor.

No wonder our board members are not more active. No wonder they sometimes hurriedly take the short way out by latching on to quick, ineffective solutions to whatever challenge is at hand. In these cases, they are not interested enough to spend the time to think through our issues and options.

We have to spend the effort to deepen their relationship with our organizations. We can evoke what they are passionate about and fan the flames of their desire to see change happen for the good. We have to be present, listen to them, offer varying ways they can become involved, and act on their suggestions. It is called cultivating their involvement —just like we do with our donors.

Engaging board members in fundraising has to start at the beginning—with the quality and involvement of your board itself. You can create partners out of your board members and have them actively participating and deeply passionate about your mission and out-comes.

We need to be sure that the *experience* that board members have is worth their time and energy. This experience gets to be meaningful at some personal level. They get to have a sense of offering something of worth to their organization. If you can create this, then their reluctance to raise money will begin to dissolve.

Board Service: A Disappointing Experience?

> *The problem with our board is that there is nothing for them to do but come to meetings and talk.*
>
> —Nonprofit Development Director

There is much talk and worry these days about what goes on in many nonprofit board-rooms—outmoded practices, conflicts of interest, holding on to the past, overlooking diffi-cult challenges, unclear accountability, and more. There is even more frustration over the lack of inspired, creative governance coming from them, not to mention board members' well-known lack of support for fundraising.

What causes a group of talented, caring individuals who join a board to slip so quickly into inaction? What is it about the experience of serving on a board that causes smart, capable, connected people who want to help their organization to inexplicably lose their fire and their motivation?

What Is Wrong with This Job?

Perhaps the problem lies in the basic setup and structure of the nonprofit board itself. The overall role of boards is not clear, particularly to board members.

What is "governance" anyway, especially in practice? Are trustees on the job just to keep order, or merely to help create legitimacy for the organization? Or are they given an oppor-tunity to live up to their potential and actually provide thoughtful leadership?

Here is the interesting question: whose job is it to give them that opportunity to lead? Will they create it themselves? Or will we have to create it for them?

What activities are we are asking our boards to undertake? Are these activities *meaningful* or *meaningless*? In actual practice, is the real work of the board detached from our organization's mission, or does it give board members the sense of actually making a difference in the world through their service?

> *I have seen new Latino boards get organized with members full of*
> *passion. Then they hear 'you have to learn how to be a nonprofit,'*
> *and suddenly the passion gets tempered with the reality of running*
> *an organization.*
>
> — Dan Moore, former Vice President
> of Kellogg Foundation

Could serving on a nonprofit board really be, as some have actually complained, an exercise in irrelevance? Do our board members even understand what their appropriate role is? Is it because they are *confused,* as some experts claim, about their duties and simply need a clearer job description to set things right?

Are Board Members Unhappy?

Instead of being unclear about their job, it may be that trustees are *unhappy* with their job. If so, I cannot blame them!

Chait, Ryan, and Taylor suggest in their provocative book, *Governance as Leadership,* that board members are not confused about their role, they are *dissatisfied* with their experience: Board members are frequently "derailed by the meaninglessness of what they do."[1]

I take the view that we do not necessarily need to give them clearer job descriptions; what we need to do is give them more satisfying work.

Chic Dambach, a BoardSource consultant and CEO of the Alliance for Peacebuilding, described this situation clearly in a recent article for BoardSource:

> Most nonprofit boards are comprised of community leaders and other people of exceptional knowledge and skill. Yet, few organizations take advantage of this remarkable resource.
>
> Committee structures impose mundane and needless tasks on busy people, and board meetings become tedious and repetitious exercises. The purpose of the organization gets lost in endless reports, while opportunities to enhance performance and produce meaningful results rarely make the agenda. The skill, talent, and resources of board members individually and collectively are wasted.[2]

One reason board time is so often spent on trivial and unsatisfying issues is the careful use of our overly structured, dispassionate friend Robert and his Rules of Order.

Just what we need to get our board members fired up: give our smart board members "mundane and needless tasks." Boring, bureaucratic meetings that follow a rigid format end up focusing members' attention on the smallest details, while ignoring pressing strategic questions. If you want to wring most of the energy, excitement, and creativity out of a meeting, then follow Robert's Rules closely and that is what may happen.

A Culture of Consensus

The challenge is more profound, however, than the way boards run their meetings. We need to look at the deeper level of how we think and act together in groups. Let's look at "group process" as an agent that can prohibit creativity and change in our organizations.

The basic nonprofit board structure itself fosters a sort of group mentality that values harmony and conformity. Like many cultural groups, boards like to hold to the status quo. They tend to discourage dissent, and resist new ideas and change.

We know well the long-serving trustees who stubbornly cling to "the way it was" when they helped found the organization. They are unable or unwilling to recognize new opportunities for change and growth.

It's like they are trying to steer a boat by looking backward at where they have been rather than forward to see if storms or funding crises are ahead.

Many boards are bastions of conservatism and reticence. People do not want to disagree; instead, they want to belong. Being accepted by the group is more important than asking the hard questions.

> *Where all think alike, no one thinks very much.*
>
> —Walter Lippman

Opinions and serious debate are rarities. Consensus can drive decisions to the lowest common denominator. I am sure we have all experienced these situations on our own boards or on boards on which we have served.

It is interesting to consider that many organizational consultants say chaos, not order, is what generates new ideas and fresh thinking. It is when you do not know what to do next that fresh bursts of creativity are brought forth.

The businesslike approach to meetings offered by Robert's Rules sets up a precise ongoing structure that inhibits healthy disagreement. There is no format to deal with surprises or chaotic conditions that might push our organizations to the breaking point.

Consider that our nonprofit organizations are like "organized systems" of interrelated—and interdependent—people and tasks. Everything that happens depends on many parts of the organization or "system" functioning properly.

Fundraising success, for example, depends on long term organizational credibility, snappy marketing, savvy strategic planning, dynamic leadership, and so on. Many of these are outside the control of the development office yet directly impact fundraising results. All parts of the overall system need to be functioning at a high level in order to produce fundraising success.

Since our organizations are organized, living systems, then chaos theory also applies. If we want creativity and change in our organizations, then sometimes we need to allow for disorganization and even chaos. Chaos theory holds that systems experiencing chaos are not completely out of control after all. They actually contain an inherent underlying organizing structure within all the disorganization and confusion.

And what is best is that a system in chaos will naturally self-correct into a new structure that is *better adapted to handle current stresses* and challenges than the earlier one. So chaos can be a good thing; not something to be avoided at all costs.[3]

Just think about an organization faced with a serious challenge—maybe it's a new competitor, or maybe it's the imminent cut off of a major funding source. No one knows what to do and everyone may be confused, uncertain, even on the edge of panic. But in the middle of the disorder, new out-of-the-box ideas come forth to offer creative solutions to the problem at hand.

Once the organization or "system" has reorganized itself, it is better prepared to handle new stresses in its future environment—for example, it may have decided to merge with the competing organization or developed an innovative new fundraising strategy. Postchaos, the newly reorganized nonprofit "system" can embrace the future with renewed vigor and an invigorated board will tackle fundraising with enthusiasm.

Can We Create Change?

If the rate of change on the outside exceeds the rate of change on the inside, the end is near.

—Jack Welch, Former Chairman and CEO,
General Electric Corporation

The trouble is, many of our organizations are sluggishly, if doggedly, conducting business the same way they did decades ago. They are burdened with an outmoded governance structure that worked in the past but can be crippling as we forge into the uncertainties of the twenty-first century.

We are operating in an environment that is changing incredibly fast, and the rate of that change is accelerating, not slowing down. The world has changed. If we are to run successful nonprofits, change is required, not optional. Our ways of doing things in the past will not necessarily be successful in the future.

When an organization starts to become a bit stale in its thinking, it first shows up in funding crises. Organizations have life cycles. A mature nonprofit can easily become "old news"—which is a real challenge for many long serving and successful organizations.

It may have begun to drop down on the community's radar screen. There are new, more "sexy" organizations capturing the hearts and minds of the community. The organization has started to lose its market position in donor's hearts and minds.

In these cases the nonprofit will call in a fundraising consultant. Invariably I will find that the problem is not fundraising; it is in fact organizational strategy, culture, marketing messages—and even the board—that are the problem.

Its leadership has been looking backward, not forward. The nonprofit will need to reinvent itself if it wants to remain relevant in its service field and/or continue to raise enough funding to flourish.

And I find that encouraging a nonprofit organization to reinvent itself can be a tall order. That's where an engaged, thoughtful, savvy board is essential—a board that looks forward, not backward. This is the kind of board that will raise money.

IN THE REAL WORLD

Once I attended a meeting as a board member of a university-affiliated nonprofit. I knew some major issues were looming on the horizon. There was a rumor that the university was considering a policy change that could pull the rug out from under this organization.

I was startled—no, I was astounded!—to find an agenda that focused on routine concerns. The order of business totally ignored the elephant in the room. How could the board members chat complacently while avoiding any mention of an impending event that could wipe us out?

We were fiddling while Rome was burning, distracting ourselves with irrelevant details. Yet the highly structured agenda gave board members a businesslike sense of competency. They left the meeting satisfied that they had dotted the i's and crossed the t's and were doing a good job managing the organization.

The Code of Nice

"The Code of Nice is pervasive in all areas of the nonprofit industry," as Pamela Wilcox writes in *Exposing the Elephants: Creating Exceptional Nonprofits*; our prevailing attitude is "do something and be hated, do nothing and be loved."[4] Of course we want a comfortable and collegial environment. But nice does not mean avoiding what is vitally important. There's nothing nice about that kind of irresponsibility.

We need to be able to deal openly, directly, and honestly with the big issues that shape the organization. Where is bold, risk-taking leadership when we need it?

Our board members' desire for consensus results in decisions that are often too safe—an easy way out for all. Audacious goals involve too much risk. Dynamic leadership can get worn down by group inertia and drag. How can the real work of the organization get done when everyone is just so very pleasant? And who will do the fundraising?

> *I worry that serving on our board is considered more of a burden than an honor.*
>
> —Executive Director's lament

THE BEST DREAM TEAM BOARD MEMBERS

There are some wonderful board members out there, who not only help in fundraising but also tend wisely to our organizations and provide all manner of moral support. They care deeply, and you can tell that they do. They bring a vision and a spirit to the cause that helps inspire other board members.

The best board members perform at a level far beyond the typical nonprofit board member's job description. What do they do that is so special? How can we capture it?

Perhaps we could start by articulating the qualities that are not even mentioned in formal job descriptions but are so very valuable; qualities that Dream Team board members share:

1. They look at the big picture (where the organization is going), and they keep a careful eye on external forces in the outside environment. They make sure our organization is adapting to a changing world, focusing on where we should be in the future.

2. They ask the tough questions that we do not always ask with a fresh perspective. They act as "outside directors" to keep us honest and focused on the important issues. They are willing to provide what you might call "a constructive friction" to our discussion.

3. They keep us accountable, and keep themselves accountable as well. They insist on results and keep an eye on the bottom line.

4. They are active and self-initiating as fundraisers, willing to use their connections, actively opening doors to create new relationships that will extend our organization's reaches into the community. In appropriate situations, they ask for funding. They participate 100% in fundraising campaigns and in all activities that support fundraising.

5. They understand our organization's needs and what we are raising money to accomplish. They are able to talk with passion and urgency about our organization, its mission, and its case for support.

6. They are wholeheartedly, actively—and pragmatically—committed to our mission.

7. They give us their wisdom, moral support, engagement, and interest. They monitor our organizations with integrity and strength and guide us to success. They look for *solutions* to problems, rather than focusing on the problems themselves.

8. They take the time to think through all our issues and challenges. They don't take the easy way out and latch on to quick solutions.

There are plenty of formal job descriptions for board members out there, but it is these qualities of leadership, vision, and commitment that make our organizations fly high, and that makes the change happen in the world that we want.

What would happen if we set these expectations out in the job descriptions we provide to board member? Would we enlist more or fewer great board members? Would we inspire them to action? I think we might just inspire them to a stronger role, even to be great in the largest sense of the word.

The Right Roles for Board and Staff

What is the board's role and what is the staff's job? Want to create confusion? Ask this question! This perennial issue about roles and responsibilities for board members is the stuff of endless discussion. We would probably all agree that defining appropriate roles for board and staff is a constant challenge for many nonprofits.

To solve this problem, many pundits offer clear, cookie-cutter divisions of roles: boards focus on policy, strategy, and governance, while staff members handle management, administration, and execution.

However, the real fact is that *much responsibility is shared* among board and staff members. Both the staff and the board have dual leadership roles that are interdependent, and many of these roles overlap.

Of course this results in conflicts about who is expecting whom to do what. That this situation occurs is understandable. The staff thinks some jobs are the board's responsibilities, yet board members do not agree—especially when it comes to fundraising.

> *Our board has been operating from the perspective that "staff" does*
> *all the work, and the board either approves that work or critiques it.*
>
> —Nonprofit CEO

Focus on Outcomes and Results

Our only way out of this potentially damaging fog is to simplify, simplify, simplify. Let's just define expectations in terms of *outcomes and results.* Who needs to do what in order to help the organization succeed?

Appropriate roles and responsibilities clear up quickly when everyone's eye is on concrete results they need to create personally. For example, the most important question to ask is: *what do I as a board member need to do this week or this month to help my organization succeed?*

Recently I facilitated a planning retreat for a local board. One of their objectives was to clarify the board's roles and responsibilities. We could have spent hours of valuable time in theoretical discussions about the appropriate role of the board.

Instead, we focused on defining what the board members needed to accomplish for their organization in the next six months. This attention to immediate action items simplified—and stimulated—the discussion.

Board members were invigorated, and they left the retreat far more excited and fired up than they had been, because they had a clear sense of how each person could be in action to help the organization. They wanted to connect their work as board members directly to their nonprofit's mission.

It is interesting that outcomes and results are so rarely discussed with board members. Staff does not typically force the issue of their expectations of the board's performance—or its responsibilities.

This can be difficult, since the staff actually works for the board: the employees cannot talk frankly with their bosses about the bosses' own responsibilities and/or their lack of performance. This is where board self-assessments and a neutral consultant are valuable.

> *My board will not fundraise; what do I do?*
>
> —Executive Director

DOES THE BOARD OR THE STAFF DO THE FUNDRAISING?

> *Our organization has a very strong board that is committed to our school. However, I believe they do not, for the most part, view fundraising (other than giving) as part of their responsibility.*
>
> —Nonprofit CEO

The issue of whose responsibility it is to bring in the money is almost always a subject of disagreement and frustration. As a consultant, one question I am frequently asked is, "What are the appropriate roles of board and staff members in fundraising?"

Allocating responsibility for fundraising is like a game of tag. The person who is "it" chases all the others until they tag someone else who becomes "it": "you're *it*; no, you're *it*," and the buck keeps passing. No one will let the monkey sit on their back when it comes to fundraising.

Everyone leading the organization wants a job description for board members telling them they *have* to raise money, and most organizations in fact state this clearly. However, even when board members actually sign agreements that they will help raise money, too many are still simply not willing to do the job. They freeze when it comes time to act.

From my perspective, if one-third of the board will shoulder fundraising responsibilities, then you have a substantial force to work with. This third can be the "tipping point" to inspire the rest of the board to action.

Board Members as Either Askers or Ambassadors

I expect my board members to fall into the roles of either Askers or Ambassadors, roles I have created so that everyone can find a way to comfortably support the fundraising program. If they are not comfortable asking, then they still play a support role by representing the organization as Ambassadors.

The Askers obviously are willing to go out and help raise money by directly soliciting. They are the fearless ones who inspire others with their energy and enthusiasm. We can't live without them!

The Ambassadors assist with everything else in the fundraising cycle. There are many, many support roles they can play: helping to identify donors, involving and cultivating donors' interest in their organization, and creatively thanking them. From my point of view, every single board member has an important role to play supporting the fundraising process.

> *The successes I've had have come from recognizing that some people excel*
> *at fundraising and some excel in other areas. While I believe that it is*
> *important for all board members to engage in fundraising, there is usually*
> *a core group who will carry the load. Expecting everybody to contribute*
> *an equal amount of raised funds is a recipe for disaster.*
>
> —Nonprofit CEO

The Three Major Jobs for Board Members

Clearly trustees have a legal duty to ensure that the organization has appropriate resources. I like to simplify all the various board roles and responsibilities into three major areas.

Their first job is to keep their organizations clean and legal. Board members are legally the "stewards" of the organization, and as such must carry out their duty to ensure that legal, financial, and reporting matters are handled honestly and accurately.

In this era of increasing public demands on nonprofits for accountability and transparency, this function of the board is more important than ever. This role of fiduciary oversight can be mundane and detail oriented, certainly not exciting or engaging.

Their second job is to serve as the link to the outside community, bringing in resources and connections. And that also means raising friends and funds.

The board members have a clear duty to ensure that the organization has appropriate resources. In actuality fundraising is interpreted in many different ways and worked out in varying structures, depending on the organization itself, its stage of development, the skills and longevity of its staff, the capabilities and interests of its board, and its fundraising history. There are as many different fundraising roles for board members as there are organizations. I treat board roles and responsibilities in fundraising in detail in Chapter 6.

Their third job is to define the organization's future. Setting organizational strategy in light of a rapidly changing environment requires a future focus, carefully observing potential outside influences.

It calls for a watchful eye on your nonprofit's position on the community radar screen; in other words, its brand and market position. It needs creative thinking and fresh approaches, not business as usual and certainly not the traditional rote fill-in-the-blank strategic planning processes we typically employ.

The Board's "Must-Do" Fundraising Duties

One thing is clear: *the board must see that the organization has a valid and realistic plan for bringing in needed funds.* Board members should play a direct role in helping to bring in these funds. They should agree on a plan with staff that allocates specific roles for board members and staff members.

Every organization executes a different fundraising program. The board and the staff together work out who is to do what to create fundraising success—with both assuming responsibility. It takes a team to raise money.

Organizations should *require* the board to play some type of role in fundraising, and this role should be spelled out clearly in a board job description or commitment letter that we will discuss later. We will also discuss the many roles board members can play to support the fundraising program.

> *We have struggled to get our board to focus on fundraising.*
>
> —Nonprofit CEO

All too often, the members agree to fundraising jobs but somehow never accomplish them. And since they are volunteers, they cannot get called on the carpet, can they?

Of course, we all know that volunteers do not react positively to being told they "have" to do something. They would rather feel guilty about letting the organization down than tackle unpleasant fundraising chores.

> *Keeping board members focused on fundraising is an ongoing problem. Most board members are already very busy, and their fundraising calls have a way of falling down their priority list.*
>
> —Nonprofit CEO

So job descriptions for fundraising simply may or may not be followed, for many reasons, human nature being what it is. Staff members privately understand that they often cannot rely on board members to come through.

Considering their lack of training in fundraising, board volunteers can hardly be expected to be wildly enthusiastic and successful at something they may have never done.

They need lots of training on how to approach fundraising and plenty of support to get their jobs actually completed. Fundraising will never be an activity that we can delegate to the board and happily go off on our programmatic way.

We will talk in detail later in this book about how to introduce fundraising to your board in a way that excites their passion and commitment for the organization—and that sets them up to tackle their fundraising roles with gusto.

IN THE REAL WORLD

Recently I was working with a nonprofit that required all board members to submit ten names to be solicited for the annual appeal. When the board members were originally recruited, they all signed a job description that plainly said they would: "provide ten names for the annual campaign mailing list."

(continues)

A problem arose, though, when some board members simply refused. They said it was not appropriate because they were uncomfortable "hitting on" their friends—regardless of what they had agreed to when they joined the board.

I recommended that the staff take a softer approach with their board. Steer clear of talk of soliciting, I suggested, and change the wording of the assignment. Instead, try asking each board member to bring ten people in for a tour. Once you get people here, you know that they become hooked and always become donors.

The staff liked this change. They shifted into asking board members to make friends for the organization rather than directly soliciting ten people.

I am waiting to hear how the board members liked this. I'll be very surprised if they do not find it both agreeable and effective.

THE REALITY OF BOARD MEMBERS AND FUNDRAISING

We all have a dream image of the ideal trustee who is able and willing to solicit with passion and energy. Consider the previous job description of the best Dream Team board member. Much of what we hope for is related to fundraising, of course, yet few board members fit this noble description.

We are holding up a "dream" level of performance as the standard and setting our expectations accordingly. However, the reality of what board members actually do is very different. Again, we must clearly acknowledge reality so we can deal with our board members as they are, not as how we imagine they are.

> Our board would talk for an hour about programs, but we couldn't get them
> to talk for five minutes about fundraising.
>
> —Nonprofit CEO

Our board members have some challenges when they are confronted with fundraising. Let us acknowledge real attitudes and real situations so we can deal with them and make things better. Here is the *reality* of the problems we have with board members and fundraising, remembering that we play a major role in solving each issue:

- *Board members are not fully engaged in our organizations.* We have discussed how they may be bored because they are not asked to do anything substantive. Or they are distracted by focusing on the wrong issues, or possibly they are too new to the organization to know what to do.

- *Board members do not fully understand their organization, the impact it makes, or its mission well enough to talk about it.* I hear too often from board members that they don't know what to say about their organization. This is our responsibility—we give our board members plenty of materials, but often it is not the right information or it is too full of jargon for board members to use effectively.

- *They do not know how to be passionate, articulate spokespeople for our organization.* Again, we can fix this: we need to help them learn what to say—and how to say it.
- *They are reluctant to open doors to their connections.* They do *not* actively look for connections in the community and potential funding relationships, because, as we have discussed, they fear the "asking for money" issue. Also, we have not made it clear to them what they will be asked to do if and when they do open doors to their connections.
- *Board members are not all making "proud" gifts to the best of their ability.* Board solicitation is frequently not done as effectively as it could be. We will talk about the right way to solicit your board in detail in the last chapter.
- *They are afraid of fundraising.* They are anxious about asking for money. They think it is unseemly and inappropriate. They are afraid of rejection. We have not educated them properly about the philosophy of fundraising.
- *They agree to make fundraising calls, but then do not do them.* We do not set them up to win with fantastic training, inspiration, and top-notch staff support.

> *I am continuously impressed by a sort of 1950s mentality that board members come in with regarding expectations for fundraising. They think if they give their time, then they are off the hook for fundraising.*
>
> —Nonprofit Consultant

Quotes from Board Members About Fundraising:

- *Let the staff do it.*
- *Isn't that the staff's job?*
- *I'm giving my time—that's enough.*
- *I'll do anything but raise money.*
- *Asking for money is dirty work.*
- *Eeek!*

THE MISTAKES WE MAKE WITH OUR BOARD MEMBERS AND FUNDRAISING

As I have said before, it is our responsibility to set up our board members in active, satisfying roles that can support the fundraising process. Too often we make mistakes that hurt, rather than help, our cause.

We approach fundraising in the wrong way. In our defense, we mean well, and we want to treat our board members nicely. However, staff fundraisers are generally overworked and overwhelmed, and all too frequently we try to tackle too many projects at once.

For all our professional skills, we sometimes rush board members through much of the fundraising process, particularly their training. Also, most fundraising training for board members focuses on the wrong thing: teaching them *how to ask for money* rather than introducing a deeper context of what philanthropy and fundraising are all about.

Most fundraising training misses the mark by jumping straight to soliciting. It eventually inhibits board member energy and excitement for the cause rather than pumping it up. Introducing board members to fundraising by presenting a seminar titled: "The Art of the Ask" is not a way to bring them gently to the table.

We forget that our board members just do not get it. And they will tend to resist until they do understand what fundraising is all about. In a too-much-to-do hurry, we as staff can make some common blunders that squelch our board members' enthusiasm and set them up for failure.

Let us look at some of the major mistakes we make with our board members when it comes to fundraising.

The Five Most Common Mistakes

Mistake One: Asking for Money, not Building and Keeping Friends   As we have discussed, presenting board members with the task of "asking for money" is not the most effective way to inspire anyone—board members or not—to help raise money. If we can get board members to change their point of view and create a conversation about their vision for a better community, not about cash, then the tone changes to one that is far more energetic and exciting.

> *I was once on a very aggressive fundraising board. I felt that we were so focused on the money that we lost sight of why we were even doing this. The conversations were always about the bottom line, not about the kids we helped or the work we were doing.*
>
> *The fundraising became almost like an end in itself. I had to force myself to remember what it was all for.*
>
> —Former Board Member

If we can shift our board members to a Passion-Driven Fundraising approach, they will focus first on making friends for our organization and then getting them on our bandwagon as donors—then everyone wins.

Recently I was doing a fundraising training for the Board of Wake Health Services. At the end of the evening, I asked the folks around the table how their notion of raising money might have changed after our discussion.

One of the doctors who cared for homeless persons came up to me later and said, *"This was so very helpful. Before, when I thought of fundraising, I immediately imagined cold calls. You have shown me that I can help in fundraising in lots of much easier ways. Fundraising is not necessarily cold calls at all; in fact, good fundraising is everything but cold calls."*

We cannot allow our good-hearted, well-meaning, but nervous board members to get away with equating fundraising with soliciting.

Mistake Two: Too Many Calls at Too Low a Dollar Level If we are going to use board members in solicitations, then it is important to plan carefully the highest and best use of their time in order to make the most of their valuable contacts and limited availability.

I have seen well-meaning but scared trustee volunteers bravely step up to the plate, willing to help make annual giving solicitations in person. And then the thankful but overly optimistic staff loads them up with far too many calls to make at one time.

Worse, the calls are for meager amounts of money. It is much better to focus our board members on fewer calls at much higher dollar levels.

> *It takes the same amount of work to get a $10,000 donation as it does to get a $100 donation—you just have to ask different people. People's own views on money tend to limit the size of the donations they solicit.*
>
> —Nonprofit Board Chair

I believe in asking board members to make only three calls at any one time. Any more will seem like too many; the trustee may set them aside until he or she has time to do it.

By contrast, making just three calls seems doable and is therefore put on the short list. When the individual completes the three calls, then you can feel free to ask for more. Loading the trustee up with too much to do at once is a recipe for disappointing failure.

My friend Michael Guillot, CFRE, Vice President for Development at North Carolina Symphony also has a simple focus. He says to "do one thing at a time. Focus on quality, not quantity. I would rather have each board member doing one task a month for our philanthropic programs than have them struggle with too many actions that never get done."

Use your valuable board members carefully where you need them most, and where they will do the most good.

Mistake Three: Cold or "Cool" Calls, Which Are Rarely Successful If you send trustees out on calls that do not have a high likelihood of succeeding, they will experience defeat rather than success. Cold calls are the worst possible place to use the energy and good will of your kind-hearted board members, because cold calls have the highest rate of failure.

Passion-Driven Fundraising will not subject your board to this kind of rejection, which will incline your board members never to venture out for you again! Preserve their fragile self-esteem and protect them from negative responses, if you want their continued help. Why would they keep beating their heads against a wall if they are rarely successful?

Send them on easy calls that will create fun, shared vision, and passion for your organization, calls that will make them happy and give them confidence. *Send them on calls where you already know what the outcome will be.*

Send them out to make friends for your organization, and engage the community with their passion. Set them to load everybody into that bandwagon that they are driving!

> *Where I have not been comfortable in fundraising is when I have been asked to send annual fund mailings or to solicit friends who are not familiar with the organization or who otherwise are in need of cultivation.*
>
> —Former Board Chair

I work hard to preserve my board members' good feelings about being involved with fundraising. I nurture their interest, starting them off with simple tasks to encourage them such as thanking current donors or taking an assignment to cultivate someone at an event.

Then, after they develop some confidence, I will bring them along on a formal cultivation or solicitation call. I will rarely send board members out to solicit alone, and only if I think they are carefully prepared, experienced fundraisers.

Mistake Four: Lack of Training, Structure, and Support   We send our trustees out with too little preparation and backup. We tend to forget that they are volunteers. They are not the pros at this that we are. Passion-Driven Fundraising will give them thorough training to correct their misconceptions about fundraising and to pump them up with confidence to venture out into scary fundraising territory.

Do not make the mistake of assuming that your board members understand fundraising, or how to talk about your organization. Be sure they have a solid understanding of the underlying philosophy of fundraising—developing donors/investors/partners who will stick with your organization for the long run.

They need—and deserve—first-rate support from staff. You will find that board members deeply appreciate this kind of backup. They need clear goals, a clear organizational structure, and inspiration to wake up their passion and deep personal commitment to your organization's success.

Mistake Five: Emergency Fundraising, Not Long-Term Relationships   I am all for a sense of urgency when setting out to raise funds. However, I have seen too many organizations wait until there is a financial crisis or emergency to ask board members for help.

At such times, board members are asked to pull in some money quickly in order to fill a budget shortfall or cover some major financial loss. Again, this sets them up for unpleasant fundraising experiences. They are sent out with little training and usually manage to approach the job from the wrong perspective.

In these cases, they will usually create a conversation about "money," not about a vision for a stronger, healthier community or a better world. This misdirection causes fundraising to be placed on the wrong plane, leaving board members with a distasteful experience that could have been avoided.

MISSION POSSIBLE—A BETTER WAY!

Of course, none of us can wait for the perfect board—or the perfect staff—to do our fundraising. I have raised a lot of money for many different organizations in my day, and most of these organizations had issues or "warts" on the inside.

We did not have the luxury of delaying our fundraising until any internal problems were smoothed out and all parts of our organizational system were working smoothly. We had people to serve and important work to do that could not wait. We had to go out there and raise money anyway.

You cannot expect to fix everything in your board and your organization, ever. You have to operate as a "going concern" and do the best you can do all the time. Don't let internal organizational challenges hold you back from your very best efforts at fundraising.

There *Is* a Better Way!

There *is* a way to engage board members' hearts, minds, and passion for fundraising. We *can* find a way to activate them and create the energy that will fuel a new passion—an on-going commitment to tackle something they deem vitally important.

With the approach of Passion-Driven Fundraising, we can overcome both major obstacles that stand between our board members and fundraising. We can transform their attitudes about money and fundraising, and we can also generate excitement about what they want our organizations to be accomplishing *now*.

The Passion-Driven Fundraising approach has four steps:

Step 1: **Focus your board** on the mission and much closer to the work at hand.

- We will learn how to re-engage your board members by focusing them on real outcomes and results, giving them substantive work and—most of all— meaningful board meetings. We will learn how to foster a sense of community and collegiality among your board members so they can work seamlessly together.

- We will give them "mission moments" to reconnect them with their passion for the cause. We will learn how to bring them back in touch with their desire to make a difference out there in their communities and in the world.

Step 2: **Inspire your board** members by literally re-defining fundraising as *making friends to change the world*. We'll show them how to start friendraising and piling everybody on their bandwagon.

- We will learn a deeper philosophy fundraising that is full of power to make anything happen—the power of a bold vision, of new, creative energy and of volunteers working only out of the goodness of their heart.

- We will learn how to overcome their fears of fundraising and introduce them to the joy that donors experience when they give to something important.

○ We will tackle head-on the attitude of scarcity that pervades many boards, and learn how the mindset of abundance will bring success. There *is* enough for everyone!

Step 3: **Ready your board** with the right tools and skills. We will learn about fundraising from the donor's point of view—when board members shift their focus to the donor, they can help keep donors happy and involved with your organization for the long haul.

○ We will take the emphasis away from soliciting and show board members all the other ways they can contribute in fundraising without "asking" but that still make a direct impact on the bottom line.

○ We will give them an experiential tour of the fundraising cycle, so they understand how we do what we do. They will begin to see just how little time is spent in the "asking" phase of the cycle, compared with all the many other activities we undertake with our donors.

○ We will equip them with the right things to say and the right way to say them. Since many board members do not know how to talk about their organization, we will discuss the all-important elevator speech in detail, and learn how to make this process fun for everyone.

Step 4: **Engage your board** members in your fundraising plan by finding specific, appropriate roles for each person. Create the right kind of support structure to help them be productive and sustain change for the long run.

○ We will discuss practical methods for setting your fired-up board members to work, opening doors, making connections, reaching out, and helping to bring new supporters into your nonprofit.

○ We will show them how to build social capital for our organization and how to be personal advocates for our mission wherever they go.

○ We will learn how to use Advice Visits to get in the door to prospective donors. Learn how board members can host Small Socials and Mission Based-Tours to build your organization's network and clout in the community.

And in the last chapter we will discuss how to set up your board members to win by enlisting a Dream Team board of the right people with the right outlook and skills.

• We will learn how to set expectations early in the game, including clearly defining the board's specific fundraising responsibilities and orienting new members appropriately so they can hit the ground running.

• We will learn how to set up a management structure for the board itself—the Governance Committee, along with the right kind of self-assessments that will monitor —and encourage—board performance.

• We will learn how to solicit your board members properly and thoroughly, so that they all make proud personal gifts to your cause each year.

Before long you will have board members who are raring to go, who, like my friends at the Ronald McDonald House of the Rio Grande Valley, love to tell their story to anyone who will listen, who are stepping up to foster relationships with donors and who *know* people will want to support them.

▓ NOTES

1. Richard P. Chait, William P. Ryan, and Barbara E. Taylor, *Governance as Leadership, Reframing the Work of Nonprofit Boards* (Hoboken, NJ: John Wiley & Sons, 2005).

2. Chic Dambach, "Good Intentions," Board Member, BoardSource: November/December 2006, *BoardSource*.

3. Margaret Wheatley, *Leadership and the New Science* (San Francisco: Berrett-Koehler, 1999).

4. Pamela Wilcox, *Exposing the Elephants: Creating Exceptional Nonprofits* (Hoboken, NJ: John Wiley & Sons, 2006).

CHAPTER 2

Passion-Driven Fundraising Step One: FOCUS on the Mission

No problem can be solved from the same level of consciousness that created it.

—Albert Einstein

If we want to create fundamental, transforming change in our board members' attitudes about fundraising, where do we start? Do we simply present Fundraising 101 and then expect our trustees to actively embrace a new role in fundraising?

Or do we start at a deeper place and go to a source that sparks their passion? A place that would evoke their deepest connection to our mission. It would engage them in the excitement and vigor of their own vision for change in the world through this organization.

How do we go from where we are now to that new place of inspiration, of excitement, energy, and creativity? How do we change our board into a true leadership *team* sharing spirit, vision, and trust—where the collective board itself is stronger than the sum of its individual parts?

If our board has lost some of its energy, how do we re-engage our trustees? How do we galvanize each person's individual vision into a collective vision based on what we want to create together? In simple terms, how do we tap the capacities of our board members so they will share responsibility for the organization's challenges and its results?

It is a tall order to create this dream board. It requires fresh approaches to dealing with group process and meetings, and especially to how we frame the issues that the board tackles. It starts by offering board members a truly meaningful experience as they serve our cause. I believe board members will react positively to even small changes in the way we handle their role.

As board members, these people should be able to act on their own personal vision of what is important to them. They are "in action" serving our cause most of all because *they care deeply about the end result.* That is where you will find a powerful, committed board—engaged and taking action on behalf of something very important.

First we have to look at how to create change in our boardrooms. We will look at the two major ways to create change: the slower incremental approach, which takes small steps over time, and the transformational approach, which offers an immediate, deeper shift in perspective resulting in dramatically improved performance.

Then we will present the first step of the Passion-Driven Fundraising model: *Focus on the Mission* to ignite your board members' passion. We will discuss how to reconnect your board members directly to the work at hand by inspiring their personal vision, and reminding them of the difference they are making through your organization.

We will look at how to offer them substantive work. I will give you a long list of ways to create cogent, meaningful meetings. We will also talk about how to create collegiality and trust among board members so they can work well together as an inspired leadership team.

Focusing on the Mission has six major components, which we will discuss in detail:

1. Emphasize outcomes and results instead of process.
2. Give board members substantive work.
3. Create meaningful board meetings with agendas that matter.
4. Let the board members do the talking.
5. Energize meetings with "Mission Moments."
6. Create a sense of community and collegiality among board members.

Creating Sustained Change: The Challenge

> *Most people change, not because they see the light, but because they feel the heat.*
>
> —Hal Williams, Rensselaerville Institute

Just how difficult is it to achieve sustained change within an organization? Think about your board's or your organization's informal culture. All those personal relationships, casual networks, and ways of working/being with each other—they reinforce a tendency to keep things as is and resist change. Your organization acts like a self-reinforcing system, a complex entity that thrives and changes based on how all the players work, think, and interact with each other.

Change management is a thriving business among for-profit concerns, yet it is not discussed often enough in the nonprofit world. However, new ideas in organizational change are directly applicable to nonprofits and particularly to our effort to engage our board members in fundraising.

> *We trained hard—but it seemed that every time we were beginning to form into teams, we would be reorganized. I was to learn later in life that we tend to meet any new situation by reorganizing. And what a wonderful method*

it can be for creating the illusion of progress while producing confusion, inefficiency, and demoralization.

—Gaius Petronius Arbiter, 210 B.C.

Change is not easy. We know that most change initiatives fail. We think some new model or fad will solve our board's inaction or our fundraising challenges. These promise to make our boards—and our fundraising—more effective, but somehow sustained change does not happen and we revert back to business (or dysfunction) as usual.

Every nonprofit organization's success depends upon the board's commitment, passion and leadership.

—Beth Briggs, President, Creative Philanthropy

Peter Senge, in *The Dance of Change: The Challenge of Sustaining Momentum in Learning Organizations,* points out the failure of these attempts to bring about new ways of working together and more powerful results: "We've seen enough 'flavor of the month' programs . . . to last a lifetime. We say privately 'here we go again' and 'this will never work....'"[1]

These scenarios sound a bit like recent efforts to reform our public education system. The program of the year is hailed as the new way to save our schools. Exhausted teachers take on another project, but only a few years later it is abandoned in favor of some new program proposed by a new crop of politicians or education experts.

Lasting change is difficult for us as individuals as well—just think of the last diet you were on, or your last New Year's resolutions. How well did they fare? And was the change permanent? What kind of reinforcement did you need to sustain your resolutions?

All people—and particularly your volunteer board members—have a natural resistance to change and a strong tendency to hold on to previously conceived attitudes, especially where fundraising is concerned. We have to address the deeply ingrained thinking of individual board members as well as the consensus-ridden "group culture" of a nonprofit board.

Often organizations attempt major transformations by attempting to implement new plans, strategies or technologies. But change doesn't happen because the messy, complex human side is ignored.

Approaches that are technical will never work unless they take into account human attitudes and dynamics. We know too well that our boards are composed of a complex set of people's emotions, energies and attitudes that all play off each other.

There is a sort of "web" of relationships among our board members, and all their work happens through these relationships. We have to recognize and work with these energies. Our challenge is to inspire our board members to put aside differences, come together as a group, and organize around the work to be done.

We have to bring our board members together to discover shared passion and values that recognizing and honor our basic values and humanity. As Margaret Wheatley said in her classic *Leadership in the New Science,* successful change has to pay tribute to deep human feelings: "our need to trust one another, our need for meaningful work, our desire to contribute and be thanked for that contribution."[2]

Creating Real Change—in People or Organizations

There are two major ways to approach change: *by increments or by transformation.* It does not matter whether your focus is people or organizations; families or corporations, these are the two major pathways. Which approach will be best if you want to change your trustees' ideas about fundraising and get them fired up to take action? Let's look at the two types.

Incremental Change

It is pretty obvious from the label: incremental change is a slow, gradual process, a series of small alterations leading toward a goal.

For example, you can help board members gain new fundraising skills and capabilities over time by repeatedly hammering away at a new set of concepts and ideas. Your consistent work will have a cumulative effect that will build toward an ultimate attitude shift.

In his popular book, *Breakthrough Thinking for Nonprofit Organizations,* Bernard Ross points out what happens when common problems are dealt with using slow, piecemeal change: the lack of a demanding deadline or a strong direction can "make the process liable to wander off course."[3]

In addition, measurable improvements can be so small that people do not understand the "significance of the change overall."[4] They may initially see an awakening to a new point of view, but then they drift back to the status quo.

This is the level of most fundraising training offered to boards today. We give our trustees a class called "Fundraising Training," or worse, "The Art of the Ask," hoping that a whole new point of view and motivation will emerge along with immediately changed attitudes and actions.

Instead of the results we want, they may dig in their heels. At best, we get small changes, increments, which may or may not hold for the long run. Inertia is at work—the tendency to stay at the current speed or stasis—and it is a serious drag on any effort to change. I call this "the drift," an undertow that drags you back to the way you have always been.

I will say often in these pages that we as staff hold much of the responsibility for our board members' lack of participation in fundraising. So often we make the mistake of presenting, in a mechanical, straight lecture format, the dry fundamentals of fundraising for board members, in a way that will not inspire real, sustained change, ignoring their attitudes and feelings about fundraising.

The Human Element   We ignore the complexity of the human element, our board members' deeper feelings and motivations. So, from all our lecturing about "how to raise money," does any learning stick? Yes and no.

I have seen board members just sit quietly through their training, appearing interested, but who knows what they are really thinking? Probably they are telling themselves, as they pleasantly nod in agreement, that nobody on earth is ever going to drag them into asking for money.

In many ways, I cannot blame them; we are not placing fundraising in the larger, more meaningful context of creating change for the good of the world.

You can take the slow incremental way to engage your trustees in your organization's fundraising programs, but a gradual approach is easily interrupted by your board members' previously conceived fears of fundraising.

The inevitable turnover of board members makes an incremental approach to change even more uncertain. When board members leave, there goes your institutional memory! Board turnover—and shifting organizational priorities—can hurt or completely stymie new efforts to involve board members in fundraising.

Transformational Change

The transformational approach requires that people examine their underlying, deeper points of view about themselves, others, or a situation, in order to create a *fundamental shift* in their perspective.

Bernard Ross calls this "sudden, exponential, discontinuous and radical change that leads to dramatically improved performance in a relatively short space of time."[5]

Transformation is a major shift in context or point of view, a great leap, a transforming leap, from one reality to a completely different mindset in a new and different place. This kind of change is exciting, although it can also be quite uncomfortable to be suddenly unfettered by previously held limiting beliefs.

Transformational change begins and operates at a deeper systemic level, based on the recognition that our organizations—and our boards—living systems. Think of your board as a complex ecosystem, for example, with all the parts constantly in play relating and reacting to each other.

Our board members are operating within a web of interdependence based on each other's attitudes and actions. If we want to foster change, we must also deal with this larger whole made of dynamic relationships.

We need to constantly reinforce the direction we want our board members to take, bolstering momentum and building on positive results. Somehow, (and we have always known this intuitively) *everyone* on the board is responsible for its challenging problems and its happy outcomes.

Opening Up Wonderful New Possibilities   When fears and discomfort are properly handled, transformational change can open up wonderful new possibilities and ways of thinking that radically improve the attitudes and performance of your board members (and your organization) for good.

Transformational change occurs when board members examine themselves and their underlying beliefs, to understand how those deeply held attitudes are affecting their current thoughts and actions. Often they discover ideas and defenses that are operating without their awareness, and they are able to discard these as false and obstructive.

Taking the transformational road is liberating; it gets people excited and creates dramatic results. As each individual examines his or her personal commitment to the organization and its mission, all kinds of new possibilities for board member involvement arise.

How do you accomplish transformational change? You have to get your board members away in a retreat, and set up an immersion experience that will open up deeper conversations about their feelings and attitudes. You create a setting that will evoke their motivations and deeper values: why they want to serve on the board, what they are passionate about, what change do they want to create in the world through your organization.

You give them the opportunity to talk and to process their feelings. You show them the inspirational side of fundraising as we discuss later in this book, how fundraising helps to create the fuel for change; how powerful and important it is. You create the opportunity for them to set their own goals for where they want to go, and how they want to get there. And then they decide what support they need to get there.

You need a skilled trainer/consultant who is deeply versed in fundraising, board development, and transformational facilitation, someone who can evoke your board members' vision, and inspire them to set "stretch" goals and go for them.

A word of warning, however, even transformative change, with its sudden new perspective, will not stick automatically. Like all change, it requires sustained perseverance, patience, and commitment over time to continually reinforce the new ideas that have just emerged. Unless your board members' new attitudes and resolutions are consistently supported, no change will be long lasting and permanent.

Passion-Driven Fundraising presents a transformational change in board members' perceptions of and involvement in fundraising. The four stages of activity (rekindling board members' passionate engagement, inspiring them with a new philosophy about what fundraising is, readying them properly with skills and tools, and engaging them in the fundraising plan with a precise matching of tasks and people) all combine to create one organic action, one sea change in board members' attitude.

You will end up with a board functioning more as a leadership team, full of spirit, committed to a common, shared vision.

STEP ONE: FOCUS ON THE MISSION TO INSPIRE BOARD MEMBERS

More than anything else, above all, I want to see passion in my board volunteers. Passion for the cause is what really counts the most.

—James May, University of North Carolina
Arts & Sciences Foundation

If we want to fire up our board members for fundraising, we first need to fire them up about our organization and the work we are doing to change the world. As we have discussed, a board that is not engaged and excited about the work at hand is not going to put itself out for fundraising.

So our first task is to focus our trustees' attention on what is really important—the mission. We have to find the answers to two deceptively simple questions. These questions sound so simple, yet are difficult to answer: What is the work we are trying to do; and what do we need to do to be successful?

We will also need to take things a step further and look at what's inspiring our board members. We have to ask deeper questions about our board members' personal motivations and reasons for serving: What do our board members want; and why are they taking the time to serve on our boards?

If we know what our board members want, then we can make sure they get a satisfying experience serving on our board.

What *do* they want?

More than anything else, our board members want to be personally involved in the central work of our organizations. They want to experience it; they want to support it; they want to feel they are directly helping to make our good results possible.

At each meeting, they need to reconnect with the real work of the organization on a very personal level. Each gathering can be like going back to the wellspring—refreshing their passion for the cause and creating new energy to tackle the work at hand.

Our board members all want to make a difference in their communities. They see serving on the board as important community service, a chance to "give back." At a deeper level, they want to be connected to something they believe in and, in some way, to make the world a better place. They join a board because they believe in the organization's mission and want to support it with their time and talent.

> *We all need to serve a purpose in life, and we find meaning every time we give of ourselves, either through time, talent or resources. Most people who sit on boards of nonprofits do not need to be convinced of this fact. Often board members simply don't know how to go about the giving in the right way. They just need some guidance.*
>
> —Todd Baker

Above all, they want the satisfaction of using their own skills to make a positive contribution. Like donors, they want to see the results achieved by our organizations. They want to see changed or saved lives. They want to experience the emotional satisfaction of their good work.

It is up to us to *make sure* that board members receive a direct experience of our real work in the world. Whether that means bringing testimonials back into the board meeting, or taking the board out to the field to volunteer and serve, it is our responsibility to make this experience happen.

The quality of board members' *experience* as board members has everything to do with their passion and their engagement in our organization's mission. Their personal experience results in either excitement and energy or inattention and disconnection. The good news is that we can control much of what happens as they participate in meetings, events, and other activities with us.

The primary experience board members want is meaningful engagement in work that matters—not just coming to routine meetings and offering opinions, or critiquing the staff's work, but discussions and activities that are substantive, which address consequential issues. Board members are not interested in just attending meetings and offering advice on "policy."

So the fundamental question of focusing on the mission is this: what is the right work for our board members to do?

> *I think the board's real job is to raise awareness and money for our organization.*
>
> —Board Member, Threshold Clubhouse

What Does Each Board Member Want?

Let us give board members the benefit of the doubt. Take a careful look at the individual trustees. What does each person want out of the experience of serving on your board? What would it take to give him or her such a quality experience that they would be engaged and excited enough to tackle fundraising?

Be sure you focus on your board members as individual people. Treat them like real people, as you would want to be treated. Just like you, your board members do not want irrelevant, unsatisfying things to do.

> *People who enjoy meetings should not be in charge of anything.*
>
> —Thomas Sowell

They want to talk about issues of substance, make contributions rather than just sitting there as if they are in grade school, and maybe, just maybe, they want to have some fun in their spare time. Board members may well be as frustrated by us as we are by them.

Let us address the causes of their boredom and inaction. If we do that, we *can* rekindle their passion.

Our Strategy for Step One: Focus on the Mission

Let us look now at our basic strategy to accomplish Step One of Passion-Driven Fundraising: Focus Board Members on the Mission. Here are specific ways you can start to fire up your board members for fundraising by connecting them deeply with the mission and giving them a quality experience as board members.

EMPHASIZE OUTCOMES AND RESULTS INSTEAD OF PROCESS

I suggest that the most interesting and engaging (and appropriate) job for the board is to cut through all the theoretical discussions of roles and responsibilities and instead focus directly on the results it needs to accomplish.

Rate Your Board's Experience

- Are your board meetings interesting?

- Do you give members the opportunity to personally experience your good work in the community?

- Do they have the opportunity to participate in robust discussions about your organization's future?

- Do you provide social opportunities for your board members to get to know each other and to enjoy themselves?

Traditional governance can have a plodding feel that deadens energy and excitement. Simplifying our focus to what needs to be done eliminates the all talk and no action syndrome that pervades nonprofit boards.

Specifically, what results should be achieved now, and what needs to be accomplished in the next 6 to 12 months? What outcomes are the board members committed to create? The most important question for each individual trustee to answer is: what do I as a board member need to do for this organization in the next six months?

I agree with Hal Williams, President of the think tank Rensselaerville Institute in New York, that we might want to forget job descriptions and instead focus on "results descriptions" for both board and staff members. How refreshing! Just focus on what each person needs to accomplish individually.

Results descriptions would simplify all the dialogue about roles and responsibilities and cut to the chase. Each board member would determine personal goals on behalf of the organization and the methods he or she will use to meet those goals, asking the question, "What do I do in the next four weeks to support my organization?" Each member would be in charge of his or her own calendar and to-do list.

How refreshing it would be to have board members decide on their own what they need to accomplish! All too often they see their responsibility to be simply an advisor, which promotes the frustrating "all talk and no action" mindset that many trustees have.

Here is an interesting example of the benefits of focusing on results and outcomes versus the more theoretical questions of strategic planning, roles, and responsibilities. I was recently preparing to facilitate a planning retreat for a local Ronald McDonald House. The CEO and the Board Chair initially wanted the retreat to cover appropriate roles and responsibilities for the board and to generate buy-in on the current strategic plan.

As I was working on the format for the retreat, I asked the CEO what she really needed the board to do for her in the next 6 to 12 months. This question dramatically shifted the focus to real outcomes instead of structure and process.

It turned out that above all else, what she needed the board to do was help nurture long-term relationships with the current capital campaign donors, so the donors would become permanent investors/partners with the House.

She thought that setting up board members as ambassadors assigned to particular donors or donor constituencies would be a wonderful asset to her plan, and we developed the retreat format to support this outcome.

We eventually decided to throw out all the theoretical conversation about formal structure and instead focus on real outcomes and results: what do board members need to accomplish in the next three months? The retreat has not yet taken place as I write, but I expect to see lots of energy and action generated around the goals we will be discussing—because they are real, concrete, and achievable.

GIVE BOARD MEMBERS SUBSTANTIVE WORK

Board members' value (and their interest in our work) can be greatly enhanced when we offer them genuine opportunities to deal with issues of real consequence, issues that matter, issues that inspire true leadership.

Skip the rote strategic planning processes that are more like "fill in the blank exercises" than occasions to generate inspired creativity about your organization and its future. Shift the focus to reality: "strategy-driven, time-specific, outcomes-oriented" issues as Chait, Ryan, and Taylor suggest in *Governance as Leadership*.[6]

Encourage the board to dream big! If your goals and aspirations are large enough, they will trigger excitement, anticipation, and a sense of great potential.

Let your board members in on the effort to identify priorities, frame problems, and develop solutions and plans, so they will commit to the results they want to achieve. Do not leave them out of the fun and exciting discussions, standing "on the outside looking in as virtually everyone else in and around the organization participates in generative work."

It is important for nonprofit board meetings to offer their members the opportunity to engage in the most important work of leading and governing the organization. Board members need to be talking about the clouds on the outside horizon where impending conflicts and challenges may be gathering. We will discuss a number of ways to use board meetings as tools for creating vision, shared passion, trust, and collegiality.

Let your board share the excitement of creating and realizing a big vision. As Peter Senge writes in *The Fifth Discipline, the Art and Practice of the Learning Organization,* if their vision is powerful enough, it will actually *pull them into action*. When board members are *enrolled* in a vision, then they have chosen to become part of it. When they are *committed* to the vision, then they are fully responsible for achieving results. The cause will be able to count on them. It's their commitment that brings excitement and passion.[7]

Help them create a vision that is "clear, urgent and challenging," as Bernard Ross describes in *Breakthrough Thinking for Nonprofit Organizations.* Show them a possibility to get really excited about. If you can create this, then you will unleash "fantastic organizational and individual energy."[8]

Give board members time to frame or define their own issues: *what is it that is really important now?* Let them identify what problems and issues they want to tackle, instead of doing the work for them.

Also, consider taking board members into the field to experience directly your organization's good work in the world. When I ran a board retreat in the Dominican Republic for the Pan American Development Foundation (PADF), the entire board spent the day before the meeting in Haiti doing field work with the local PADF staff. This is a powerful reminder to board members of why they are involved in the first place.

CREATE MEANINGFUL BOARD MEETINGS

Down with Robert and his Rules! Let's bring back the passion to board meetings!

> *The largest waste of human talent and brainpower in the world today is a nonprofit board meeting.*
>
> —Richard P. Chait

If we want our board members to tackle fundraising willingly and enthusiastically, we need to start with their principal point of contact with our organization—the board meeting itself. These meetings are more important that we realize; they are key moments that create either enthusiasm or boredom.

Boring Meetings = Bored Boards = No Passion = Lackluster Fundraising Participation

The way we typically structure our meetings and agendas is almost a perfect way to drive the passion out of any organization. Too often agendas are pulled together routinely or hurriedly with no thought given to creating an interesting discussion or the important issues really on the plate.

> *Our board meetings are boring . . . snoring.*
>
> —Board Member

As I mentioned earlier, Robert's Rules of Order is a major culprit here. If we want to focus our passionate and powerful leaders on boring and unimaginative material, then we can follow Robert and his Rules closely. Robert often encourages a focus on the trivial and unimportant; the more important issues can remain untouched.

This traditional system may create a balanced, democratic format for running a meeting, but it can also be your enemy. Parliamentary procedure is not known for creating a sense of urgency to correct serious problems in the world.

On the contrary, it creates highly structured meetings that deal in abstractions too far removed from the vital business at hand, feeding hungry children or teaching reading to the jobless or solving urgent health problems.

You may be surprised to read this in a fundraising book, but often too much meeting time is spent on money. These days financial oversight is an important priority for all boards. But laborious, agenda-driven meetings focusing on the specifics of financial and legal reporting tend to drain the energy and creativity from board members, as Chait, Ryan, and Taylor point out.[9] A meeting spent entirely on picking over expenditures drives board members away, thinking, "Why should I be here?"

If your board is bored, will they be willing to tackle fundraising? NO!

I have a vision of a group of people urgently meeting around someone's kitchen table, all deliberating about a new project they are developing to solve a pressing problem, one that is important to everyone there. I can feel the palpable energy around this small table, the passionate sense of urgency that is compelling these people to commit themselves to a bold plan.

Compare this scene with the typical dry nonprofit board meeting. Where is the material that will spark a board member's passion for the cause? We need to create a sense of intimacy and energy, of shared commitment to something important, to a vision that is bigger than the individual. I challenge you to bring that "back room" energy into the front room, and then enjoy the payoff!

I have a dream . . .

—Martin Luther King, Jr.

Set Up Meetings with Agendas That Matter

The act of framing the board's order of business is a powerful task. What will they choose to address in their limited time? What will you suggest that they discuss? Will it be routine, or will it be issue oriented, innovative, and creative? Will it focus on results and outcomes that really matter?

If you pose interesting questions to board members, you will be pleased to hear new ideas (from *them*) that they will own and work hard to implement. Why? Because they came up with the idea and thus have a stake in its being a big success. Look for ways to interrupt their routine ideas and encourage robust discussions that engage trustees' energy and creativity.

Hal Williams of the Rensselaerville Institute suggests that we might want to eliminate our standard meeting agendas and instead set targets for each meeting's accomplishments. In fact, I am currently experimenting with this idea right now. While I continue to prepare traditional agendas for a client's Campaign Committee meetings, I now add at the top of the agenda a list of "desired outcomes" from the meeting.

This clarifies our work and helps us focus on the results we need to achieve in a short time. It has been surprising to me that the committee chair is the person most pleased with this approach—because he knows where to focus his energy as well.

Williams also suggests that, in place of formal minutes, we might want to consider simply summing up verbally who is going to do what and immediately send an e-mail confirmation to everyone right after the meeting.

In a recent address to the North Carolina Center for Nonprofits Conference, Williams offered a startling perspective on board meetings: *Your board should never meet just for the sake of meeting—only when there is something to be done.*

Williams shared that he works hard to be sure his own board members are personally engaged in the Institute's mission. At every meeting, his board spends quality time on a real project, getting their feet muddy so to speak.

They get the chance to interact directly with participants in the organization's programs and to experience the results of their work directly. Williams feels that this experience is by far more valuable to his board than sitting in a meeting, because at the end of the day, he wants his board members to be in action out in the world making friends and connections for the institute.

> *I didn't say it was wrong. I said it was dull. Its sheer competence was staggering. Interest nil. Oddity nil. Singularity nowhere.*
>
> —Alan Bennett

Roberta's Rules of Order: More Fresh Ideas

Alice Collier Cochran has written a wonderful book outlining an alternative to Robert's Rules: *Roberta's Rules of Order: Who Is Robert and Why Do We Still Follow His Rules Anyway?*[10]

A seasoned facilitator and student of successful meetings, Cochran has assembled many useful field-tested techniques and practices for creating interesting, compelling board meetings. Cochran suggests creating a mission-based agenda format that has you identifying the purpose of the meeting and its needed outcomes right from the start.

She points out that traditional procedure has people offering solutions to problems (motions) before the problem is even identified or discussed, and she suggests a more informal format of "proposals" that allows problems to be defined, several options brainstormed, and then the range of options narrowed until a decision is made.

She also suggests such techniques as "straw polls" (which are not allowed under Robert's Rules) to test for agreement in the middle of a discussion. The book provides sample templates for proposals and innovative meeting rules.

Roberta's Rules also call for two additional steps in meetings that would greatly enhance and sustain momentum and enthusiasm: a "wrap up" to the session, centering on "what did we accomplish and now what do we need to do?"

Second, she suggests concluding the meeting with time for off-the-record out-loud reflection on "how well did we do in this meeting, and how can we improve?" These two steps can dramatically enhance a sense of accomplishment—and the board's true owner-ship of the action items they have agreed to in the meeting.

WAYS TO LIVEN UP YOUR BOARD MEETINGS—AND YOUR BOARD

- *Focus the agenda on results.* Look for ways to structure real discussions among board members that will elicit commitment and leadership. Decide what is needed most out of this meeting, set your agenda accordingly, and tell your board members at the beginning of the session why they are present and what you need out of them: "By the end of this meeting, we need to accomplish x, y, and z." That will get their attention.

- *Be creative with the agenda.* Look for ways to tweak the meeting plan to evoke your board members' passion for your cause. Perhaps there's a way of presenting a report that is more song-and-dance and less a dry recital of figures. Think of ways that you can humanize any presentation and really give the board a feel for what the agency is doing.

- *Consider occasionally throwing out the agenda altogether!* Although this may seem a radical approach, consider the benefits: the board can create its own order of busi-ness by consensus at the beginning of the meeting. That way everyone is immediately paying more attention to the work that needs to get accomplished in the meeting. They are not just meeting for routine reporting and discussing; action needs to be taken on real issues *now.*

- *Focus on problems, challenges, or ambiguous issues.* Clearly discussions of this nature will activate your board members' various backgrounds and skills sets, not to mention their interest. It will allow you to draw upon a deeper reservoir of their talent and energy, and will give them more interesting work.

- *Look at trends within routine reports.* Identify larger, big-picture issues that are reflected within routine reports. For example, along with the financial report, consider a discus-sion of long-run implications of certain revenue or cost trends. What are three impor-tant questions anyone might want to ask about this month's financial report? Identify these questions yourself and introduce them to the board as discussion topics. (You will see more on this subject in the discussion of Mission Moments later in this chapter.)

    Also, along with the regular fundraising report, you could schedule a big-picture discussion of the pros and cons of particular fundraising events, which we know to be high cost to everyone, providing a lower financial return than efforts that concen-trate on cultivating major donors. Or you might have the board brainstorm ways to double the funds raised from the annual event. (Wouldn't you love to hear your board grapple with that one?)

- *Plan big.* Bring big-picture strategic planning issues into regular board meetings. For example, you could take the standard strategic planning issues focusing on organizational strengths, weaknesses, opportunities, and threats, (SWOT analysis). Divide the four subjects over four board meetings and at each meeting, take your board through a discussion or update of one of these issues.

- *Look at your board meetings as cheerleading sessions* designed to fire up your board members and put them into action. For these meetings, switch your view to seeing the board as the team that is out on the field, with the role of the staff being to encourage and congratulate them: How would you stage such a session? Identify who would need to speak in order to rev up the energy of your board.

- *Use consent agendas* for routine business items that do not require much board discussion. The list of items can be mailed out in advance and approved in one vote. Any member can ask that a consent agenda item be moved back into the regular agenda for discussion. Good items for handling in this manner are routine committee reports. Provide written reports in the place of lengthy oral reports to save time. Your board has too much important work to do to spend a lot of time listening to routine reports.

- *Interview the CEO.* Occasionally consider allowing time for the board members to interview the CEO about what is on his/her mind. What keeps the CEO up at night? How about a relaxed "fireside chat" with him or her for about 10 minutes at each meeting? What an interesting discussion this could be, and how engaging for board members!

- *Always choose one interesting item and set it up for a discussion.* If you are nervous about turning your board loose and are not sure where the discussion might go, then let a couple of trusted board members know in advance about the planned discussion. Tell them your perspective and what you need from the board's conversation on this issue.

- *Select a theme for each meeting.* For the Alliance for Peacebuilding, CEO Chic Dambach likes to select a theme for each meeting based a particular need or issue facing the organization. He says that this "allows ample time for in-depth analysis of that topic. For particularly important issues, the theme can be repeated over the course of several meetings until the issue has been adequately addressed."

- *Create "mission moments" in every board meeting.* Give your trustees a personal experience of your mission in action. We'll discuss mission moments in depth in just a few pages.

- *Break into groups.* Instead of reporting to board members about an upcoming challenge, present the issue as a question and ask them to discuss it in small groups. Then the board chair can facilitate the full group discussion afterwards. Having small groups enables everyone to speak, encouraging shy people to participate, those who typically avoid speaking to the full board.

> ## TIPS AND TECHNIQUES
>
> **Hint:** Work hard to eliminate handwringing; it is not effective and can backfire, causing board members to back off. People want to be associated with success.
>
> Long-winded discussions about problems and how bad they are will be deadening for morale. Many board members will quickly drift toward pessimism, exercising the "scarcity mentality" that we discuss later in the book. Do what you can to frame conversations in terms of opportunities, without stifling discussion. Create agreement among board members that they will not belabor problems unless they also focus on solutions.

LET THE BOARD MEMBERS DO THE TALKING

Many board experts are recommending a new twist on the traditional board meeting: let the board members themselves do most of the talking.

Consider constructing an agenda that has board members spending 70% of the meeting in group discussions of issues and only 30% of the meeting hearing presentations from staff or committee reports from other board members. I know it is a challenge, but what an interesting and empowering experience this type of meeting would be for your board members!

If your goal is to create participation so that the members will feel valued and involved, then take the initiative to set up ways for them to participate.

If *you* were a board member, would you like to come to a meeting in which your input was not only wanted, it was expected? A meeting in which you actually had something to offer, and could create change and results, rather than just sitting, listening to other people talking? I think it might be an interesting experience, even enjoyable.

I do not know about you, but if I sit through a meeting saying nothing, I wonder if it made any difference whether I was there or not. I think to myself, *"Why did I come? No one would notice if I weren't here, since I have nothing to say and they apparently are not interested in hearing from me."* My next thought: *"I am very busy, and I have better uses of my time. I'll just slip out early."*

We can bet that our disconnected board members are thinking these thoughts, or some that are very similar. That is why they are not showing up in the ways that matter! If the staff does not want to hear what they have to say anyway, if the group culture emphasizes decorum and agreement, and the meetings are nothing but reports, why bother?

> *The least productive people are usually the ones who are most in favor of holding meetings.*
>
> —Thomas Sowell

Think about the important community leaders you would love to have on your board. I will warrant that the more important and busier they are, the less likely they are willing to sit through meetings.

That is why so many of our top leaders will only join advisory boards: they are "too busy" for regular meetings. What they do not say is that they are not willing to attend meetings in which no one wants their ideas.

IN THE REAL WORLD

My client, Wake Education Partnership, had an advisory board of trustees composed of the top leaders in our community. We wanted to bring them together for a session that I would facilitate to get them fired up for fundraising, but we knew if we called this meeting "fundraising training" or "a presentation from a consultant," they would steer clear and not attend.

I suggested that we instead call it "A Conversation about the Future of Wake Ed," expecting that they would want to come to a gathering that was set up for their input and discussion. The members of this panel are too important in the community to simply be "talked at" and instead should be "listened to" (which you could also say is true of anyone).

ENERGIZE MEETINGS WITH MISSION MOMENTS

Our board members need a set of vivid, very personal encounters with our organization as it is actively at work—and with the lives that are being changed or saved in the process.

These Mission Moments are demonstrations, beyond the power of words, of the real meaning of our efforts to fill urgent human needs. They are experiences of personal connection to a greater good.

Mission Moments are the most powerful reminder of the reason an organization exists; they are also reminders of the reason a board member is spending his or her time in service.

We all know the power of testimonials and personal stories. Remember the fundraising rule: If you only have five minutes in front of a donor, you should tell a story. This rule also goes for board members. Just as *donors* are moved by real stories to make gifts, *board members* are moved to action by those same experiences.

IN THE REAL WORLD

A Mission Moment at the Raleigh Rescue Mission

There was a homeless little boy in the day care center at the Rescue Mission who simply would *not* keep his shoes on. It was quite a problem because there was a firm rule that all children must wear shoes in the center. But this cute little kid would take his shoes off, over and over, several times a day.

(continues)

One day a staffer decided to measure the boy's feet. Guess what! His shoes were three sizes too small for his feet! Everyone was stunned, and saddened that they had not realized his plight.

As a fundraising consultant, all I had to do in front of donors was tell this very simple, short, and heartrending story. It perfectly illustrated our case for support and our mission to build a new wing for homeless women and children. One donor even wrote me a $1,000 check on the spot to the Rescue Mission for shoes for the kids.

It is crucial to bring the mission right into the board meetings. Every time there is a significant gathering of board members, let's be sure they have a direct experience of the good work the organization is doing. Better yet, we can bring those who benefit from our organization's work to meetings and let them share their experience directly with our board members.

Try beginning each meeting with a message from the heart that connects board members with the mission and with their own personal passion for that important work.

Designing the Mission Moment

The brief experience of the mission at the start of a meeting—which is essentially a moment of dedication—should connect the board directly to the cause at hand. A story or a letter from a participant or client can set the right tone, creating a transition from a board member's busy life to a different place of a higher calling.

It can remind everyone of why they are serving and, most of all, renew in our board members' hearts and minds the true, deep desires that fuel their passion. The moment can be educational at the same time that it motivates. Let them all learn something at each meeting to help them remember why they are there:

- Share a testimonial or story about how the organization has made an impact in the community.
- Share a success story: have a staff member describe an event that demonstrates how the agency's work has actually affected someone's life.
- Tell a story with a statistic that has a major impact. We should always provide board members with a statistic or two about our work that is powerful enough to blow somebody out of a chair. Be careful of using too many statistics, however; we should remember that a colorful story is easier to remember than a fact or a number.

A board member's personal mission-moment story may tell of the exact time when she realized how deeply committed she was to our cause. I will warrant that they all have such a moment they will never forget. How about asking them to share their personal mission moments? Just imagine how powerful that conversation would be.

> *A mission moment imprints the hearts of those who witness it with an indelible image that expresses, beyond words, the true meaning of the March of Dimes efforts to improve the health of babies by preventing birth defects, premature birth, and infant mortality.*
>
> —Nancy Kennedy[11]

Setting Up Powerful Mission Moment Conversations among Board Members

The most powerful (and empowering) conversation of all is when board members share among themselves why they care enough about the mission to serve on the board. When they share their vision of what speaks to them most personally about your organization's mission, the board members see that they all hold a common vision toward a goal that they all want to achieve.

When visions are truly shared, they lift everyone up and pull them toward some goal. As Peter Senge says in *The Fifth Discipline: The Art & Practice of the Learning Organization,* "a shared vision is a force in people's hearts, a force of impressive power . . . . It is palpable. Few, if any, forces in human affairs are as powerful as shared vision."[12]

This is the conversation to have over and over with your board members. Senge reminds us that talking about their vision is like watering the tree of their passion. They get hooked in again to something they care deeply about. And when board members discover that they share a common vision, they create a true sense of "team."

Help them remember what they are all ultimately trying to accomplish, and you can quickly reinvigorate even the most routine meeting. Or better yet, let them remind themselves why they care. Let them reconnect with "what do we want to create?"

It's best when you have a leader who can inspire your board and galvanize their attention. As Jon Jaworski says in *Synchronicity: The Inner Path of Leadership* (one of my favorite inspirational books) a good leader has the "capacity to inspire people in the group: to move them and encourage them and pull them into the activity, and to help them get centered and focused and operating a peak capacity."[13]

Sometimes I begin meetings or retreats with a simple informal conversation. I ask board members to share why they care enough to be sitting here around the table today, or to say what it is about the organization's mission that speaks to them most personally.

I may ask them to turn to the person next to them and talk about what moves or inspires them. Or I break them into small groups to tell others about their personal perspective on our organization's work. Or I simply go around the room, asking each person to share their story.

If you want to set up this powerful and empowering conversation, you may want to designate someone to lead or facilitate the experience. It is a surprise move: board members are expecting a formal business meeting, and they are very rarely asked to relax and share emotions or personal perspectives.

I contend it is more important to have them talking about their personal passion for the organization's work than it is to hear report after report. You may be amazed to find out what people believe in and what they are willing to do as board members.

TIPS AND TECHNIQUES

Discussion questions that will help reignite your board members enthusiasm for the cause:

- What excites you the most about our organization's work in the world?
- Why are you on this board?
- What do you want to accomplish by serving?
- What are you, as a board member, committed to creating?
- How is this board service helping you achieve your own personal goals?
- What legacy do you want to leave by virtue of serving on this board?

These types of discussions can be a valuable source of information for the staff. Be sure to pay close attention to what really turns board members on and where their personal interests are. Remember: if fundraising is about developing relationships, then it is a smart move to be working hardest and first on developing relationships with your board members.

Create a Sense of Community and Collegiality

Social time helps to develop healthy relationships and a sense of collegiality among board members. Your board is, in fact, a social unit, not unlike a small community. It is a team in many ways. Its work requires members to create interrelationships with each other as they work together toward the common good.

The board's informal social time together may be *more valuable* than the formal proceedings. Often the casual conversations during breaks or lunch can foster deeper discussions of important issues as well as closer relationships among board members.

Michael Guillot of the North Carolina Symphony suggests that we should build social time into our "meetings and retreat planning from the start. It's time to abandon old-fashioned ways of agenda preparation and create some open air-time for informal discussions. And during your retreats, use the overnight cocktail/dinner time to put board members at the same table who do not often talk—give them plenty of time to discuss what really matters."

A strong sense of community will bolster your board members' ability to coalesce around critical work. It will also help engender a common bond and passion toward their goal, supporting your organization's mission.

When the board members share this sense of collegiality, they create a positive atmosphere that helps to find common ground, promote thoughtful discourse, and foster trust and respect for each other. Now that is a powerful team!

When your board members feel a clear sense of "we are all in this together, united for an important purpose," they will be more willing to put their shoulders to the wheel and raise some money.

They will not work well together if they do not know each other. How can they wade through difficult discussions, honoring all viewpoints to create consensus, if they do not know who is doing the talking?

Pity the poor new member who does not know everyone, and pleasantly sits through meetings, wondering who all these people are and how he or she fits into this group. Does he or she feel truly welcomed and socially supported? Will this new board member feel welcome to offer his or her input? How much talent are you wasting when board members hang back because they are unsure of their acceptance in the group?

Once I joined the board of a prominent "old-school" organization associated with the Episcopal church. The doyenne who enlisted me to take her place said, "of course you know, the first year, you shouldn't say anything on this board." Unfortunately (or fortunately) I offered my opinion sooner than the first 12 months!

Scheduling social time among board members is an absolute must that is too often ignored in the effort to use board members' time expeditiously and wisely. It is important to be focused and efficient, but the down time is equally vital. The coffee time before the meeting can be as essential as the real business meeting of your board.

In fact, this same organization routinely held a most valuable coffee hour before each board meeting. Trustees worked hard to get there in time because that was the opportunity for informal socializing. I would always find out the background on the hot issues at coffee or lunch, certainly not at the formal meeting!

Noreen Strong, CEO of the Ronald McDonald House of Durham, NC, has a challenge just getting her board members to know each other because her board only meets four times a year. Additional social time after meetings helps make this happen:

"Our trustees look forward to networking with each other over lunch following each meeting. We have found a donor who provides lunch after each quarterly meeting—the meetings begin at 11 A.M. and end at 12:30. Some members rush out, but most typically have an after-the-meeting 'agenda' of their own with their peers or with staff."

Help Your Board Members to Enjoy Themselves

Life is short and volunteer hours are precious. Your busy board members have many, many other demands on their spare time. The time they are spending with your organization could otherwise be spent with their families or their friends, on their hobbies and interests, their health, or simply relaxing. But they are choosing to spend these valuable hours with your organization.

We must always keep in mind that people want to have a good time whenever they possibly can! If your organization can offer pleasant social experiences, your board members might come to meetings, not just out of duty, but also out of enjoyment. You will find that, when they are having a good time, they are happier to spend time with you—and they will work more effectively together as a team.

IN THE REAL WORLD

I have to admit that when I serve on a board, one of the main reasons I like to come to meetings is to see some of my friends. We are all so hopelessly busy that at least I know I will be able to spend some time with them there. I look forward to meetings because I like helping the organization, and I like the people on the board!

Board members should have an experience of actually enjoying their volunteer experience with you. They also deserve the opportunity to have a pleasant time (certainly not an unpleasant time!) in their valuable time off.

Make Sure All Board Members Get to Know Each Other

Remember, as we have discussed, board members like to get to know the other members of the board for many reasons. *If they are strangers to each other, how can they work effectively as a group to make wise decisions guiding your organization?* How can they approach fundraising as a shared team experience and not as lone rangers? How can they support each other as teammates?

Remember to acknowledge the reality of what your board members really want—and try to give it to them. Don't forget the social aspect of board membership. Remember that your board members want to meet each other and make new business and social contacts.

IN THE REAL WORLD

When I was Director of Development at the Kenan Flagler Business School, I made a real point to always introduce board members to each other and help foster relationships among board members. I would introduce the real estate developer from Atlanta to the investment banker from New York, knowing they may even want to do some business together. The board members understood what I was doing for them and always appreciated this. Our board meetings became quite important events, not only for their content but also for their social aspect.

HAVE SOME FUN!

Fun is not what board members expect. Our sector typically approaches "doing good work" as an obligation rather than for enjoyment. The term "do-gooders" is not a particularly positive descriptor. However, there is no rule that says nonprofit work has to be dreary, difficult, and no fun.

Creating some enjoyment would be an unexpected and much appreciated benefit. Life is busy and stressful enough as it is and people desperately want to enjoy themselves.

Also, there is a benefit to creating a sense of fun: you will be surprised at the energy and excitement people will bring to your cause. You may find that it is easier to recruit new board members if the word is out that your board is a "congenial group."

Someone told me recently about a board that shared a great sense of humor. They had established a rule that no one could speak for more than three minutes. The board chair, who clearly had a sense of play, obtained some Nerf balls that she could shoot with a Nerf gun. When someone on the board got long-winded, she would shoot them with the gun! This created much glee—and camaraderie—among her board members!

How to Create Social Experiences for Your Board Members to Get to Know Each Other

- Routinely have a coffee time for half an hour before the board meeting; it can be coffee with staff and volunteers or an appropriate constituency your organization serves. Make coffee time important by including it in the meeting notice for board meetings.

- Schedule down time during board meetings or retreats. One of my clients invites members to dinner before every evening meeting. The board members enjoy casual, collegial personal time with each other before they do business together.

- Schedule "simply socials" once a year. But you must make them special so that board members will want to come—perhaps even dinner or cocktails at someone's home or at a restaurant. (Find a board member who is willing to underwrite this.)

At the Alliance for Peacebuilding in Washington DC, CEO Chic Dambach has started arranging dinners or receptions for his board the evening before board meetings. Dambach says, "It builds a sense of community, and it breaks down potential animosity before the meeting even begins."

Dambach also mentioned that, as a consultant, he once had a client whose board went to the theater together the night before every board meeting! It was a church-based senior citizen service organization. "Everyone loved it. It helped the board work well together, and it made board recruitment much easier."

Name Tags Are Absolutely Essential

Providing name tags is good manners; it is simply a courteous thing to do. However, I am continually surprised at how often it is overlooked at board meetings.

It is a particular boon to new members of the board so they can get to know the others. When staff members also wear name tags, it helps board members know who the employees are and be more willing to ask them questions.

Recently I was meeting with two new board members of a local rape crisis center. They had volunteered to head up the all important Development Committee, and they offered valuable new talent to the board. These new members revealed to me that they actually had no idea who all the people were on the board, because no name tags were used at meetings.

Name tags, however often neglected, are an absolute must for every board function. There should not be any excuse for ignoring this essential aid to your board.

TIPS AND TECHNIQUES

Name Tags as Conversation Starters

"I never realized what a fabulous conversation starter a name tag could be; my board members now ask where the name tags are when I don't bring them to board meetings. To some degree, they laugh at the tags—but I know they use them. I've caught them craning their necks to read new members' names!"

—Andrea Farage, Executive Director; Ronald McDonald
House Charities of Northwest Florida

Status Is an Unavoidable Issue with Some Nonprofit Boards

Being invited to sit on some boards conveys a certain social status. It is a fact of life in our business and we need to be realistic about it. Just be careful that people joining your board have a passion for your mission as well as a desire to make social connections.

If social prestige is associated with your organization's board, then accept it and use it as a tool to enlist active, committed, and engaged people to serve. Be glad that your board carries the cachet that allows you to attract the people who can make a difference for your organization in the community. You can get a lot of good work for your mission out of the fact that a position on your board is considered an honor and not a burden.

Remember, fundraising is all about gathering influence and power to make good things happen for your community. You want folks with access, affluence, and connections, who have the clout to help solve pressing problems and make your community a better place. If social status is a factor, recognize it and let it work for you to create more good for your community.

YOUR ROLE IN GENTLY LEADING YOUR BOARD

Regardless of how strong or weak your board is, you as staff can take responsibility for helping to develop a more active board that is deeply engaged in the mission. Leaving it all up to the board chair can bring disaster, as staff members reading this book already know.

Too many CEOs carefully shy away from what they consider the "board's arena." However, it is important to remember that busy board members often count on staff, who are closest to the organization, to point out challenges and opportunities proactively that the board may be missing—and to help bring the board members together as a team.

Don't abdicate your responsibilities where the board is concerned. Practice leadership; just make sure to practice it behind the scenes.

The suggestions about boards in this chapter require the CEO and Development Director to take an active leadership role in helping to develop the board. It is up to all of us as staff to help identify new board members, to arrange board social time, and to help create interesting board meetings and offer satisfying experiences for the board members.

In fact, each of us can have a great impact on how the board members individually perceive their experience of serving. If we choose to make the effort, we will be rewarded with a board that is active, interested, and much more willing to tackle fundraising.

In contrast, the staff members who take a hands-off approach to managing their board are frequently disappointed with the results, especially in recruiting new members. Again and again, I find myself encouraging staff members not to hold back, and to bring their suggestions for new board members front and center to the nominating committee.

Staff members are in an excellent position to find good board candidates, in the course of their days representing the organization out in the community. They may have a better sense than many board members of potential new members who are both passionate about the nonprofit's mission and powerful in the community. Don't hold back!

The CEO and other staff should exercise leadership, but, again, offer it carefully and behind the scenes, where the board is concerned.

HIGHLIGHTS OF STEP ONE

Focus on the Mission

- What it takes to create real change—in people or organizations.
- Incremental change is slow, representing small steps toward a goal.
- Transformational change is a sudden major shift leading to dramatically improved performance.
- Focus on the Mission to Inspire board members.
- Consider what each board member wants out of his service.
- Emphasize outcomes and results instead of process.
    - What do we have to do this month, this year?
- Give board members substantive work to do.
    - Let them deal with the exciting discussions of consequence.

(continues)

HIGHLIGHTS OF STEP ONE (CONTINUED)

- Create meaningful board meetings with agendas that matter.
  - Shift away from Robert's Rules.
  - Bring big-picture strategic issues into board meetings.
- Let the board members do the talking.
  - Let them talk 70% of the time in board meetings.
- Energize meetings with "mission moments."
  - Set up powerful mission-moment conversations among board members.
- Create a sense of community and collegiality among board members.
  - Be sure all board members get to know each other.
  - Have fun whenever possible.
  - Name tags are essential.
- You have an important role to play behind the scenes in gently leading your board.

NOTES

1. Peter Senge, *The Dance of Change: The Challenges to Sustaining Momentum in Learning Organizations* (New York: Doubleday, 1999).
2. Margaret Wheatley, *Leadership and the New Science* (San Francisco: Berrett-Koehler, 1999), 164.
3. Bernard Ross, *Breakthrough Thinking for Nonprofit Organizations* (San Francisco: Jossey-Bass, 2002).
4. Ibid.
5. Ibid.
6. Richard P. Chait, William P. Ryan, and Barbara E. Taylor, *Governance as Leadership: Reframing the Work of Nonprofit Boards* (Hoboken, NJ: John Wiley & Sons, 2005).
7. Peter Senge, *The Fifth Discipline: The Art & Practice of the Learning Organization* (New York: Doubleday, 1990).
8. Bernard Ross, *Breakthrough Thinking for Nonprofit Organizations.*
9. Richard P. Chait, William P. Ryan, and Barbara E. Taylor, *Governance as Leadership: Reframing the Work of Nonprofit Boards.*
10. Alice Collier Cochran: *Roberta's Rules of Order: Who Is Robert and Why Do We Still Follow His Rules Anyway?* (San Francisco: Jossey-Bass, 2004).
11. Nancy Kennedy, "Saving Premature Babies Is a Mission with Passion at the March of Dimes," *Western Pennsylvania Hospital News,* July 2006.
12. Peter Senge, *The Fifth Discipline: The Art & Practice of the Learning Organization.*
13. Jon Jaworski, *Synchronicity, the Inner Path of Leadership* (San Francisco: Berrett-Koehler Publishers, 1998), 66.

CHAPTER 3

Passion-Driven Fundraising Step Two: INSPIRE Your Board Members with a New Philosophy of Fundraising

How wonderful it is that one can start doing good at this moment.

—Anne Frank

FUNDRAISING IS CHANGING THE WORLD FOR THE BETTER

When we ask board members to help with this activity called fundraising, what are we really requesting of them? What do they think they are being asked to do? Do they really understand how powerful the act of raising money can be? Do they know what good they are creating through their efforts to build friends and connections for their cause?

In the largest context, fundraising is an effort to make the world a better place. It is some of the most important work anyone can ever do. When we come together to raise resources in order to serve others in need, we are putting ourselves right there on the front lines causing change for the good.

I believe fundraising is one of the noblest and most altruistic activities a human can undertake. Everything we do as fundraisers is for the betterment of mankind. I wish everybody on our planet would dedicate some of their time to raising resources to make their communities and the world a better place.

But as we have discussed, many trustees of our nonprofit organizations are caught up in self-defeating myths and stories that they are making up about fundraising. They are stuck in what Kay Sprinkel Grace calls, in her book *Beyond Fundraising,* "the tin cup" attitude—equating fundraising with begging.[1] Instead of the highest form of human activity—they make it into one of the lowest!

We have to understand that those who hold the "tin cup" view aren't trained like we are; they have no exposure to the philosophy and methods that we know and practice so well. Let's identify their myths and mistaken assumptions so we can blow them up, and set up these good-hearted, well-meaning, and powerful board members to approach fundraising from a whole new place.

Since board members equate fundraising with asking for money or worse, with begging for money, we need to turn their ideas completely around. We need to give them a whole new perspective about raising money that is on a much higher plane, with a far more empowering and inspirational point of view. When we change their perspective about fundraising, it also shifts their sense of themselves as board members and what they can or cannot accomplish.

We forget the deeper purpose of fundraising: it is really helping to create good in the world—making the world a better place. Fundraising is emphatically *not* begging or taking advantage of people.

Fundraising is actually inspiring others to join with us to help create positive change in our world and our communities. We are taking action to solve important problems and make things better.

> *Without deep reflection one knows from daily life that one exists for other people.*
>
> —Albert Einstein

If we want to turn around our board members' point of view about fundraising, we will need to present this persuasively. This is the way to take board members from fear to *understanding* and open the door for *willingness*. We will completely transform their point of view. Fundraising is *not* about asking for money at all; it is about the board members' vision for making their communities a better place. Fundraising is really "making friends to change the world." And it can be exciting, engaging, even fun.

In this chapter, we will first look at our board members' myths and worries about fundraising. Then we will the cover five major ideas that will help transform a board member's negative perspective on fundraising and awaken new energy for your organization.

First: Fundraising Is Changing the World for the Better. We will redefine fundraising into an entirely new and much bigger philosophy: changing the world. We will introduce a new, much more comfortable fundraising role for board members who are afraid of soliciting: *being ambassadors and making friends.*

Second: Fundraising Need Not Be Scary. We will deal directly with their fears. We will give them the opportunity to get over their mental blocks by having an honest, open discussion about their nervousness or anxiety about fundraising.

Third: Giving Is a Joyous Experience. We will introduce them to the joy and pleasure donors feel when they make a gift that can create a change for the better. How did the board members themselves feel the last time they made a contribution to a nonprofit organization? Was it pleasurable? Was it powerful or joyful? We discuss the perennial question, "why do people give?" from the perspective of educating the board members.

Fourth: Fundraising Is Full of Power. We will move them to action by using a number of tools already at hand: the power of a shared vision; the contagiousness of excitement; others' admiration for those who work (as they do) without pay, motivated by the desire to help; and the tradition in the New World democracies of citizens banding together to solve community problems.

Fifth: The Expectation of Abundance, Not Scarcity, Will Bring New and Greater Resources. We will shift their expectation of what is possible with a new point of view about abundance instead of scarcity. There is enough! We will tackle head on the perennial, self-defeating scarcity conversation with board members—and change their perspective permanently.

BOARD MEMBERS' MYTHS AND PROBLEMS WITH FUNDRAISING

These stories include many unpleasant thoughts I'm sure you have heard or, on a bad day, even personally felt:

- "Fundraising is nothing but genteel begging."
- "Fundraising is distasteful and unpleasant."
- "Asking for money is invasive."
- "Asking takes advantage of people and friendships."
- "Fundraising is scary—I don't understand how to go about it."
- "I am afraid of rejection."

Fundraising Is the F-Word to Many Board Members

We all know who these board members are. They are the ones who, to our frustration, say, "I'm giving my time and that is enough." We all know of the wealthy board member who can open every door in town yet who, as one once told me, say "I'll do anything but fundraising; don't even talk to me about it."

These folks are so fearful of fundraising that just the mention of the F-word causes their automatic blocks and defense mechanisms to jump up. They sometimes shy away when the development director just opens his mouth for help.

Can you picture what happens when that staff member asks the board, for example, to help bring in sponsors for an event? Because the words are coming out of the development director's mouth, a lot of board members automatically think: "Yuck, fundraising, I can't do that!"

I've seen the same request come from someone not associated with fundraising, and the board members were more apt to respond freely and enthusiastically offer support and help.

I've had to work hard to focus our board on what they can do in fundraising instead of what they feared they couldn't do.

—Linda Reynolds, Director of Development,
Children's Theatre, Charlotte, NC

The "Nice" Issue Is Particularly Hard to Counter

Remember the "code of nice" we discussed earlier? For better or worse, niceness pervades nonprofit boards—and board members! Many board members think that polite people do not talk about money. Above all, they want to appear appropriate and seemly, never, ever obnoxious.

In nice company, it has always been considered bad form to talk about other people's money, how much they make, or how much they are worth (although there sure are a lot of people who love to talk about that subject anyway!). I have often joked that my mother would be embarrassed to know that in my fundraising role, I have been known to talk about other people's money all day long.

What board members do not understand is that the conversation is not about money *per se*; it is really about the important work you are trying to accomplish in the world and what resources you need to succeed. Let's change their point of view about what fundraising really is.

My board members have trouble overcoming their own fears about asking people for money. These range from not wanting to be rejected to not wanting to 'damage' relationships. When people enter into their fundraising overcome with these fears, they are rarely successful!

—Rob Katz, Chair, The Legacy Foundation

In the book *Boards that Love Fundraising,* Zimmerman and Lehman zero right in on board members who view fundraising with fear and trepidation, who think it is "invasive and obnoxious."[2]

(By the way, I think this excellent book may be misnamed, because the title perpetuates what is, in my experience, an unreachable ideal. I doubt that there will ever be boards that really love fundraising. They do it because they want to help their organizations make a difference and carry out their missions, not because they love the fundraising in itself. But I highly recommend the book itself as an excellent guide.)

Our work is so very important that *"we mustn't let embarrassment about money get in the way,"*[3] as these authors so aptly put it. We cannot possibly let embarrassment stop us, because we are trying to solve urgent problems in the world that must be dealt with right now.

I'm sorry, but if children are dying in our streets, then saving them is too important and urgent to be set aside because of politeness.

Many Board Members Worry about Taking Advantage of Their Friends and Contacts

Many trustees feel it is inappropriate to bring money up into the conversation. They think, as Zimmerman and Lehman describe, that it will be "trading unethically on a friendship."[4]

They forget about their dear friend Joyce, who biked for muscular sclerosis and e-mailed hundreds of her friends and contacts to sponsor her for the ride. They forget how quickly they followed the link to support their friend. They forget what a pleasure it was to help her, and the important cause as well. They forget how much they celebrated with her when she was successful, and how pleased they were when she won the prize for the most funds raised. Did they think they were being "used" for their friendship? Of course not!

Instead, board members mythologize that it is weird to ask their friends and contacts for help. But if they act strangely about it, they will certainly come across as awkward and inappropriate.

Remember, you bring your perspective into everything that you do—what you envision becomes true for you. So if you envision something to be awkward and embarrassing, you will certainly appear awkward and embarrassed to your friend.

However, if board members make fundraising conversations into something important, urgent, and positive, full of passion and excitement, then they will experience those efforts as important tasks with energy and momentum of their own.

> *Become a possibilitarian. No matter how dark things seem to be or actually are, raise your sights and see possibilities—always see them, for they're always there.*
>
> —Norman Vincent Peale

Board members are worried about the quid pro quo: if they venture to ask a friend for a contribution to their organization, they expect that the friend will counter by asking them for a contribution to his or her favorite organization.

Yes, that is how business is done these days by powerful people who tackle worthy causes. If you do someone a favor by supporting their cause, this will, in fact, set you up as someone who takes action to support people and who cares about your community.

Yes, you can expect to be asked to support other worthy causes. And then, guess what? You will be viewed as a powerful person in your community who makes things happen, the kind of person who can help solve urgent problems, who makes a difference in valuable ways, who is influential. Exactly the kind of person your cause needs on its board.

Board Members Do Not Know What to Say about the Organization

In spite of all the help we give them—messaging practice, fact sheets, materials, brochures, talking points—board members are still tongue-tied and do not know what to say. Their knowledge of our case for support is often weak, to say the least. No wonder they are shy about talking up our organization in the community.

*I just don't know what to say when I try to talk about our organization
to my friends! Do I talk about what it does, or the impact that it makes,
or my experience as a board member supporting its mission?*

—Nonprofit Board Member

We need to give our trustees *practice* talking about our good work in the world, including positive results that happen as a result of our organization's mission. The elevator speech exercise, which we take up in the next section, is a fun way to practice messaging, liven up a board meeting, and reengage everyone's passion for the mission.

The Biggest Myth of All: Fundraising Is Just Asking for Money!

- If we can understand that board members deliberately equate "fundraising" with "asking," then we can counter by reminding them that they are up to something vitally important: making a powerful difference in the world.

- If they have a fear of "asking," and are stuck in their negative energy about it, then we can introduce them to the inspirational aspect of fundraising that transcends personal fears and hesitations, and focuses on the worthiness of trying to change the world.

- If they think that bringing the money discussion into a friendship or business relationship is inappropriate and even unethical, then we can remind them how rewarding it is to help out a friend and colleague and how much they naturally want to help their friends.

I agree with Lynne Twist's point of view. In her audio-video course, *Fundraising from the Heart,* Twist (author of *The Soul of Money*) has it right on: Fundraising "is a joyous, honorable, thrilling and brilliant way to use your time."[5]

Why? Because when we raise funds, we are gathering the resources to take care of a problem that needs solving—and the problem usually centers on something vitally important, kids, the elderly, families, students, animals, nature. Or it may be something that we human beings value and treasure, such as our history or our future.

Fundraising has a profoundly important philosophical base. Why do we do our work? Because nonprofits provide, as Kay Sprinkel Grace says, "Meaning and hope and social change, offering people an opportunity to become involved with something that is purposeful and powerful."[6]

Lynne Twist is a passionate advocate of the inspirational power of fundraising: "if you bring joy, privilege and honor to fundraising, it will always be productive and fulfilling."

She goes on to say: "When you ask people to invest . . . in a new future, you honor them by asking them to risk, to take a stand, to cause something unpredictable to happen." I particularly like the way she values the act of soliciting, describing it as "asking people to invest." Her definition really does raise the bar and makes it an important, powerful, even transforming act.[7]

Many people say that soliciting is a transformative act because it dramatically converts a conversation of ideas to an action that will cause positive change. The act of giving is a transforming experience, because the donor does take a stand, as Lynne Twist says, participating with the solicitor to create a change for the better.

We know that people want to make a difference, and they want to use their time, their money, and their energy to help create something of value. Donors want that, and board members want that. It is our job to show them the way, to give them the opportunity to unlock their power, energy, and money to fulfill this dream.

Give me a place to stand and I will move the world.

—Archimedes

Proud to Be a Fundraiser!

Here's my personal point of view: I know that I am making a difference. My personal mission is to change the world for the better in any way I can. The mission of my business, Gail Perry Associates, is to empower and inspire as many people as possible to change the world through their nonprofit organizations.

The way I carry out my mission is to equip nonprofit leaders with fundraising and management skills and inspire them with new energy and confidence to make a difference. I can have a stronger influence for the good by working through other people. I feel I am doing something that matters in a huge way.

Board members want to make a difference too. If you can get them to understand that fundraising is a powerful activity, that it creates ways to solve very important and urgent problems in the world, then those board members will start to shift their perspective.

Becoming allied with something important in life is a wonderful aspect of giving—and of soliciting. Contributing and raising money, and becoming part of important causes is a vital and important activity, one that gives meaning to many people's lives.

The Healing Power of Doing Good, by Allan Luks with Peggy Payne, talks about the largeness of spirit that helping others confers on the helper. The study of religions shows "what so many of us have learned for ourselves: that giving to others is the farthest thing from self-denial. It is an enhancement of the self. As we give to others, we give also to ourselves—physically, emotionally, and spiritually."[8]

As fundraisers, we are offering donors an opportunity to be part of something bigger than they are. Something that will live on after they are gone. Something with profound meaning that touches the heart.

We offer this unique and important experience to our donors. When a donor makes a gift, he or she becomes a partner in a cause that is bigger than just one person's life. That donor's life and legacy are enhanced.

To work for important purposes, to take part in solving problems of great magnitude gives deeper meaning even to daily routines. People want to be involved in something with meaning.

Board members are surprised to hear this, or at least they have not thought of fundraising in this way—it is giving others a very special opportunity to connect with something deeply important.

Putting fundraising on this high a plane is a new idea to them. It gives them fresh inspiration and energy to take action for their own organizations. You would be surprised to see their attitudes shift after this discussion.

> I do not want to talk about what you understand about this world. I want to know what you will do about it. I do not want to know what you hope. I want to know what you will work for. I do not want your sympathy for the needs of humanity. I want your muscle. As the wagon driver said when they came to a long, hard hill 'them that's going on with us, get out and push. Them that ain't, get out of the way.'
>
> —Robert Fulghum, It Was on Fire
> When I Lay Down on It[9]

Lynne Twist says that when people are in touch with their own vision of the difference they make, and if they see that an organization's work really does make a difference, then they are happy to respond to an opportunity to invest.

I love the way she talks about a fundraiser's role in empowering donors to be "prime movers—to generate, catalyze, found, invent; to make possible a beginning of something."[10]

Forgive me when I get on my soapbox, but I feel deeply that we are engaged in a significant and powerful activity, one that is meaningful beyond all measure. When I think about homeless children, kids who want an education, people who have never seen a play or felt the heart-expanding touch of good art, the elderly in need, you name it—I am concerned and glad to help any way I can. And I will ask others do to so in a heartbeat. What a far cry from thinking that fundraising is obnoxious!

TIPS AND TECHNIQUES

What Is Fundraising?

- It is about getting the community behind your mission.
- It is making friends for your organization.
- It is about solving important problems.
- It is bringing in resources to help change the world.

Fundraising is *very* important work. Board members are sometimes startled to hear it presented in this light. When I explain that it is all about making something important happen, then they start to shift away from their fears to a more empowered, inspired point of view.

GET EVERYBODY ON YOUR BANDWAGON

I tell board members that their job is not necessarily to solicit — it is to get the whole community on their bandwagon, and they instantly understand this image. They smile and nod when they visualize their friends all hanging off that wagon—and they start thinking about how to get everyone they know on there with them! They start to think: If that is what fundraising is all about, then maybe I can do that.

Charge up the mountain! I tell board members that they are like leaders charging up the mountain, carrying a flag for their cause. They are making friends, rallying folks, and rounding up the troops to join them. Their cause is urgently important. People will help them because they want to see the cause addressed.

Board members forget that people (donors, their friends, community leaders, politicians, potential donors) all actually *want* to help. These folks are just as concerned as board members about community problems.

People will help if they are shown a way and asked for their help. People want to align their financial resources with what is meaningful to them, with what Lynne Twist calls "their deepest commitments."[11]

Board members immediately understand these metaphors and start to remember that they *are* the leaders in the community for their organizations, and it is *their job* to load up the bandwagon.

When I tell a board that the community is looking to them to solve the problem at hand, the members are surprised. In other people's eyes, the board members are the community representatives who "own" the mission of the organization. The community actually *expects* board members to ask them to support this important issue.

TIPS AND TECHNIQUES

Fundraising Is More Than Asking

- It is supporting a vision of a better world.
- It is about your mission, not money.
- It comes from the heart.

The people in our towns do not want to see, for example, the local Ronald McDonald House turning away children and their families; they do not want to see their water quality deteriorate; they do not want needy people in their own community to be neglected. They are counting on the board members of nonprofit organizations to lead the way and let them know what resources are needed to solve these problems.

These board leaders are more powerful to the community than they ever realize!

Get Your Board Busy Raising Friends

A friend may well be reckoned the masterpiece of nature.

—Ralph Waldo Emerson

As fundraisers, what we really need our board members to do, above all else, is to be active in the community on behalf our organization. This can mean lots of things: talking up the organization; introducing new people to its work; bringing in friends and volunteers to help in different ways; and, yes, helping to acquire money and resources.

It is easy to assume that the real work is the direct solicitation of funds, but "the talking up" part of the job is equally important. If a nonprofit is a bright spot on its community's radar screen, so to speak, then that visibility will make the fundraising so much easier and more successful.

The larger the number of people who have been personally introduced to the work we do, the better we fare. The more friends our board members can make for our cause, the stronger and more successful our work is.

I agree with Hildy Gottlieb's perspective in her inspirational new book, *FriendRaising: Community Engagement Strategies for Boards Who Hate Fundraising but Love Making Friends.* "When you engage with members of your community in real friendship—not that euphemism for wanting their money, but true friendship—your community will never let your mission die. . . . You will have a community working together (with you) to build a better place to live."[12]

Let us focus our board members on FriendRaising. The point of FriendRaising, Gottleib points out, is to engage your community by creating friends. In an article on her Web site, Help4Nonprofits.com, she says, "If you have friends, they will help in ways you never dreamed possible. They will want to see good things happen. . . . Friends share all their gifts with the organization, and are thrilled that the organization sees value in those gifts! They give what they have, whatever that is—and yes, quite often, it is even money. But it is not only money. It is usually far more."[13]

I say we take soliciting out of the picture and get our board members hard at work developing friendly relationships for our organization all over the community, state, region, world—wherever our mission takes us. There are so many activities related to fundraising (outside of soliciting) in which we need their help.

For those on a board who are not ready to take on solicitation, we can ask them to do everything else in the fundraising cycle: help create new friends and supporters, and help thank and involve current donors. FriendRaising is something all board members like to do, and are proud to do—and it is a *most* valuable and needed fundraising function.

If you set up a committee and call it the FriendRaising Committee, board members will probably be enthusiastic, and the effect of the group's efforts will be powerful and lasting.

As Hildy Gottlieb says on her Web site, "The only road to sustainability is to engage the community in your work, to turn that community into an army of friends, spreading the roots of ownership of your mission and vision throughout."Your army of friends "would not dream of letting your mission die. And as the link to the community, that is a job board members can do without fear."[14]

A nonprofit organization called Interact, a rape crisis center and battered women's shelter in Raleigh, formed a committee called the "Fun Raisers."Their job was to organize a series of "Friend Raiser" events designed to introduce new friends to the organization. Their major objectives were to increase the size of their mailing list and to secure some new donors for the organization.

The Fun Raisers committee had lots of fun. They also created six Friend Raiser events over a six-month period that drew well over 100 attendees each, none of which cost Interact a dime. As a result their fundraising mailing list grew from very few names to ultimately several thousand. And gifts to the organization went up!

> *The energy of the volunteers on this committee was fantastic. They had ownership of each event, which led to incredible creativity and efforts on their parts.*
>
> —Adam Hartzell, Executive Director of Interact

Let us make all our board members "friend raisers" —regardless of whether they are soliciting—and train them to be ambassadors representing our organizations.

FUNDRAISING NEED NOT BE SCARY: DEAL WITH THEIR FEARS DIRECTLY

Putting fundraising on a much higher plane is not the whole solution. Some board members may still be hanging onto the "cringe factor" when we raise the topic of the F-word. What will it take to handle these deeply harbored, unpleasant feelings of dread that can keep your board members stuck and afraid of anything that smacks of fundraising?

Changing these stubbornly persistent attitudes takes specific conversations with your board. It takes an open and honest discussion of feelings. It also needs a special environment, probably a retreat, to encourage these board members to let go and speak freely.

Sometimes, particularly for grassroots organizations, it is important to have an open conversation about money and power. Again, laying personal feelings and points of view out on the table is critical if your board members are going to get over their private blocks and on to becoming active ambassadors for your organization.

This section shows you how to set up an opportunity for women and men on your board to talk—head-on—about their fear and discomfort with fundraising. You will learn how to counter the fear with a discussion about the joy of giving, the joy of making a difference, and the powerfully transforming experience of giving to support something important.

Included here is a discussion of why people give. As experienced fundraisers, we all know this basic information—but your board members do not. We will talk about how to

TIPS AND TECHNIQUES

When board members see fundraising as both a means of improving the world and a source of profound joy and satisfaction, they will view this work from a whole new perspective.

present this information to them, as a happy and positive follow-up that counters the "fear of fundraising" discussion.

In the course of this multipart, highly focused conversation with your board, you will first lead them deep into the dark forest of their anxious feelings about asking, and then back out to the sunshine where they are more comfortable and at ease, possibly more at ease in some ways than ever before. They will emerge from this experience in a more powerful place because, with your help, they'll have rid themselves of a hindrance to fundraising, to asking, and to receiving.

Psychology 101: A Fundamental Principle That Underlies This Work

There is an important concept in psychology about dealing with feelings that are blocked. If you hold unpleasant feelings suppressed and bottled up inside, these emotions never dissipate. They may even grow. However, if you bring them to light and discuss them openly, then they are likely to fade away and dissolve. Certainly they will become less intense.

Think of the last time you were angry with someone. If you stuffed the feeling in, then the anger stayed with you. It simmered. It bothered you. It kept cropping up. You may have tried to ignore your feelings, but since you had not sorted them through and aired them out, they lingered and festered.

However, if you had the confidence, courage, or boldness to bring up the hot topic and discuss it with the person who offended you, then your anger dissipated. If you cared enough about the person to talk about it, then you worked through the situation.

Sounds easy, but it takes guts. This is why there are so many shrinks in business today. People who want to work through old, stuck feelings are *talking* about them in order to process them and let them go.

It is crucially important to the success and growth of your nonprofit that your board members have an open, honest talk about their fundraising feelings. Encourage them to get all their bad energy about fundraising out on the table, every bit of it! In fact, encourage them to "throw up" if they need to—to rant and rave, if they want to.

You MUST Allow Your Board Members to Speak Bluntly about Their Fears and Objections

Please note that I am not saying that *you* should talk to them about their fears, I am saying that you will allow *them* to do the talking about how *they* feel.

This is how you can successfully handle these fears: by going straight to the source of their discomfort. Bring the painful problem out on the table and into the light of day. Tackle this in the time-honored way of talking through any tough subject—by staying with the conversation.

Remember all the advice earlier in this book about letting your board members talk? Well, here is a perfect place to begin.

> *Often, when people have their feelings and opinions acknowledged*
> *respectfully, then they can move on.*
>
> —Debbie Grammer, Development Services
> Director, Wake Health Services, Inc.

In my retreats, if we do not deal directly and successfully with fears of fundraising, then some trustees will sit through the training all day, with their inner voices loud in their ears, saying, *"I just can't do this. I'll pretend to go along."*

We are not dealing with a logical situation here. We all know that feelings too often do not make sense. The head is saying one thing: *"Sure, that's okay."* And all the while the gut is saying: *"No, not me!"*

I remember how relieved I felt when I read Thomas Moore's *Care of the Soul,* which discussed how deep feelings are often not completely logical. I was not the only one! Not only are deep feelings often conflicting, Moore wrote, but they can be inherently contradictory and inconsistent.[15]

So, my own inner jumble of opposing thoughts was perfectly appropriate and normal. However, and importantly, I do need to be aware of them, and, as needed, unburden myself.

A CONVERSATION ABOUT DISCOMFORT WITH FUNDRAISING

IN THE REAL WORLD

Here is how a retreat can set the stage for frank talk about fundraising fears.

A retreat with the board of the Pan American Development Foundation:

"How do you feel about fundraising?" I asked. "No, really, how do you personally feel about raising and soliciting funds? Most people are nervous about it. Let's do an exercise just for fun. Turn to the person next to you and share for a minute or two how you really feel. This is your chance to get it all out on the table. You can vomit if you want to." Big laugh.

They start the exercise, sharing their feelings about fundraising with a neighbor. More smiles. They're starting to like this, having the chance to talk. How unusual. Clearly not board business as usual.

(continues)

Animated conversation begins among staff and board members. I start to see some brows furrow. A look of urgency on some faces. Distaste showing. People are gesturing with their hands as they speak. Folks are pretty passionate about this. They are doing more talking than most of them have had a chance to do at a board meeting so far. They like this talking to each other. The room is full of the power in this conversation.

As we move to full group discussion, people all around the room speak up. The members representing Latin American and Caribbean countries talk about how fundraising does not fit with their culture. A tough-talking American businessman says he has no problem at all. A former Foreign Service officer says that, for him, "it depends" on who is doing the asking and what they are asking for.

They toss back and forth a huge joke about "depends"—not Billy Crystal-level humor, but we are all in giddy good mood at this point and the moment offers comic relief around a tough subject.

We come back to that subject, and one board member says she always hated to say no to people. The businesswoman from Chile says she had no problem ever saying no. Some speakers are analytical. Others are emotional. People are responding to each other.

This international group of people from all over the hemisphere is starting to bond. Something is growing in the room, a feeling of collegiality. A feeling of shared responsibility or power, as if to say:

"We are all in this together. We do not have to be in agreement about everything, but we all like each other and care mightily about our organization. We are nervous and are not sure how we can actually help in fundraising but we can plow through this okay while we are together today."

I remind them that it is perfectly fine to feel awkward and nervous about "all this." They laugh when I tell them that many people think of fundraising as "the F-word." They really like it when I acknowledge that it is inappropriate and unseemly in some cultures to ask for money. They feel acknowledged.

They seem to get a kick out of my jokes about what fictitious board members typically say about fundraising: "Isn't that the staff's job?" or "I'll do anything but ask for money!" or better yet, "I'm giving my time, that's enough."

Their resistance has begun to diffuse. The subject itself is no longer disturbing. Tensions have released. Their attitudes say: "Okay, she is talking about these things that I feel inside. She understands that I think this is awkward and inappropriate. Okay, so maybe I can listen to her because I like where she is coming from. She is not trying to stuff something down my throat and lecture to me."

At dinner that evening, a former ambassador tells me about his surprise that the whole training had been a teambuilding experience for the entire board. I was surprised as well: I had never thought of this work as "teambuilding," but it certainly was!

You may very well have a board member who is passionately devoted to your cause but who is petrified of "asking." Let me get hold of her in a retreat, and I bet that, with this approach, I can stir her to change her feelings about fundraising, and her thoughts and actions as well. Here, in more detail, are the exercises that can help to turn your reluctant board members into willing and effective fundraisers.

FEAR OF FUNDRAISING EXERCISE

Part One: Let the Board Members Put Their Feelings about Fundraising Right on the Table

If board members are really so uncomfortable with fundraising, then here is an exercise that offers an opportunity to let them get rid of all the unpleasant feelings. Let them put all their discomfort out on the table for an open acknowledgment and discussion. It's a chance for them to do the talking.

Ask board members to talk about how they feel about soliciting and asking for money. Have them pair off, two by two, and ask them to take a few minutes to share with each other how they feel about fundraising and soliciting.

You will suddenly see them pouring out their hearts to each other. They will be animated, passionate, engaged, and sharing their perspective from the heart. It is almost like a dam breaking; finally they can talk about the elephant in the room.

The next step is to process the discussion with the entire board. Choose a discussion leader and ask board members to share their feelings briefly. Write key phrases up on a board, so everyone can see all the negative feelings that many of them share.

For each negative feeling you write, ask how many people feel that way at least part of the time. You can highlight each phrase to represent each person who shares that feeling. You will probably end up with lots of highlights on the chart!

This exercise is an amazing opportunity to clear the air. By this point, there is often a feeling of new freedom in the room.

This is what you are likely to hear your board members say: *I'm embarrassed; don't like it; don't know what to say; worried about the quid pro quo; worried about infringing on my friends; don't know how to do it; find it distasteful; unpleasant; don't like talking about money.* And plenty more for sure!

When I am conducting board training, I openly acknowledge that many people feel these things when thinking about soliciting. Board members are surprised sometimes when I tell them that I also have felt nervous in tough situations.

Those were the times when I lost my hold on my vision and my passion and let the conversation deteriorate to one about money. It is important for board members to know that it is not unusual to have some of these feelings.

Sometimes I share stories of when I was a young fundraiser just starting out. I tell them about those days when there was a "scary" phone call to make and I felt intimidated and had to wait until my energy was up before I could pick up the phone.

Board members feel a lot better when they learn that a seasoned, thick-skinned professional fundraiser has also gotten nervous and uncomfortable on occasion. I often see relieved looks on their faces. However, note that when I felt awkward, it was when I had lost my sense of vision, of the change I wanted to see in the world. I was getting too close to a discussion about money.

Frank Talk of Issues about Money and Power

Many good-hearted board members, particularly those associated with grassroots organizations, hold personal biases against money or people with money and power. These issues, too, must be dealt with head on, because they will hold your board members back.

You can create a discussion in the same way as you did the one about fundraising. Put the words "money" and "power" up on the board. Encourage people to share their feelings about these two highly charged words. Then let everyone go at it, while you write the comments, for all to see.

Some people feel that people with money and power are not "pure." Some very personal stories and comments, with strong emotions attached, may arise in response to this part of the exercise.

In your discussion, try to create an opportunity to show that money is just money, and what matters is how it is used. Remind them how dramatically it can help your wonderful organization to serve more people and do more outstanding work. In a way, money is the lifeblood of your organization. If it is the primary resource to make your work possible, how can it be dirty? How can it be something to be avoided?

And consider Lynne Twist's inspirational take on money: "The moment you ask for money, you raise the quality of the dialogue. You elevate both your relationship with the donor/investor and the work you are doing, and you will be taken seriously." Twist says that money given to make a difference is "blessed money."[16]

Power is another difficult concept. It is easy to make up a story in your head that that wealthy, powerful folks are unreachable. I used to imagine sometimes that my potential donors were high up on a hill and I was a miniscule person way down below. They were far, far away! How could I possibly put myself high enough to approach them for help with my important cause?

> *I like to encourage free association about what it means to have money, give money and ask for money. Generally, folks welcome the opportunity to talk about this taboo subject and to put their societal and family baggage on the table for honest discussion. The discussion tends to de-mystify the whole notion of asking and giving and segues nicely into the associations between money and power in our society. Those with money tend to have power and there are so many preconceived notions about what that means in terms of access to both money and power.*

> —Susan Sachs, Starfire Consulting, Inc.

If we are going to get the world on our bandwagon, we have to consider *everybody* as a potential supporter. We cannot avoid people just because they are wealthy and powerful and we have made up off-putting stories about such people. We must be willing to approach the people who can help our cause.

This means cheerfully finding ways to develop connections with powerful wealthy people; sometimes this can take special effort and strategy. Our board members need to be willing to approach these people, who, regardless of their money, are just folks—but folks who happen to be able to help us out a great deal.

THE JOY OF GIVING

Immediately follow the discussion of fundraising fears with a look at the other, much more positive point of view. If fundraising can be so uncomfortable, then what is the experience from the other side, from the person who is making the gift? Here is this exercise in action with the Pan American Development Foundation, picking up where I left off earlier.

IN THE REAL WORLD

"OK," I say, "we have talked about the bad stuff in fundraising. We have all our discomfort out on the table and up on this poster. Let's turn to the other side and look at fundraising from the donor's perspective."

"How do you feel when you make a gift? Think for a moment, of the last time you wrote a check for a contribution; maybe it was the Boy or Girl Scouts, a school or hospital, whatever it was. Think to yourself how you *felt when you gave*. Now turn to the person next to you and share how you felt."

They take off at top speed, smiles this time on their faces. They are dying to talk about this! Words pour out; they are talking heart to heart this time.

I like this two-by-two discussion because it gets everyone talking, sharing what they think or feel. Board members who are more vocal do not take over and overshadow the others. Having everyone involved makes the topic come alive. Also, power and bonding arise when they discuss these very positive feelings among themselves.

IN THE REAL WORLD

As before, they share their reactions to this question. Here is what they are saying: "I feel proud." "It depends on who is doing the asking." I stop and thank that person, telling him that he has just pointed out a very important factor in whether a solicitation is successful. Who is doing the asking makes the most difference. Someone pipes

(continues)

up: "I feel pressured sometimes." (Not what I was hoping for, but I write it up there anyway.)

Other comments:

- I feel powerful. I am happy to make a difference in the community.
- I am glad I can make a gift.
- I am grateful.
- I feel the need to give back.
- There is a sense of obligation in my sharing with others less fortunate.
- I am doing something meaningful.
- I feel joyous!

I remind them that these emotions are pretty powerful. There are not many things we can do in this world to experience such positive feelings. We all are looking for meaning in our lives.

We want to be part of something that is bigger than we are, something that will live on beyond our small human lives. Giving is a chance to experience joy and connection, to join in work that is powerful, positive, and enduring.

The board members are sitting back, taking all this in. The light is dawning on their faces: maybe fundraising is not so bad after all. They are shifting. They like what they are hearing.

I stop and ask them to take a minute and think, what is most meaningful to them? We are starting to get more personal here. I want them to think of fundraising as something that is connected to a sense of higher purpose in their lives. They are getting it.

As they are talking in pairs, you will be seeing smiles instead of furrowed brows and tense faces. Let them revel in the nice feelings they are remembering of times when they have made a gift. They are talking about their favorite causes, about their organization, about important work in the world that they are a part of through their giving.

As your board members talk, note the views that most people share, as you did earlier. If you step back and look at these wonderful, powerful feelings, it may occur to you that this particular constellation of feelings is hard to find in life.

Certainly such emotional experiences occur, but they may not be frequent or easily arranged. Think about it—these are the higher human feelings that make us happy!

Consider the experience of doing something meaningful. In this 21st century of separateness fostered by working round the clock, the barrage of ever present electronic media, and too-busy families, heading in different directions, the experience of "meaningfulness" can be rare.

Yes, we are all looking for meaning in our lives. We are looking for a connection to something more important than our own individual experience. Finding meaning in life — and having an immediate sense of it—is a precious, rare experience.

As Jerry Panas says in his book, *Mega Gifts,* "Man transcends death by finding meaning in life. To count for something. To make life meaningful. To serve mankind. To provide life and renewal from one generation to the next. This is the drive and desire among those who give."[17]

The Healing Power of Doing Good documents the profound effects on the helper of helping others, including a "helper's high" that either is or mimics an endorphin rush. Not only is stress reduced and health improved through the practice of doing good, but a sense of meaning and largeness can result.

Volunteers report again and again a set of responses to the experience of helping another: "a sense of unity, an uplifted feeling, a feeling of reaching beyond the usual definition of self."[18]

Also, consider joy. We talk a lot in fundraising about donor joy, the wonderful satisfaction that gift-givers receive when they see their contributions making a real difference in the world. When we offer someone the chance to participate with us in something important and meaningful, we also offer them the experience of joy and satisfaction because they, personally and individually, are helping create change for the better in this world.

Board members begin to transform when they consider that fundraising can actually be "ennobling and empowering," as Zimmerman and Leeman so nicely put it.[19] The expressions on their faces—and their attitudes toward asking—will start to change.

Giving Is a Joyous Experience

Return to the previous discussion and compare the two sets of feelings: the "yuck" about "asking" and the joy from giving and making a difference. Board members begin to see that if they can get over their feelings of distaste and fear, then they can bring important and positive experiences to their friends and associates.

With the "yuck" feelings on one sheet of poster paper, and the "joyous" ones on the other sheet, it is easy to contrast them to make your point. Here is a discussion worth having!

Tell the board members that if they can get over themselves, get out of their own way, stop being stuck in discomfort, and instead focus on the experience of giving that they are offering to potential donors, then they *can* change the world! They *can* make a huge difference in this very organization.

You will see a clear shift in your board members at this time. Now they are almost ready for some serious fundraising training. We have cleared the decks by wiping out their inner distaste and opened the door in their hearts and minds for the possibility of some involvement in fundraising.

We have put fundraising on a much higher plane: it is not about money, it is about vision and making the world a better place. Soon they will be ready to understand more about the how and why of fundraising.

WHY DO PEOPLE GIVE?
LESSONS FOR BOARD MEMBERS

One of the great advantages of having money is the joy of giving it away. What other thing can you get as much joy out of—helping other people and a cause you think is important?

—Lewis Cullman, Philanthropist

As fundraising professionals, we all know the motivations inside donors' hearts. This is, again, Standard Fundraising 101. However, our board members have labored long under their own misguided fears and notions about raising money. They do not know the basics. They are not trained professionals who understand the whole ball game. They are like ball players who have made up their own offbeat sets of rules that will never allow them to win.

The question of why people give is fundamental because we must understand the donor and his or her motivations before we can construct coherent fundraising techniques and strategies.

Usually it is a constellation of factors that inclines someone to give. Jerry Panas, author of *Mega Gifts: Who Gives Them, Who Gets Them,* found that million dollar donors were motivated by a sense of civic pride and community responsibility. These mega donors also considered the organization's financial stability and the quality of its leadership much more than they did other matters, such who was doing the soliciting.[20]

Your board members need to review and understand the various kinds of donor motivation, which is the basis for all we do to encourage philanthropy. This thought-provoking discussion will be another step in awakening your board members to Passion-Driven Fundraising. When you stage a fundraising retreat for your board, make these points one by one, and land them directly in your board members' hearts and minds.

People Give to Improve or Save Lives

This fundamental fact colors everything, every technique, every "best practice" we use in fundraising. That is why we emphasize our good work, our results—the real change in people's lives—which come to pass as a result of the money raised.

All cases for support, all direct mail copy, all proposals (if they are good), start off emphasizing the greater good that will come of the donation—the *impact* on the community that this gift will make. This motivation is a clear, deep river running through every aspect of philanthropy.

Donors want to make a difference in the world. With every gift, every check written, comes the hope for change for the good. As Penelope Burk has pointed out in her book and many presentations about *Donor Centered Fundraising,* donors are writing that check with a sense of excitement and anticipation that the contribution will have a positive impact.

People Give to People

I am usually moved by the passion of the solicitor.

—Lewis Cullman, Philanthropist

Above all, fundraising is a relationship business. It is one person talking to another, working with another, involving another. Relationships are like a web: many interlocking people and circles of friendships that overlap.

Relationships are the most valuable asset in any fundraising situation. The person with the right relationships can get the door open, get in to see the decision-maker, get the power players in a room to hear the pitch, and even get the legislative appropriation passed.

As Zimmerman and Lehman put it, "Like it or not, 'who knows whom' is at least as important as what an organization is doing to benefit the world."[21]

This is why cold calls so very rarely work. Cold calls are not based on a prior relationship. They are literally a cold approach to a potential donor. They are like throwing your body against a locked door, hoping it will open. It is not successful and it hurts! Cold calls are a waste of your valuable energy and time.

Instead of your making a direct approach to a stranger, you should instead spend your time working to get the right person to open the door to this person. Don't attempt to charge through the door by yourself. Board members are happy—and relieved—when I tell them I do not believe in cold calls.

People Give the Most Money When They Are Involved

We all know that donors' investments follow their personal involvement, but our board members may not. Moreover, there is a direct correlation between the number of times a prospective donor has contact from the organization and the ultimate size of her gift.

Volunteering is a vital element in the decision to make a gift. Donors who are involved with an organization are more likely to give and will give at higher levels than people who are not engaged as a volunteer.

When I am trying to develop a relationship with a potential donor, I ask him or her to do something to help move the cause forward. If that person will take some action on our behalf, even if it is just a phone call, then suddenly he or she becomes part of our team.

The prospective donor has stepped onto the bandwagon with us and now has a vested interest in our success. The best way to cultivate and involve a prospect in an organization is to get him or her on board helping in some way as a volunteer. That person will soon have a new sense of ownership in our cause.

People Give Because They Believe in the Mission of the Organization

Clearly donors choose one organization over another based on what impact it is having out in the community or the world. Frequently donors give to nonprofits that support issues they have personally encountered in their lives.

One donor may prefer the Girl Scouts because of her early childhood experience; another will give to her women's college because of its impact on her education. Others may give to hospice because of an experience with a loved one's death. Others may give to veterans' organizations because of their military service.

People have natural affinities to one cause or another. It is our job to find those folks who are likely to have an affiliation with our issue and develop that interest into some type of active involvement.

Gifts Are Investments That People Make to Create a Better World

I love the idea of a gift as an investment. When a donor gives, the money is supposed to yield a return on that investment. The return is, of course, change for the better in the community or the world. And a change for the better ultimately affects us all.

Fundraisers have the pleasure and responsibility to be sure that the donors receive meaningful information about the results their gifts have created. We are finding that donors want information on the good work their contribution has accomplished, more than they want recognition, naming opportunities, or public acknowledgment.

People Give Out of a Personal Responsibility to Others

Many people feel a desire to "give back," to return something to the larger community for the greater good. Often those who have abundant resources feel a strong obligation to share some of those resources. This is a powerful altruistic motivation.

Donors Give Because They Want To

If we would remember this precept, maybe we would not be so afraid to approach them for help. Board members are also relieved to hear this. No one *has* to write that check or make that gift!

Donors Do Not Give Unless They Are Asked

This statement is self-explanatory, but board members will not think of it unless you put it squarely in front of them.

Donors Experience Joy When They See the Results of Their Gifts

In his *Mega Gifts,* Jerry Panas identified joy as an important influence on mega gifts. "Each donor spoke about the joy they experience in their giving. The magical and glowing ecstasy."[22]

We would be well served to remember carefully the "exhilaration and the joy" that donors experience. Too many nonprofits, in their efforts to more forward vigorously with more donors and greater dollars, tend to ignore this all-important factor, forgetting to honor the donor's very special experience.

We talk a lot about donor joy in our business. We must be sure that all those we work with in our fundraising efforts take care to cherish this profound and moving reaction of donors to their act of giving. Those who do will be inspired fundraisers.

FUNDRAISING IS FULL OF POWER

Fundraising is all about empowerment; of thinking we can actually enlist people to join in our cause. If we—or our board members—are not feeling enlivened and empowered, we will not go far to create change for the good. However, the energy we need is within us all; it needs only to be unleashed and inspired into action.

We will talk here about several kinds of power, several ways of "charging up" board members and staff as well:

- *The Power of Vision.* A big plan, an overall view, helps to keep the social change for the good that we want to create in front of us. When we speak from a vision of what can be, we are taking the conversation far away from money. When the vision is clearly communicated, the fundraising will be more like fundgathering.

- *The Power of Energy.* Excitement is contagious: when one person is full of energy and inspiration, others are stirred to action. And the action leads to real results. Your board members who are "organizational spark plugs" help inspire others and ensure success.

- *The Power of a Volunteer.* When a board member works without pay, he or she is persuasive in a way that staff can't be. The volunteer sets an example; he is already giving, and demonstrating his own commitment to the cause he represents.

- *The Power of Our History.* We come from a barn-raising tradition, neighbors working together to solve problems, rather than relying on government to solve most of them. This is a powerful tradition in North America, and it creates deep, fertile ground for our fundraisers today.

The Power of Vision

We know that fundraising is about having a vision of a better world. We—both board volunteers and professional staff—need to be fully grounded in a deep sense of urgency to solve an important community, regional, national, or international problem.

This is where we stand. We are agents of change for the good. We act on behalf of peace, justice, the honoring of those who have fallen, helping those in need, curing sickness, providing education and opportunity, righting wrongs. We are on the front lines of vitally important causes, tending to urgent needs.

You can call us visionaries if you want. We stand squarely in our vision of change, of a solution to these problems.

An important step to warming up board members to fundraising is to reconnect them with their vision for the real work at hand. If they are in touch with their vision for what your organization needs to accomplish and can accomplish, then they *will* be willing to venture out to get the needed money.

If they are fully grounded in the importance of their mission, of the sheer urgency of the need, then, yes, you will be surprised at what board members are willing to tackle.

That is why the first step in this model is to focus your board on the work to be done; they change they want to make in the world. A passionate, committed, active board can create incredible results. Such engaged board members will be willing to go places that scare them because they care about their vision.

New research into what really motivates people is pointing this out. Margaret Wheatley, in *Leadership and the New Science,* observes, "in motivation theory, attention is shifting from the use of external rewards to an appreciation for the intrinsic motivators that give us great energy. We are refocusing on the deep longings we have for community, meaning, dignity, purpose and love in our organizational lives."[23]

When someone is fully grounded in a great vision of what the world can become—and the difference her organization can make—that someone becomes a powerful person on behalf of the cause.

This is a person who makes change happen. A person who attracts others to join with them to solve problems. A person who can raise lots of money.

IN THE REAL WORLD

"Our fundraising results have been tremendously enhanced because of a dynamic new board member with a passion for the work and a gift for connecting people with like suited causes. Our Vice Chairperson, Louise Coggins, has naturally woven her gift of caring for disadvantaged and oppressed people into a practical approach to telling their stories and inspiring others to take action on their behalf.

Through her ordinary encounters each day, Louise has recruited three new board members already this year. Each new board member has been eager to encourage their own centers of influence to become involved and therefore, Louise's efforts have been exponential."

—Kimberly Smith, Make Way Partners, Birmingham, Alabama

If, on the other hand, a reluctant fundraiser carries with him his fear, embarrassment, and self-consciousness about asking for money, then he will get nowhere. If any of us approach potential friends and donors hesitantly and apologetically, if we are "all about" ourselves and our discomfort, then we stay in an unpleasant place—and we're not going to be successful!

Again, the retreat with the board of the Pan American Development Foundation (PADF):

I introduce a theme that I will amplify throughout the training. I take the conversation about raising money to a higher level. "We don't want to equate fundraising with 'asking.' There are so very many ways to help in fundraising that do not involve asking." (The board members look surprised).

I remind them that their fear and discomfort come from thinking that the conversation is really about money. I introduce a new perspective: "true successful fundraising is about a vision for a better world. It comes from the heart, not from fear. If you are stuck in your fear, you will not be a passionate advocate for a better world! You will be talking about money, which is a much lower place."

I show them my clip art cartoon of two men talking. One man is talking about a light bulb idea and he is in a green background—he is smiling. The other man is talking about dollars and he is in a red background—he is not smiling. He looks tense and hard. The smiling guy is talking about exciting ideas that will lead to money. He's happy.

The board members start to get it. I tell them about my life and my volunteer work. I am a nonprofit missionary. "I am passionate about lots of causes, and I really want to make the world a better place. I am like the person charging up the hill holding a flag, encouraging as many people as possible to join me in something really important."

They can be like that in their organization, PADF, trying to find friends to join with them to make a huge difference in our hemisphere.

I tell them about the bandwagon. "Let's get everybody on our bandwagon to make something happen. When you approach fundraising like this, you are really making friends first for the organization."

They are relieved when I tell them that I would rather have a friend for my organization than a donor. A friend will come through with lots of help, perhaps in-kind, perhaps introductions to others, perhaps as a volunteer, and this friend will also give money. "Let's look for friends for PADF, not donors."

Smiles and nods all around. An important shift is beginning. It will take all afternoon, but they will be in a totally different place in just a couple of hours.

They are starting to think that fundraising may be something different than they had thought.

The Power of Energy: It Is Catching

If you read the new books on quantum physics, you will be surprised to learn that energy is contagious. Of course we fundraisers knew this all along. In fact, scientists now tell us that at the subatomic level, we all vibrate at different frequencies. Sick or scared people vibrate at lower frequencies; healers and people who meditate vibrate at higher frequencies. Everyone has an energy field, which others can often sense.

We all know people who seem to be energy drains on us. We also know people who give off such positive energy that they lift us up. We want to be around them. We are drawn into what they are up to. We want to be part of their energy—and their causes.

Leaders who are up to vitally important work easily attract people to join with them, because their energy is *contagious*. This is why it is so important to pump up your board members and spend valuable board meeting time not reviewing dull reports, but getting them in touch with their passion and vision to change the world. Awakening your board members' energy is the most important activity you can do.

I like the way that think tank Rensselaerville Institute emphasizes energy as a vital asset to people within a nonprofit organization: "Energy, which builds on focus, optimism and vitality, is the key resource leaders generate and harness. Energy is scarcer than knowledge" in a nonprofit organization.

"Energy is the predictive characteristic of successful organizations and communities, as well as individuals."[24] Wouldn't it be interesting to value energy in your volunteers more than know-how and expertise?

Hal Williams, President of the Rensselaerville Institute, recommends identifying and nurturing the people who are the "spark plugs" in an organization, whether staff or board members. These are the people who lead change by example; they create the results in a fundraising program and in an organization.

Williams recommends that you bet on your spark plugs to pull people together and fire them up. Frequently your board is an extraordinary group of people, but their energy is not tapped, and they are encouraged to be passive. Your spark plugs can be the ignition.

As soon as you walk into a room, you know what a group's energy level is. Organizations have energy levels that we can feel. How does the energy feel when you walk into your board meeting?

THE POWER OF BEING A VOLUNTEER

> *This is the true joy in life, the being used for a purpose*
> *Recognized by yourself as a mighty one . . .*
> *I am of the opinion that my life belongs to the Whole community, and*
> *as long as I live, it is my*
> *Privilege to do for it whatever I can.*
> *I want to be thoroughly used up when I die.*
> *For the harder I work the more I live.*
>
> —George Bernard Shaw

Board members do not understand their power as volunteers. Too often they see their role as small instead of powerful. Volunteers create much more credibility for the organization than staff or consultants, for several reasons. But our trustees forget that they wield such influence.

Why are volunteers so powerful in the fundraising arena? Why do they command respect?

- They are working for their organization only because they *care* about the community or the agency's mission.

- They are showing up only out of the *goodness of their hearts,* and not for any other reward.

- They do not *have* to be helping our organization; they are doing it because they *want to help.*

Your board members could do many other things with their valuable spare time—spend it with their families, their hobbies, relaxing, catching up on myriad projects. Instead they are serving as our board members, and they are out in the community trying to make a difference by supporting their organization's important mission.

Your board members may have varying reasons for serving: devotion to the cause, making business and professional contacts or new social friends, or perhaps a personal experience of your organization's mission. Whatever their motivation, they have chosen your cause for their time and attention, and they will receive respect in the community for their service.

Unpaid worker/leaders automatically get attention from people they ask for help, and board members forget this. Generally, the person being asked will be willing to listen to the volunteer and will want to help. The one asking and the one being asked are peers: both are representatives of the community, conferring over a problem they are interested in solving.

Of course, big problems require many people to solve them. A board cannot solve them alone. Bringing friends and supporters who care about your mission is vital to your success.

As Andy Robinson, said in *Big Gifts for Small Groups: A Board Member's 1-Hour Guide to Securing Gifts of $500 to $5,000:*

> "Let's be honest—when we're raising money, we are asking for help. If we individually had enough money or energy or power to solve community problems alone, we'd probably just do it ourselves.
>
> Unfortunately, big challenges such as poverty, disease, and injustice require big solutions. None of use can solve them individually. We need each other. (We have to ask.)
>
> Given your passion and the power of your cause, some will say yes. I promise you that they will be grateful for the opportunity to participate."[25]

As we have discussed, people in your community expect board members to be asking them for help. Remember, the board members are seen as the representatives of the organization out in the community. Of course they are asking everyone to jump on the bandwagon. That is what they are supposed to be doing. The community does not want them to be shy.

I was training our local Habitat for Humanity board recently, and I told them that the folks in the Raleigh community were absolutely expecting to hear from the Habitat board—about what Habitat needs to be successful in our city.

Who would not want to support something as vital and important as Habitat? Of course the people in our area will want to invest in such a successful community enterprise with Habitat for Humanity's kind of track record.

But somebody has to ask the citizens for help. Somebody has to tell them exactly what they need to do, how they can help—and then they will.

If a community member cannot help at the moment, that does not mean that they do not care about the Habitat mission. They might love to help build a house, or help in some other way until they have the funds available to contribute.

It is vital to point this out to your board members. People will respond to them. They are "clean." They are not being paid like us hired guns.

They are coming from the clear, high moral ground of being people who simply care. Who want to make a difference. Who are taking a stand to cause important change.

Of course, they will be respected, welcomed, listened to, and assisted.

This thought really resonates with board members. They are surprised to learn this distinction about being a volunteer. The idea of volunteers occupying the high ground empowers them and helps pump up their energy and courage.

They begin to perceive themselves in a different light, as community representatives doing something very important. At this point in their education, they have become much more open to learning the techniques of fundraising.

The Power of Our History

There is a wonderful philanthropic tradition in the United States and Canada. Remember Ben Franklin, one of our republic's very first fundraisers? Philadelphia urgently needed a hospital, and a good friend of his came up with the idea of establishing a public medical facility.

Ben Franklin managed to get the Pennsylvania legislature to agree to fund half of the cost of the hospital—*if* he could raise the same amount of money from private citizens. This became the very first matching public-private partnership in our country. He was so pleased at his success that he later said, "I do not remember any of my political maneuvers, the success of which gave me at the time more pleasure."[26]

This is how democracies work. The government is not expected to take care of everybody and everything. We believe in individual initiative and in the community taking care of its own. We believe that we should all look out for our fellow citizens.

There is a great tradition on this continent of people seeing a community need and responding to it. No matter what the need—protection for lost animals, shelters for the homeless, access to art and great cultural experiences, care for the sick and elderly—there are nonprofit organizations, and their energized board members, at work at all levels of society, doing their best to solve these problems.

Our countries are filled with energetic, passionate people who have a dream, a vision of a better world. These people are actively involved in important work. They are doing something huge!

When I remind board members of how important the work is that they are doing, they light up with a new enthusiasm. The quiet ones start to forget their innate shyness. For a fundraiser, a staff member, it's exciting to see them remember their original passion and commitment—the energy that got them started in the first place and that brought them to commit to the mission of the organization.

Our job as fundraisers is to reconnect our board members with their passion and then get out of their way.

EXPECT ABUNDANCE, NOT SCARCITY

Abundance is, in large part, an attitude.

—Sue Patton Thoele

"There are so many hands out there asking for funds; how can we ever be successful?" worried board members complain.

"I get so many solicitations a day, I am overwhelmed."

"There's too much competition for the dollar. We will be just one in a million requests."

"All these other organizations are out there in the public eye; we are a nobody. How can we ever raise money?"

I have only one word to say when anxious board members bring up the subject of scarcity and competition. The word I say is, "Katrina."

Hurricane Katrina proved that the money was out there beyond a shadow of a doubt. The money—and the last count was over $5 billion—came from the American public out of nowhere.

Prior to the hurricane, that money was just sitting in people's pockets. Those people were already giving to many worthy organizations; but when they saw what was happening on the Gulf Coast—the trapped and desperate people—they were deeply moved to make generous gifts quickly and expeditiously.

And giving studies now show that all those gifts to Katrina victims did not hurt giving to other nonprofit organizations: the Giving USA report found that giving totals went up in 2005 in many sectors. Even after removing the disaster relief funds from the overall giving totals, total giving went up 3.2 percent.[27]

One thing Katrina had that we do not have, as I say to my clients, is that the Katrina victims had the media telling an effective, emotional story of urgency, with the capability of asking a national audience for donations.

This one landmark example reminds us all that the only thing standing between us and lots of financial contributions is the ability to tell an effective, emotional, and urgent story, and to *ask* for support. If you are out there being cheerfully aggressive, telling your story with impact and urgency, there will be plenty of funding for your organization.

There is so much money everywhere! Ask your friends who deal in investments, or attorneys who are settling estates. The multitrillion dollar transfer of inherited wealth from the savings-oriented Depression-era generation to their baby-boomer children is in full force right now.

So let's skip the worrying about competing nonprofits. Instead, focus on telling the particular story of need to the community, and loading friends onto the bandwagon. If we all do that, there will be plenty of funding for every nonprofit organization.

As marketing guru Robert Middleton said recently in his online newsletter:

> If you put your focus on what everyone else is doing, you'll miss the greatest resource of all—your own creativity and your commitment to making a difference.[28]

> *The more we develop an abundance mentality, the more we are genuinely*
> *happy for the successes, well-being, achievements, recognition, and good fortune*
> *of other people. We believe their success adds to . . . rather than detracts from*
> *. . . our lives.*
>
> —Stephen Covey

Abundance versus Scarcity: You Choose!

We have a choice of whether we will operate from a mentality of abundance or a mentality of scarcity, in life as well as in fundraising. Which way we have chosen shows up in the way we approach people, new challenges, and our fundraising opportunities.

Abundance: "There Is Enough! And There Is More Than Enough!"   Abundance says that there is plenty for everybody. The glass is always half full (or more), rather than half empty. There is enough of everything for everyone. Dollars are not scarce; in fact, there is plenty of money for every good cause.

And how luxurious abundance feels! Plenty of time, plenty of love, plenty of money. And a positive future in which everyone is taken care of. Many people correlate abundance with feelings of trust, safety, and freedom. Philosophers have been saying for eons that abundance is a state of mind—a way of living that inspires the creation of even greater plenty.

> *Abundance is not something we acquire. It is something we tune into.*
>
> —Wayne Dyer

A strong sense of plenty leads to greater creativity and expansion of energy, to developing productive momentum, and to good work. Abundance creates cooperation; we share, and we benefit each other.

A sense of abundance is born of optimism; it tells us that the more we share, the more we have. Think of the loaves and fishes. Spiritual texts teach that giving and receiving are one and the same. When you make a gift, you are also giving to yourself. The energy you give out comes back to you three times over.

Life is a field of unlimited possibilities.

—Deepak Chopra

The philosophy of abundance also fully recognizes that we are interdependent with each other. All people are linked. When one nonprofit organization is successful and highly visible in the news, the positive publicity permeates the town and benefits all nonprofits working in that domain.

If I keep a green bough in my heart, the singing bird will come.

—Chinese Proverb

Scarcity is based on the view that "there's not enough to go around" and we have to compete fiercely for funds. We must grasp and hoard in order to be safe.

Scarcity is an attitude of taking, not giving. Scarcity is at work when we feel that we *are not* enough or do not *have* enough. It's based on an outlook of judgment, anger, and even destruction. Scarcity creates fights, competition, and even wars.

> *The first lesson of economics is scarcity. There is never enough of anything to satisfy those who want it.*
>
> —Thomas Sowell

The scarcity mentality permeates a lot of Western civilization. Capitalism itself is based on competition. Darwin's "survival of the fittest" has its roots in this mindset. This mentality is fear based, and it results in selfishness and greed. The basic supposition is: "If I have it, then you can't have it." Or, "If you have it, you're keeping me from having it."

> *The "beat your competition" mentality is, at best, severely limiting; at worst, it's evil and destructive.*
>
> —Robert Middleton, Marketing Expert

Scarcity is built on pessimism. The scarcity mentality can hold us down; it can sap energy and momentum and leave us paralyzed. It fosters the attitude of: Why bother trying, when the effort is so great and success is so unlikely?

The old ways of thinking, à la Darwin, are shifting in many realms to a more positive, abundant outlook that allows for considering the greater good. We have created technologies that are virtually unlimited in the problems they can solve and the quality of life they can create.

While some worry about not enough water, food, or land in the future, others talk of a transition to abundance at a whole new level on planet Earth.

> *People with a scarcity mentality tend to see everything in terms of win-lose. There is only so much; and if someone else has it, that means there will be less for me.*
>
> —Stephen Covey

How could we fundraisers possibly go to work every day if we did not live from an abundance mentality? Every morning as we get up, we have to expect that the world will be our oyster.

We must think and believe in our potential success—that problems can be solved, that people can be helped, that funds can be raised to make this important work happen.

What we do know for a fact is that successful organizations deliberately choose to operate from an abundance outlook. Approaching fundraising, and life, as a "win-win" proposition is the only possible way to be successful—and perhaps to be happy too.

This means that we do not need to be threatened by competition for the dollar. Since there is enough for all, we can even cooperate with our sister organizations. One organization's success breeds a successful environment for all.

> *Life is just a bowl of cherries.*

Time after time I have seen board members wringing their hands in desperation over competition for money—and sabotaging themselves from the beginning. We have to inspire them to take the "glass is half full" perspective of fundraising. Nonprofits need boards that share our positive outlook.

The "power of positive thinking" is an absolute underlying law of fundraising success. Board members can and must shift their perspective from pessimism and scarcity to celebrating all the nonprofits in their organization's realm and understanding that there is plenty for all. In fact, there is strength in making alliances; several organizations banded together have a much better chance of getting the funding they seek.

> *Never talk defeat. Use words like hope, belief, faith, victory.*
>
> —Norman Vincent Peale

HIGHLIGHTS OF STEP TWO

Inspire Your Board Members with a New Philosophy of Fundraising

- Fundraising is so much more than asking for money—it is all about changing the world for the better.
- Board members' myths and problems with fundraising:
  - They worry about taking advantage of their friends.
  - They do not know what to say about their organizations.
- Get everybody on your bandwagon.
- Get your board busy raising friends.
- Fundraising need not be scary.
  - Deal with your board members' fears directly.

HIGHLIGHTS OF STEP TWO (CONTINUED)

- Giving is a joyous experience.
    - It gives meaning to our lives.
    - Donors experience joy!
    - People give to change or save lives.
- Fundraising is full of power:
    - The power of vision.
    - The power of positive energy—it is catching!
    - The power of a volunteer coming from the high moral ground.
    - The New World tradition of people looking out for each other.
- The expectation of abundance, not scarcity, will bring fundraising success.

■ NOTES

1. Kay Sprinkel Grace, *Beyond Fundraising,* 2nd ed. (Hoboken, NJ: John Wiley & Sons, 2005), 17.

2. Robert M. Zimmerman and Ann W. Lehman, *Boards that Love Fundraising: A How-To Guide for Your Board* (San Francisco: Jossey-Bass, 2004).

3. Ibid.

4. Ibid.

5. Lynne Twist, *Fundraising from the Heart Audio-Video Course* (Edison, NJ: Produced by Woman Vision copyright © 2001 Woman Vision and Lynne Twist), 9.

6. Kay Sprinkel Grace, *Beyond Fundraising,* 2nd ed.

7. Lynne Twist, *Fundraising from the Heart Audio-Video Course,* 9.

8. Allan Luks and Peggy Payne, *The Healing Power of Doing Good* (New York, iUniverse.com, Inc., 2001).

9. Robert L. Fulghum, *It Was on Fire When I Lay Down On It* (New York: Ballantine Books, a division of Random House, 1989).

10. Lynne Twist, *Fundraising from the Heart Audio-Video Course.*

11. Ibid.

12. Hildy Gottleib, *FriendRaising, Community Engagement Strategies for Boards Who Hate Fundraising but Love Making Friends* (Tucson, AZ: Renaissance Press, 2006), p. 30.

13. Hildy Gottleib, "FriendRaising and Your Board," help4Nonprofits.com, copyright © *ReSolve, Inc.,* 2003, 2005, 2006.

14. Ibid.

15. Thomas Moore, *Care of the Soul* (New York: Harper Collins, 1992).

16. Lynne Twist, *Fundraising from the Heart Audio-Video Course.*

17. Jerry Panas, *Mega Gifts: Who Gives Them, Who Gets Them* (Chicago: Bonus Books, Inc, 1984).

18. Allan Luks and Peggy Payne, *The Healing Power of Doing Good* (New York: iUniverse.com, Inc. 2001).

19. Robert M. Zimmerman and Ann W. Lehman, *Boards that Love Fundraising: A How-To Guide for Your Board.*

20. Jerry Panas, *Mega Gifts: Who Gives Them, Who Gets Them.*

21. Robert M. Zimmerman and Ann W. Lehman, *Boards That Love Fundraising: A How-To Guide for Your Board.*

22. Jerry Panas, *Mega Gifts: Who Gives Them, Who Gets Them.*

24. Margaret Wheatley, *Leadership and the New Science* (San Francisco: Berrett-Koehler, 1999).

25. Andy Robinson, *Big Gifts for Small Groups: A Board Member's 1-Hour Guide to Securing Gifts of $500 to $5,000* (Medfield, MA: Emerson and Church, 2004).

26. *The Autobiography of Benjamin Franklin* (IndyPublish.com, December 2001).

27. *Giving USA 2006,* publication of the Giving USA Foundation and is researched and written by the Center on Philanthropy at Indiana University. www.givingusa.com.

28. Robert Middleton online newsletter (actionplan.com service@actionplan.com).

CHAPTER 4

Passion-Driven Fundraising Step Three: READY Your Board with the Right Tools and Skills

A ship in harbor is safe, but that is not what ships are built for.
—William Shedd

We have already introduced board members to a startlingly different perspective on raising money and inspired them to take action so they can make a real difference in the world. These two steps made up the important first half of their fundraising training, and they did not even know they were being "trained!"

Now it is time to take them deeper into philanthropy and fundraising with the right tools and methods. We need to cover some key principles that will make them more comfortable with the process and continue to build their confidence. We will cover three major topics in this section:

Topic One: Fundraising from the donor's point of view. Board members must come to understand the donor's point of view on all this asking and giving. We will show them how to be focused on the donors and not on themselves—and they will understand how much easier it all is when they shift the focus to the donor.

We will discuss Penelope Burk's groundbreaking studies about what donors want so that we can find new ways to make donors happy and generous.

Topic Two: No-ask fundraising. *Take the emphasis away from soliciting* and show board members all the other ways they can contribute in fundraising without "asking." Give them an experiential tour of the fundraising cycle, so they understand how we do what we do. They will begin to see just how little time is spent in the "asking" phase of the cycle, compared with all the many other activities we undertake with our donors.

We will take a detailed look at how board members can support fundraising by serving as Ambassadors assigned to cultivate specific donors and by helping with the Ask Warm-Up and the Ask Follow-Up.

Topic Three: Equip them with the right things to say and the right way to say them. Since many board members do not know how to talk about their organization, we will discuss in depth how to train them to produce the all-important elevator speech easily and gracefully. We will learn how to make this process fun for everyone.

Fundraising from the Donor's Point of View: What Donors Want

Educating your board members about donors and their expectations will orient them in the proper direction—towards the *donor*. We have heard plenty in recent years about customer orientation of businesses; now it is time for *donor orientation* at nonprofit organizations.

Just as customer satisfaction is key to making a business successful, when we make asking sure that our donors have a satisfying experience of giving, it will pay off immeasurably for our organizations and the people we serve.

For-profit companies work to please their customers for one simple reason: they want repeat business. We need to give our donors plenty of positive experiences associated with our organization in order for them to stay with us. The goal of any good fundraising program is to create solid, life-long relationships with donors; this is the foundation of sustainable funding.

> *Hopefully, the first gift is never the largest!*
>
> —Michael Rierson, my mentor at my very
> first fundraising job at Duke University

Treat your donors well, and they will give and give and give again. And they will be happy about it every time they give!

> *The first gift should be such an occasion of joy and celebration that it is
> the beginning of a long and happy relationship between the donor and the
> institution.*

What DO Donors Want? Approach Fundraising from the Donor's Point of View

People are wonderful to make their gifts to our organizations so we can carry on with our missions. We learned earlier why the donors gave, but what do they want from us now that they have given? Now that they have become donors/partners/investors in our organization?

Put yourself in a donor's shoes and think what you would want as a result of your gift. Donors want to be appreciated as *people, not pocketbooks.* This means that they want to be treated like a real person, just the way you would want to be treated.

They want to be thanked for their gifts appropriately; they expect to receive meaningful information about the results we achieve with their gifts. Most of all, they are looking for a long-term relationship with an organization they believe in.

The Conversation Should Never Be about Money   If we give donors what they want, then they will be happy and satisfied. They will be glad that they gave to our organization, becoming joyously connected to the wonderful good work we are doing to make our community a better place.

Of course everyone wants to be wanted for themselves, not just for their money. When we approach them with a conversation that is just about money, guess what? It turns them off and makes us uncomfortable. As we have discussed earlier, the conversation should never be about *money*.

Donors Want to Be Treated Like People, Not Pocketbooks   In treating donors like real people we need to be *personal*. For example, that means they get personalized communications, such as letters that say, "Dear Mr. Smith," rather than "Dear Friend."

In his essay, "Death to the Dear Friend Letter," Todd Baker points out that if you do not call donors by their names, then you give them the impression that you do not know who they are. You treat them as if they are anonymous.

Why should donors continue giving when the organization doesn't even know who is giving the money? I don't think I would! Treating them impersonally becomes "death" to the stream of contributions from this donor.

Baker reminds us once again that loyal donors are looking for personal fulfillment through their giving:

> Your charity must inspire donors to loyalty. This is best accomplished when donors truly feel they are part of the effort—when they can envision themselves standing side-by-side with you to carry out a worthwhile cause. Let donors in. *Your mission and their mission must become one. You'll soon hear them refer to your charity as "we" and not "you."* [1]

✿

A one-minute phone call (to say thank you) can represent the equivalent of a year's worth of solicitations. You never know why or what someone might give.

—Penelope Burk [2]

Donor-Centered Fundraising   Fundraising pioneer Penelope Burk has published groundbreaking research on what donors want and what they need from organizations in order to keep giving. Her work forms the basis for a new fundraising approach that focuses directly on the donors themselves, and offers interesting possibilities for board members to play a greater role in thanking donors.

If we can identify what donors expect as a result of their gifts, then we can satisfy them. If we can keep them happy, then they will become partners with our organization for the long haul, providing valuable ongoing support.

In her book, *Donor Centered Fundraising,* Burk quotes startling statistics about donor retention and attrition. We are losing too many of our donors after they make the first gift, because they are not renewing:

- The attrition rate between the first gift and the second gift is 50%. That means there is only a 50-50 chance that a donor will renew their initial gift.
- After five fundraising appeals, the chance that a donor has continued to make subsequent gifts to the organization is only 10 to 15%.

This statistic is quite concerning! We fundraisers spend a great deal of effort trying to find new donors, but we are not focusing enough energy or attention on our current donors. Yet it is easier to secure a renewal gift than it is to bring in a brand new contributor.

TIPS AND TECHNIQUES

When you need funds, go first to your current donors who are standing with you as your investors/supporters, who have already bought in to your mission.

Why are we talking about this in a book about board members and fundraising? Because board members can do the very important work of nurturing current donors, making sure they are appreciated as people, not as wallets. When donors are personally appreciated by board members, then donor attrition does down, donor retention goes up, and the size of gifts goes up.

If board members are personally involved in thanking donors, then they will be able to impact the bottom line directly without actually having to solicit! And that is a job all board members can do, especially those suffering from the "cringe factor" with fundraising.

IN THE REAL WORLD

Let us look at one of Burk's landmark studies to see how this works:

Burk ran a test for the Canadian Paraplegic Association to study whether phone calls to donors that simply say "thank you" might impact their decision to give again.

She worked with a standard direct mail acquisition campaign for the association. The average gift was $26. Every tenth donor was singled out for special acknowledgment by board members, who phoned to say thank you to the donors within forty-eight hours of the gift's arrival at the organization. Nothing else special was done for these donors.

What were the donors' experiences when they were actually phoned by a board member? Burk says they were incredulous and thrilled. The donors expressed amazement that

(continues)

board members, who were the highest authority of the organization, took the time to phone them to simply say thank you!

And what was the board members' experience in this experiment? They loved it! The donors profusely thanked them for taking the time to phone their thank-you. The board members had a lovely time receiving all those compliments. They had a rewarding experience and felt wonderful about the project.

What was the long-term impact? About four months later, the association resolicited both groups, with the same appeal letter. Amazing results: Donors in the test group who received personal phone calls from board members gave gifts averaging *39%* *higher* than those in the control group who were not called.

After 14 months, the group that received phone calls from board members was making average gifts valued at *42%* higher than the control group.

Best of all, during the phone calls, 4% of those called expressed an interest in making a major gift or "doing something more." This means that there are plenty of potential major gift donors hiding in the ranks of your most modest contributors.[3]

Moral of the story? *The board members were able to bring much-needed dollars into their organization simply by "saying thank you!"* We can learn a lot from this experiment. *All* board members, whether they are involved in soliciting or not, can help in personally thanking donors—and can bring in money as a result!

Why are board members the best ones to make the thank-you calls? They are the highest representatives of the organization; they are people who are generally perceived as being important, having clout. Better yet, they are volunteers, and they are doing this out of the goodness of their hearts, not for any other gain.

When board members spend their time with donors—the people whose contributions are making such good work possible—it is a major compliment to the donors.

"As the top authority in the organization and as the group of people who embody the highest ideals of volunteerism, there is no substitute for the Board of Directors," Burk comments, "The single greatest honor that can be bestowed on a donor is recognition from the board . . . When a board member acknowledges a donor's gift and does so immediately, the donor knows that the organization as really made an effort."[4]

And why shouldn't board members want to communicate with such an important group—the people who are so generously giving to support the organization's good work?

The Value of the Personal Touch

Penelope Burk also found that donors want three things from an organization before they make a repeat gift. Her studies showed that when nonprofits do these three things, then retention and gift value increase: the list of three is simple. Donors want:

1. A prompt and personal thank-you.
2. Reassurance that the gift will be used as intended.
3. Meaningful information about the results the organization achieved using the gift before the donor is asked for another contribution.

Let us take a look at these three factors.

Prompt Thank-Yous   Why would a donor be impressed with a prompt thank-you? One reason: it tells her that the organization quickly noticed and appreciated the gift. Donors do like the idea that their gifts get immediate notice. Otherwise, the gesture does not seem appreciated, and the thank-you note can seem no more than a routine piece of paperwork, rather than a real response.

When a contributor gets quick positive attention and thanks for a gift, this positively reinforces the giving experience. Then that contributor is more likely to give again!

A second reason that quick thanking is important: this sign of efficiency tells donors that the nonprofit is well run. When the response comes quickly, donors think that if the organization can turn out a good thank-you note fast, it probably will do a good job of using the gift for its good work.

Personal Thank-Yous   Why would a donor like a personal thank-you? We have already talked about how donors want to be treated like *people,* not *pocketbooks.* A warm, sincere thank-you letter makes a donor feel not only like a real person, but a wonderful person who is making a big difference by sending a gift.

Never send out a boring, stale, uninteresting, formal letter like this one: "On behalf of the board of directors of the xxx organization, we are pleased to thank you for your generous contribution of $xxx." No, no, and no again!

Instead, send something warm and wonderful, like Burk recommends in *Donor Centered Fundraising:* "We needed you and you were there. We are so grateful for your donation which has been allocated to our new literacy program for street youth . . . "[5] Let your personality come through and show up as a real person.

Penelope Burk lists 20 attributes of a good thank-you letter, which are listed in *Donor Centered Fundraising.* Take the time to study the fine points of thank-you letters, even if you think you already know how to write a good one. Any little detail you learn or relearn will pay off handsomely in your fundraising efforts. And encourage your board members to employ these thank-you techniques!

Meaningful Information on Results   Burk's research found that giving donors meaningful information on your organization's results and outcomes was more important to the donors than recognizing them through donor walls and honor rolls. Most of all, donors wanted assurance that their gift had an impact—that their gift made a difference. That is when they experience *joy:* when they see the good work that they were able to accomplish through their contribution.

The information we provide donors matters a great deal to them. They "are giving to achieve results through a cause that is personally important. To give again to that cause, the donor needs to be confident that the original gift satisfied the obligation he made to himself and to society."[6]

Burk found that particularly corporate donors felt they did not get the information they needed to justify their contributions to a specific organization (pg 108). We are not doing a good enough job of communicating our results from our donors' gifts at work.

Don't rely on your newsletter to communicate with donors about your organization's results. The Donor-Centered study found that 66% of respondents said that nonprofit newsletter content is not particularly exciting or compelling, *and* 69% do not have time, or take the time, to read it thoroughly.[7]

From my perspective, I worry that nonprofit newsletters are often not compelling, interesting communications vehicles. They can appear stale when compared to the snazzy communications coming out of the for-profit sector. Too often, nonprofit newsletters are too wordy and focus on the wrong things. We forget that the newsletter is a marketing tool designed to be interesting to the reader.

Newsletters are quite impersonal, anyway. I believe they are not as effective as a personal letter written directly to the donor that provides an update on the organization and the results it is creating with the donor's funds.

IN THE REAL WORLD

Here is an experience of my own—when I received a personal update letter, and the rush of pleasure and joy when I learned about the results of my gift.

A friend of mine, Katie Early, was past chair of an international organization called IPAS, that fights for access to birth control and abortion rights around the world.

I made a casual gift to IPAS, largely in support of my friend Katie. I got a nice thank-you note. That was fine, but it made no huge impact on me.

Then one day much later, my attitude toward IPAS shifted dramatically. I received what looked like a personalized letter from that organization. There was no label, and it looked personally typed.

Upon opening the letter, I read: "Dear Gail, I am writing to thank you for your support over the past year. Your gift is being used to further our shared vision that no woman should have to risk her life or health because she lacks safe reproductive options . . . ." Three articles of interest were enclosed, one of which highlighted the organization's work.

What was my response? I was very impressed with the letter (and I am hard to please!), so much so that I started looking for the solicitation envelope that came with it. I was

(continues)

IN THE REAL WORLD (CONTINUED)

stunned to find out that there was *no* solicitation envelope; they had written me personally just to give me an update.

I was floored. I was flabbergasted. I was amazed. I had never received a personal letter like this solely to give me an update. The next time I saw Katie, I told her how impressed I was with the note; and the next time IPAS asked me for support, I sent a check gladly, knowing what a great, well-run organization I was supporting.

Results of Donor-Centered Fundraising: If you put into practice all three things donors want that Penelope Burk recommends, what kind of results will you achieve? Consider these statistics. In Burk's research, she found that when a donor received a prompt, personal thank-you that was followed up with meaningful information on the results the organization achieved with the gift, then:

93% would definitely or probably give again they next time they were asked

64% would definitely or probably give more,

And best of all, 74% would continue to give indefinitely as long as they continued to receive meaningful information.[8]

Board members' main role should be to contact donors and build relationships.
They don't necessarily have to ask for money. Properly developed relationships
should take care of that.[9]

TAKE THE EMPHASIS AWAY FROM SOLICITING

There are so many important ways that board members can aid fundraising directly without having to ask. They need to understand that fundraising is very much more than simply soliciting. The actual process of developing a relationship with a donor, particularly for a major gift, is a lengthy process with many delicate steps.

Let's take a closer look at the basic Fundraising Cycle and how board members can fit in. Let us introduce our board members to the other myriad activities of the process, when we are simply making friends and building relationships, which of course leads to giving, and long-term giving, at that.

Let's give board members a visual picture of the many activities of the fundraising cycle —outside of "asking"—in which they can make a real difference.

The Only Way to Approach Major Gifts: Cultivating Relationships That Matter

As experienced fundraisers, we know that the more emphasis we put on cultivating, thanking, and informing donors, then the easier, and more natural the "asking" will be.

Terry Axelrod, in *Raise More Money,* compares cultivating a donor with the metaphor of an apple ripening on a tree. With each act of cultivation, the donor's interest ripens a little bit more. With enough proper care, a donor's gift is a natural act. It just drops down from the tree—right into your hand—like a ripe apple, without having to be picked. The giving is easy and organic; it happens as a result of involving the donor in a close relationship and developing/growing his or her interest in the organization.[10]

This is how all successful fundraisers approach major gift activity. We know the old axiom that successful major gifts require spending about 90% of the time cultivating and less than 10% of the time asking. Or perhaps it is 95% on cultivating and 5% on asking. The "ask" is one tiny moment within the whole fundraising cycle.

If the relationship with the donor is properly developed, then the gift will take care of itself. What a relief to scared solicitors, to scared volunteers, and perhaps to nervous staff members as well!

Show Board Members the Fundraising Cycle

A sophisticated fundraiser knows that there are many, many ways board members can support fundraising. In fact, we would be quite pleased just to have board members in action outside of soliciting Of course we know that if board members are actually involved in helping to cultivate a donor, then they are much more willing to help with a solicitation.

> **TIPS AND TECHNIQUES**
>
> A friend of mine, who chairs our local community theatre board, said recently, "I just can't stand fundraising and won't do it. But if I were involved in helping to develop a relationship with a funding source over time, well . . . then, I think I might be willing to help approach them for a gift."

Let's take a closer look at the basic Fundraising Cycle and where board members can fit in. We professional fundraisers live this process every day. This diagram (see Exhibit 4.1) encompasses—and perhaps oversimplifies—just about everything we do to raise money and bring in resources for our organizations.

- IDENTIFY: We *identify* who we think would be a likely prospective donor to our organization because of the person's involvement, affinity, or possible interest in our mission.

- CULTIVATE: We *cultivate* their interest in our organization by involving and informing them—developing an ongoing relationship.

- ASK: We *ask* for their support when we think they are ready to consider a gift.

- THANK: We *thank* them repeatedly, in many ways, particularly by giving them meaningful information about the results our organization has achieved as a result of their gift.

EXHIBIT 4.1   FUNDRAISING CYCLE

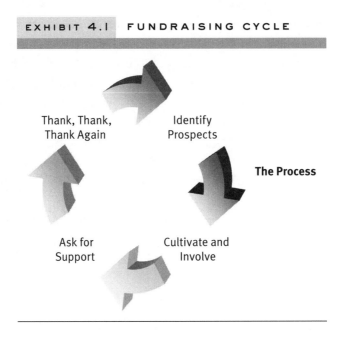

Although we perform this process continuously, this diagram and the overall process is news to many board members, especially to those suffering from the "cringe factor," who are stuck in an uncomfortable place about money and soliciting. Explaining these steps in detail is an important part of teaching these uneasy students the basic processes of fundraising. Such an education will help remove their fear and distaste for the whole process.

In the next chapter I will treat in detail many ways board members can help identify and cultivate prospects—the fun "courtship" part of the fundraising process. These are the activities in the fundraising cycle in which board members are loading new friends onto the bandwagon, getting them involved, and turning them on to the mission of your organization.

Perhaps paradoxically, I want to begin with what would appear to be the final step: the thanking.

The Important Role of Thanking

> *Find seven ways to thank your donors and they will give quickly when you ask again.*

Appropriate thanking, as we all know, is vitally important. We have already discussed the board's crucial role in thanking donors, and how that simple action alone directly contributes to increased gifts from your donors. Good fundraisers know that if you do a great job of thanking your donors, then thanking becomes further cultivation.

It is possible to shortcut the fundraising cycle with powerful thanking. You can go directly from the Thanking Stage into the Soliciting Stage and back again, but only if you arrange for the donor to have such a joyous experience of giving that he or she then becomes a close partner and friend of your organization. And only if you provide your donor with information that the gift was used as intended and you accomplished good work through the donor's generosity.

The donor's first gift becomes one step in the process of building that long-term relationship. The cycle goes round and round, as the donor keeps giving to a cause she is personally interested in, and the organization thanks and communicates back to the donor what great things are happening because of her gifts. Then she gives again, glad to be a part of change for the good, deeply satisfied that she is part of something important

We professionals spend far too little time in the Thanking Stage, and we miss so many opportunities to create long-term relationships with our donors. We all know that it is the donors who stick with us for the long haul who form the foundation of sustainable fundraising programs that yield gifts year after year.

As I mentioned earlier, we are usually out there looking for new donors more that we are focusing on our current donors, what they want from our organization, and how to involve them more deeply in our organization.

As I write, I am for the first time in about 10 years not making my annual $1,000 gift to a certain organization that has been important in my life. Frankly, I have been feeling neglected by this organization. No one seems to care if I give or not. Maybe they have taken me for granted by now, and are just assuming I will renew my gift as usual. But I am simply not motivated this year to give again.

I imagine that we have all had these feelings as donors ourselves. Let's take a lesson from our own personal experiences when we establish our daily priorities as nonprofit leaders. Just consider again the power of a personal phone call to thank any donor. I believe if this organization actually had a board member phone me to say thanks that I might not feel so neglected or ignored.

Living and breathing the Fundraising Cycle—and taking each step seriously—creates deep and sustainable long-term funding for our organizations. And ultimately, it is sustainable fundraising that we are all after—contributed support that our organizations can count on annually, year in and year out.

The goal of fundraising programs is to raise needed revenue for our organization's mission, but also *to build a core of people/donors who really care about what we are doing.* It's all based on communicating with your donors.

THE ACT OF SOLICITING IS ONE TINY INSTANT IN THE CYCLE!

I have done a lot of thinking about how much time we spend in each of the basic stages of identifying, cultivating, soliciting, and thanking prospects, especially when we are confronted with board members who are nervous about that one point in time in which we do the asking.

As I mulled this timing issue over, I decided to redraw the Fundraising Cycle flow chart into a pie chart (see Exhibit 4.2) to show the amount of time we typically spend in each stage of the fundraising cycle. I wanted to show scared board members that the act of soliciting that they were so afraid of was only *one tiny moment* in the whole long-drawn-out process of cultivating and soliciting a gift.

If you look at this graph, you can see that the small red sliver representing "asking" is a tiny point in time within the whole continuum of the fundraising process. We spend endless hours, days, months, even years, outside of the Asking Stage, while we are identifying and cultivating our prospects, and then thanking them.

The feared Moment of the Ask is only a brief part of the whole continuum of fundraising activity. As we know, after the Ask, we spend plenty of time thanking and reporting back to our donors, until they are ready to give again.

Many Roles for Board Members

If you show your board the diagram in Exhibit 4.3, then your trustees can better understand how complex and lengthy good fundraising—Passion-Driven Fundraising—typically is. They will start to see roles they can play, somewhere in this process, that are comfortable for them.

The graph shows board members that they can perform an important role doing many vital tasks, without having to solicit. *They can serve at all levels and get as close to or as far away from the actual moment of solicitation as they want—and still make a huge difference.*

This is really an eye-opener for many board members. When I present this material in retreats and trainings, I see amazed and interested expressions, as if an entirely new idea is dawning upon them.

EXHIBIT 4.2   FUNDRAISING CYCLE

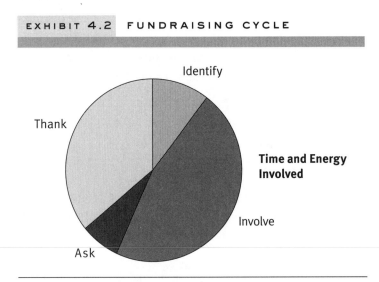

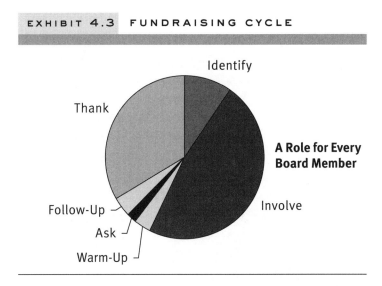

EXHIBIT 4.3   FUNDRAISING CYCLE

You can almost see the tension draining out of their faces and bodies. There is a palpable sense of relief in the room. They are thinking, "Yes! I can make a difference for this organization that I care so much about, *and* not have to solicit. What a relief!"

Use the Graph with Your Board Members

I urge you to use this graph, which is available to book purchasers from my Web site, gailperry.com. A picture paints a thousand words for scared board members. Show them how they can fit in and still make a difference without having to solicit.

Show them the many activities that your fundraising program undertakes in order to create powerful relationships with people who want to support your organization. All these activities support the Moment of the Ask, when you make a powerful request of someone to step up and help out in a meaningful financial way.

In fact, I'll guess that your board is not even familiar with all the various strategies and activities of your organization's fundraising program: what you do, what is successful, where you put staff energy, where you are challenged. Do they know the stats on your mailing program? Do they know the results of your fundraising events? Do they know where you could use their help the most?

Break Up the Ask into Three Stages

Taking the analysis of time spent in the cycle of fundraising even further, I broke the "ask" moment into three parts: the Ask Warm-Up, the Ask Moment, and the Ask Follow-Up. Nervous board members are sometimes even willing to participate in the Ask Warm-Up and the Ask Follow-Up, as long as they do not have to "ask."

The Ask Warm-Up: How Board Members Can Help   Here is an example of an Ask Warm-Up: The head of an Arts Council made an appointment with the CEO of a local bank to solicit the bank's support to sponsor its annual arts festival. The bank CEO happened to be a social acquaintance of several board members, but they did not want to go on the solicitation call. However, they did know that the appointment with the bank CEO was set and when it was to take place.

The board members made a point to "run into" the CEO the week before the solicitation visit. When they saw her, they said, "Arts Council folks are coming to see you this week. We just wanted to let you know that we are board members. This is an important organization that impacts the entire community. We would really appreciate your help as a sponsor."

Now, did the board members solicit the CEO? No! Did they pave the way for a successful solicitation? You bet! Was this easy for the board members? Yes!

Did they put themselves in an awkward distasteful role? No! They were working to get the bank CEO on their bandwagon. They could, in addition, have asked the CEO to come over for a tour or join them to volunteer at the organization.

A well-coached, smart board member could even go a bit further and initiate a conversation with the bank CEO about the Arts Council, probing for her opinions and thoughts, and gently making some important points about the Council's good work in the community.

Then, freshly armed with new information on how the CEO perceives the organization and the questions she asked, the board member can convey this useful material to the staff, who then can use it to craft a stronger solicitation appeal.

The Ask Follow-Up: How Board Members Can Help   The time I am most nervous in fundraising is not the solicitation visit, but the period after the gift request is made and before I receive a commitment or answer to my request for a contribution.

This time—while the gift is possibly pending and the donor is getting around to considering the request and coming to a decision—is fraught with anxiety for me. I find myself pondering, while I brush my teeth in the morning, *exactly how I can stack the deck to ensure a favorable reply? What can I do to help sway the decision to positive?*

I like to arrange for opportunities in that period to touch base gently with my potential donor, reminding him that we are here and hopeful that he will be generous, and that this is a very worthy cause. I also want people who know both our organization and the potential donor to get in touch with this prospect and help nudge him toward a favorable decision. Sometimes it is in the follow-up that the tide can tip toward my organization.

If board members can do this gentle touching base with solicited prospects, even better. If they are friends, acquaintances, or customers of the prospects, they can add a powerful boost to the previous solicitation.

An Ask Follow-Up could go like this: The bank CEO is in the same Rotary Club as a board member, who knows that the solicitation visit has just taken place. The well-briefed board member knows the amount that was asked for, who made the call, and what the CEO's initial response was.

She sees her friend the bank CEO at the Rotary Club, and simply says to her,

"Hi! I know the Arts Council came to see you this week. I wanted you to know that I am a board member there. It would be great if your bank could sponsor the auction this year. It's a social highlight for our community, and it will give the bank good visibility. I will personally make sure that you get all the recognition you may want. It's a really important cause. Thanks for considering the contribution."

This board member was well briefed on exactly what the "selling points" were to appeal to the bank CEO. As a business, the bank is looking for maximum exposure with every community contribution, much more so than an individual donor.

Now, did this board member have to put herself out in an uncomfortable place where the conversation is about money? No! Did she have to "take advantage" of her relationship with the CEO? No. All she had to do was back up the solicitation team, nicely paving the way for a more favorable response.

The board member could go a step further and ask a most important question: "what was your impression of the solicitation?" This open-ended question will find out where the CEO is in considering the gift. It will point out any issues they can address in order to tip the scales in their favor. It can identify important follow up activities or questions that need to be answered.

It's a better question that asking, "do you have any questions about our Arts Council?" because this is a yes or no answer. An open-ended question like "what was your impression" is a golden key to finding out what is in your donors' hearts and minds. It treats them like a real person with real thoughts and opinions, taking the entire conversation to a deeper level.

Listen, listen, listen your way to the gift.

The Ask Warm-Up and the Ask Follow-Up are great places for board members to shine. Even reluctant board members, if well briefed, are usually comfortable helping in these stages of the cycle, and they can make a huge difference. These steps are vital and important functions, and your board members can take the lead, sometimes being the only ones who can sway the decision in your direction.

Board Members as Ambassadors to Cultivate Major Gifts

We have looked at some interesting ways board members can support the actual solicitation of a donor. Now let's examine additional roles for trustees in other phases of the fundraising cycle—how they can cultivate potential and current donors.

Consider the benefits of setting up your board members in formal roles as Ambassadors for your organization. Board members can shine as Ambassadors, where they are assigned one-on-one to be in charge of specific donor prospects.

The board members who serve as Ambassadors focus on the pleasant tasks of cultivating and communicating with donors. The board members do not have to be involved in soliciting unless they want to. This is a perfect format for hesitant board members not only to participate in fundraising but even to enjoy it.

To me, cultivating donors is all about focusing on wonderful people who believe in my cause; it is usually lots of friendly fun. We always need more personalized communication with our donors. What better way to put board members to work!

Specific Framework for Action

To ensure an Ambassador project's effectiveness, you need a well structured framework for your board volunteers. As we know, sometimes getting board members to actually do what they say they will do can be a challenge.

If you set up specific time frames and clear responsibilities, board members will know exactly what they need to do when. As busy volunteers, they want and appreciate a precise structure that will both support them and spell out clear expectations.

Who would not relish the dignified role of "Ambassador?" As we know, many board members are better suited to handle the courtship and cultivation of potential donors than the actual solicitation. Let us give them this very important role: developing long-term relationships with potential donors.

Ambassadors can leverage the energies and talents of your board members and put them to use in an appropriate area where they can do the most good. As we have discussed, board members who are afraid of soliciting can handle "friendraising" and concentrate on encouraging donors' interests in our organization. This is an essential first step toward a major gift.

It also lets our board members get involved in the creative and fun side of fundraising. I like this delicate and more subtle side of our work. It is all about developing strategies to strengthen relationships with our favorite people, figuring out how to increase a special someone's involvement, how to bring lost donor friends back to our organization, and/or matching up our organization's needs with our donors' visions and interests.

Ambassadors as "Relationship Managers"

My approach to Ambassadors is based on the for-profit model of an "Account Manager" in business who manages relationships with key clients. We follow this format by setting up board members to become a "Relationship Manager" for key funders of our organization.

Each board member who participates in the project is assigned to manage and foster the relationship with one to three major donors, either past, current, or potential future donors. Board members typically understand the concept of an Account Manager, borrowed from the business sector.

We know that, if the relationship with the donor is fostered correctly, then the actual solicitation and asking for gifts will almost take care of itself. In this approach, everybody wins:

- The board members win because they finally have a comfortable and highly productive way to promote gifts to their organizations.
- The donors win because they get more attention and personalized communication from an organization they care about.
- The organization wins because it leverages the resources of board members' talents to cultivate long-term relationships with funding sources, ensuring financial stability over time.
- The staff wins because they are receiving help, at the highest volunteer level, in developing deeper and more extensive relationships with important donors.
- The organization's constituency wins because more resources will flow into much-needed services.

Customer Relationship Management for Donors

This type of Ambassador role program sets up a donor-centered approach to cultivating a gift, because the donor's interests guide the whole process. It builds on Customer Relationship Management (CRM) techniques used by many for-profit companies.

CRM holds that customers—with their needs and wants—should drive business strategy. It holds that businesses should keep focused on their customers above all, watching for and constantly adapting to trends and changes in customer behavior and interests.

However, in the nonprofit sector, we do not actually want donors driving our organization's mission just because they are donating. But we do need to know why our donors care about our cause and why they are giving to us instead of another organization. What do our donors want to accomplish through their giving? Why are they giving to us? What is their personal passion? What are their values?

I personally think we need much more of a donor orientation in our business. We usually focus in the wrong direction, on what our organization needs from donors rather than why our donors care about us. Our communication is one-way, often focused too much on money rather than change for the good.

In fact, what happens when a nonprofit's gifts level off? In business terms, the organization's sales—its contributions—are flat. Why is this happening? It may not be the fundraising program failings. It may be the organization's strategy and positioning itself. Could it be losing relevance in its field? Could it be in danger of becoming "old news" in the community, overshadowed by newer "sexier" organizations that have captured the donor public's interest?

I read last week in the *Wall Street Journal* that The Gap's sales were flat for yet another year. What is The Gap going to have to do? This fine retail company will have to "re-brand" itself to become more relevant and competitive in the marketplace. It is about to become old news in the retail market.

What do we often do when our "sales" are flat? We focus on fundraising, and bring in a fundraising consultant. More often than not I will find that the problem is not the fundraising program, it is that the organization has lost its hold on the passion and vision of its donors. The nonprofit may need to "re-brand" itself too, and look at its position in its nonprofit service market. It may need to reinvent itself to recapture lost energy among its donors.

Listen to your donors. They will tell you what you need to know! Ask them why they are giving and what they want to see your organization doing. Assigning board members to important donors as Ambassadors will help you create ongoing consistent communications with them. And your board members can be important earphones out in the community—finding out what is exciting—or unexciting— about your organization's work in the world.

Implementing Ambassadors

When you first set up board members to be Ambassadors, make the purpose of the board member's first meeting with the donor a special one: to thank her personally and find out exactly why she is giving to your organization. The Ambassador's only charge is to focus on the donor's vision and giving interests. I cannot think of more valuable input, can you?

We can give our Ambassadors a set of questions to guide them through their interview. I love the idea of my board members systematically collecting vital information about donors, information that we urgently need to know.

Best of all, when we start board members off with the task of information gathering, it gives them a comfortable framework for the first meetings, and a good way to begin developing a personal relationship with the donor.

Ambassadors Are Perfect for Major Gift Programs

Board member Ambassadors can be assigned to all types of potential major donors, individuals, corporate or foundation representatives, or government officials. Frequent personal contact should be made. This is the perfect way to help foster a friendly, close relationship that is personal and sincere.

Major gift donors usually start by making small gifts to their organizations. They also want to know more about us. We know there will be plenty more gifts in the future if we create the right kind of relationship. Since these donors already have some level of involvement, they are at a perfect stage to be cultivated by a caring, committed Board member.

Setting Ambassadors Up to Win

As I mentioned earlier, Ambassadors need a solid structure and great staff support if they are to be effective. First of all, they must have a specific time frame for everything they do. I like to see a systematic pattern of monthly contacts, in the tradition of the major gifts program, called Moves Management.

Moves Management is a way to manage activity with your top prospects. You want to make a "move" or create some type of connection to the donor once a month. You track your activity with this group of prospects on a monthly basis. Good fundraising practices hold that getting in touch with an important donor monthly will cultivate that donor quickly and ready them to a major solicitation.

When Ambassador board members connect with their assigned prospects monthly, they will offer deep and broad support to your major gift program.

Your Ambassadors will also need help defining the cultivation activities they will engage in with their assigned prospects. Above all, they need hand-holding, moral support, coaching, and encouragement.

Ambassadors definitely require smart staff support or they will go nowhere. You should examine carefully what benefits Ambassadors might offer your fundraising program.

On the surface this project may appear to be a revenue loss, because of the drain on staff time. But if you look more carefully you will find that it can bring in major gifts with little effort while also cultivating your board members for their own gifts. Ambassadors can be an integral part of your major gift and stewardship programs.

One way to support Ambassadors is to create *small groups* composed of board members themselves who check in with each other regularly for peer support and coaching. The small groups give board members a way to support each other without overly taxing the staff.

Clustering Ambassadors together in teams for training sessions, review meetings, and/or conference calls provides an efficient framework for coaching; the group can be dealt with as a whole. The small groups can also help to:

- Create a team spirit among board members.

- Create a sense of fun.

- Foster new relationships among board members who do not know each other.

- Provide indispensable moral support and friendship.

Do consider the benefits of creating a formal Ambassador role for your board members who are nervous about actually soliciting. They can bring a lot of benefit to your fundraising bottom line by helping to cultivate important relationships with your key funders.

HOW TO MAKE USE OF A LUCKY MOMENT: TEACHING THE ELEVATOR SPEECH

Suppose one of your board members finds himself standing next to Bill Gates in an elevator. They are the only two people in the car for several floors. Your guy is on his way to a meeting of your board.

Bill Gates makes a pleasant conversational comment. The way is open for a comment about the good cause that the board member passionately supports and cares about. In this once-in-a-lifetime moment, what does he say?

Over and over, I find that board members do *not* know what to say about our organizations! They are even a bit confused about the mission, and they are really unsure how to articulate the case for support.

They urgently need training on exactly what to say and how to say it, not just for elevator moments, but for all the professional and social conversations in which the subject of the nonprofit might easily arise.

One of the most important roles our board members can play is to represent us cheerfully and enthusiastically in the community, building social relationships as advocates for our organization. So, more than anything, we *must* be sure they know the right things to say and how to talk about our mission with passion and impact.

We have a tendency to give our board members our fundraising materials and then expect that they will know the key points to make when they go out to talk about our organization. Wrong!

For one thing, they do not read our materials carefully. Also, do our materials really convey the guts of how we make a difference in the world, or do they talk in jargon about "programs of work" as opposed to our real results?

Can a busy board member skim our materials and immediately have something persuasive and compelling to say about our organization and its mission? Again, we can and must take the responsibility for their preparation for this situation. We need to train them to make the most of the moment in the elevator.

TIPS AND TECHNIQUES

Give board members these materials:

- Easy to read fact sheets
- Success stories or testimonials
- Conversation starters
- Ideas on three key points to say about your organization

It is important to give board members practice on what to say—live, real-life practice. Do not forget the power of involving your board members in a verbal conversation about your organization, which is something that we rarely do.

The Mingle Exercise: Helping Them Express Why They Care

To get them started thinking about their own elevator speech, try a "mingle exercise" to get them warmed up. This is an exercise in which board members mingle around the room and share their own perspective about the organization with four or five different people.

Here is how to set this exercise up.

- Have them think to themselves what they might say to someone about why they care enough to sit on the board. Then ask them to share with other board members why they are on the board and what speaks to them personally about the good work of your nonprofit.

- Give them a few moments to write down some notes to themselves.

- Then have them stand up, go around the room, and share their perspective briefly with four other board members, one after the other.

When they do the mingle exercise, they will find themselves saying over and over why they really care about this organization and what is deeply meaningful to them about your mission. The mingle exercise brings out exactly what they should be saying in their elevator speech to their friends and acquaintances: something personal and from the heart.

The mingle exercise has a very special added benefit: it is also a "re-kindling" conversation. As your board member talks again and again about what sparks his enthusiasm or interest in your organization's work, he is re-igniting his own passion as he speaks. He is reminding himself about the difference you make; and why it is personally important to him.

Re-inspired by their own passion for the cause, board members are now ready to share their own excitement about your organization. They are often surprised and relieved to hear that it is perfect if they just talk about their own personal excitement and passion for the organization's work.

They do not need to memorize case statements and lots of facts. Just send these people out to be passionate and share their enthusiasm.

You can go far with enthusiasm alone.

The All-Important Elevator Speech

Exercises in creating an elevator speech are a fun way to liven up board meetings and give your board members real practice in talking persuasively and passionately about your organization.

What is an elevator speech? It is:

- A "speech" you might give about your organization if you were in an elevator with someone and only had 30 seconds to tell them about your organization.

- A mini sound bite of information that will inspire the person you are talking with to want to know more.

- A "teaser," designed to encourage more involvement with your organization.

> *Gail's training on the elevator speech worked miracles; I have used it over and over ever since she helped me understand the concept: simplify, simplify.*
>
> —Betsy Buford

IN THE REAL WORLD

In North Carolina, we do not have that many elevators, so I tell folks to imagine that this is a "check-out line speech" when you meet someone in the grocery store. This always gets a good laugh.

I had a successful experience once with a "check-out line speech" in the local Harris Teeter grocery store. I had just started working on my new ideas about board members focusing on cultivation rather than on solicitation and was interviewing nonprofit leaders for their perspective.

I saw Betsy Buford, former Deputy Secretary of Cultural Resources for the state and Director of the Division of State History Museums, in the check-out line. She had been on my list to interview but I had not yet reached her. I knew her, but not very well, so I was a tiny bit hesitant to call her on the phone. I could have been shy and apologetic about approaching her, but instead I ran right up with a big smile and said enthusiastically:

"Hi Betsy! I've been wanting to ask you about something! I'm working on some new ideas about setting up board members as ambassadors to cultivate prospects. I'd love to bounce these ideas off you and see what you think about them. Can I get together with you for a cup of coffee?"

Betsy Buford, wonderful lady that she is, looked me straight in the eye, and said, *"Absolutely yes! Let's get together! In fact, I may have a museum that needs this idea right now."*

Now this was a surprisingly successful elevator speech. Not only did Betsy Buford meet with me, but she engaged me to work with a museum to enlist a group of community leaders who would serve as ambassadors to lay the groundwork for a capital campaign. That project helped to get many new community supporters talking enthusiastically about the museum, and it also gave me a chance to expand my ideas, which in turn led to this book.

Elevator speeches are more difficult than you might think. They must be more than just a recitation of your mission, which is probably written in a formal, high-brow fashion, in words that would never come out of someone's mouth unless it were a formal "speech."

What you say in the elevator speech must be personal and from the heart. It must be conversational and even casual, the way you naturally talk. The elevator speech needs to be free from jargon or "nonprofit-ese," language that a layperson might not understand.

For example, I am working with a medical clinic that provides medical services for the underserved. Somehow the word "underserved" does not carry the same impact as the phrase "people in need" or "needy." If you try to talk passionately to someone about the "underserved," they simply will not feel the same sympathetic response that is stirred when you talk about people who are seriously ill and cannot afford to see a doctor.

Far too much of our marketing literature is written in noncompelling language that is abstract and distant from what it describes. Consider the difference in the emotional impact of "wife beater" and "batterer." When did we remove the horror from this issue by using the abstract word "batterer?" This word leaves out the wife, and thus feels more removed from the scene of shouts and physical struggle. It makes me think of punching a boxing bag rather than the awful situation of a husband beating his wife.

When we talk to someone about our mission and our good work, each word we choose to use must have passion and impact. If we pussyfoot around, or apologize, or are timid, then we will not be effective messengers for our organization.

TIPS AND TECHNIQUES

Once a client asked me, *"What exactly do we say in our 30-second elevator speech?"* I responded, "Tell about the impact you are making in the world." The client, surprised, said, *"Oh! That's it! Of course!"*

The elevator speech is a serious exercise in discipline. If you only had 30 seconds, what would you choose to say, out of all the things you possibly could address? Would you use a short anecdote as a testimonial? Would you talk about your personal passion and experience and why you feel so strongly about this issue? Yes and yes. Both are highly effective.

What You Say is very important. It is up to us to refine our message so that it is quick, easy to understand, easy to deliver, and has high impact. What a job! And we are not professional marketers! I urge you to work and rework your key message that you want your board members to share. Simplify it and make it easy for board members to deliver.

However, we must remember that board members are more often than not uncertain volunteers—they may forget the speech we have so carefully honed. If and when that happens, we need to keep right on encouraging them and continuing to make it fun for them. We will cut them all the breaks they need in order to keep their momentum going. Even if they end up "blathering" it is OK by me.

In my training sessions, I tell board members that the most important thing is to say something directly from the heart that reflects their personal feeling and point of view about their organization and its cause.

I remember one training session I was doing with Ronald McDonald International that included many board members from around the world learning about fundraising. The folks in the room were working earnestly on their elevator speeches. They were all concerned about getting their facts just right.

These good-hearted board members were worried about doing a good job on the elevator speech, and they were in fact struggling to come across as natural and passionate. I found that they were trying to recite facts and mission statements instead of talking from the heart with passion. Their delivery was too stiff.

We had been having a good time that afternoon with our training session. The biggest surprise hit of my seminar was when we were working on the elevator speech, and I told them that as long as they were passionate and enthusiastic, then it was okay to "blather." What fun we had with that one!

Why can it be OK to blather? Even if the board member ends up making no sense in the elevator speech, the person who is listening will pick up on his excitement, commitment, and enormous sense of urgency about families with sick children who are being turned away for lack of space. The listener will understand that this is something important to understand; he or she will get the passion that this friend has for this organization.

Studies show that the most important component of personal communication is not what someone says but how they say it.

When I presented the "OK to blather" concept, the audience had a big laugh: they were immensely relieved —that they could just be themselves and share their passion, which would then mean they would be successfully communicating about the mission.

> I always tell my volunteers that they can go far with their enthusiasm and passion alone. It is passion that injects life into what we are doing.

The importance of enthusiasm cannot be overemphasized in this business of fundraising. We have to be passionately and cheerfully aggressive in sharing our story every time.

Key Components of an Elevator Speech

An elevator speech has three distinct components. The first is What You Say. The second is How You Say It. The third is a Request for Follow-Up. If your conversation does not have the key information (What You Say) and a warm personal natural tone (How You Say It), and a way to Follow-Up, then it is not a complete elevator speech.

Note my check-out line speech above with Betsy Buford: it had all the components. I was enthusiastic, I said something compelling about my project, just enough to tweak some interest, and then I asked for a follow-up visit.

When people focus on the first component, What You Say, they often forget the other two parts of the speech. In practicing the elevator speech, many board members find they are so busy talking that they can appear far too serious or come across as if they are reciting a list of facts. Sometimes they are too intent on what they are saying, so they forget to watch the listener for cues to stop talking and listen to something the listener has to say.

When they focus too much on what they are saying, something important is missing. It is their humanity, their passion, their excitement, their sense of urgency. That is why I tell board members to focus more on *how* they are talking rather than exactly what they are saying. I think *how* they say it may be more important than what they are saying.

Do not make your elevator speeches overly complicated. Let your board members play around and have fun. Let some folks role play if they want. Or role play with them.

Here is an easy way to introduce the elevator speech exercise to your board members.

IN THE REAL WORLD

Here is another example of a successful elevator speech: I was getting ready to work with a new client, the Partnership for Children on the Outer Banks of North Carolina. I had much to learn about the organization, as I had not yet started my engagement.

By chance, I ran into a major developer from the Outer Banks at the high school graduation of our respective daughters. I barely knew him, but I wanted to mention I would be working with this important group soon, and I wanted to see if I could get him involved.

I said, "You know, I am going to be working with the Partnership for Children down in Dare County next month. I would love to pick your brain about this group and its opportunities."

And then I said the only thing I could think of, without any detailed knowledge of the organization's priorities or needs. I looked right at him, put my hand firmly down on the table, leaned over to him and said intently, "You know, we have *got* to do something about the kids in Dare County."

You know what? He put his hand right down on the table too. Leaned over to me and said, "You are right, we have *got* to do something," echoing my exact intonation. "Call me when you come down."

That was my short and sweet elevator speech. It had a compelling teaser (What You Say); it had emotion and personal passion (How to Say It), and it had a Follow-Up, all in three sentences.

The Elevator Speech Exercise

1. Ask your board members to think about what they would say if they had only 30 seconds to tell someone about their organization. Give them a few minutes to make some notes to themselves. Or they can discuss this with the other people sitting near them. Ask some members of the board to share with others what they think is important to say. It may be useful—and interesting—to put a few key points up on the board, or provide a fact sheet to board members with some suggested facts or issues to emphasize.

2. Have them stand up, and ask them to find a partner. When they are paired off, tell them to decide which person will be Partner A and which will be Partner B. Partner A will go first and Partner B will be the listener. Set the background for this "conversation." Tell them to pretend that they are acquaintances but that the listener does not know a lot about their organization.

3. Use a stopwatch, and give Partner A 30 seconds to tell Partner B his elevator speech.

4. When Partner A finishes, ask Partner B to provide some feedback to Partner A. It is important to provide feedback, so each board member can understand how he

is coming across. Board members will take feedback more easily from another board member than from staff or their trainer. Having them work together helps make this a teambuilding exercise as well. The board members will start to have fun at this point!

5. Ask Partner A to go again, using the feedback to polish up the first elevator speech. Allow 30 seconds again.

6. Let Partner B give Partner A some feedback again. This time you will find that Partner A is getting a lot smoother and that the two partners are beginning to bond.

7. Next it is Partner B's turn. Ask her to give her own elevator speech a try for 30 seconds. Partner A can provide feedback and then let Partner B try again, providing feedback on her second try.

8. Ask for volunteers to come to the front and try their elevator speeches for the whole group. If no one will volunteer, either drag the board chair up there, or volunteer to give the elevator speech yourself to a board member. Then the group discusses the example. There should be lots of laughs by this point.

9. Then bring the whole group together for a conversation. Ask everyone for their impressions of this exercise. Let them share their insights and learnings. The energy in the room will be high at this point. Your board members will be having fun while they are practicing an essential skill for being community ambassadors, friendraisers, and fundraisers. What a great teambuilding experience for your board members!

Hardcopy Materials

A board member going out to make a call or visit will feel more confident with information in hand. These are also useful for preparing the elevator speech. Volunteer fundraisers really rely on them!

Whether or not board members read the materials, they often feel they *have* to have them. I have seen board members hang on to their materials like a crutch. There are board members who will do *nothing* until the materials are complete. Talk about delaying tactics! However, if providing the information in hardcopy form gets the fundraising done, then let us give our volunteer fundraisers the comfort they think they need.

Fact sheets. I like fact sheets the best, because they contain the important points and are easy to read. Remember, everything must be written at the fifth grade reading level for easy skimming. Few people read for detail any more. Busy people scan for the important points. Fact sheets can also have diagrams and pictures.

Statistics. You need to teach your board members one or two statistics about your mission that are *amazing!* You need a number that really shows, with impact, what you are doing, or how great the need is. If you do not have a statistic like this, then figure out how to take your data and create one. I like to have one statistic that can knock somebody out of a chair!

Be careful, however. A sheet with too many statistics will stultify your reader, and glaze over their eyes. Do not make it boring!

Success stories and testimonials about your organization are of the greatest importance. If you only have five minutes with a prospective donor, you should tell a story with a testimonial.

A powerful Mission Moment story is all you really have to present in many situations. One story can have more persuasive power and energy than any campaign case statement we could have written.

Be sure your board members have a good story to tell.

HIGHLIGHTS OF STEP THREE

Ready Your Board Members with the Right Tools and Skills

- Fundraising from the Donor's Point of View
  - Donors want to be treated like people, not pocketbooks.
  - The conversation should never be about money.
  - What donors want: prompt personal thank-yous and meaningful information on your results.

- No-Ask Fundraising: Take the Emphasis Away from Soliciting
  - The Ask is only one tiny moment in the entire fundraising cycle.
  - The only way to approach major gifts is by cultivating relationships that matter.
  - Board members can help with the Ask Warm-Up and the Ask Follow-Up.
  - Board members can serve as Ambassadors assigned to cultivate specific major donors.

- The elevator speech helps you make use of a lucky moment.
  - Equip your board members with the right things to say and how to say them.
  - There are three parts to the elevator speech: What to Say, How to Say It, and Request for Follow-Up.

NOTES

1. Todd Baker, "Death to the Dear Friend Letter," *Fundraising Well* newsletter, November 2003 (www.blackbaud.com/files/Newsletters/FundraisingWell/2003/fundraisingwellnovember-2003.pdf).

2. Penelope Burk, *Donor Centered Fundraising* (Chicago: Cygnus Applied Research, Inc., 2003), www.donorcentered.com, 77.

3. Ibid.

4. Ibid., 76.

5. Ibid., 48.

6. Ibid., 115.

7. Ibid.

8. Ibid., 23.

9. Ibid., 80.

10. Terry Axelrod, *Raise More Money* (Seattle, WA: Raise More Money Publications, 2002).

CHAPTER 5

Passion-Driven Fundraising Step Four: ENGAGE Your Board Members in Your Fundraising Plan

If I could just get my board members to open doors and introduce me to key people, I would be thrilled.

—Nonprofit Executive Director

We may affirm absolutely that nothing great in the world has ever been accomplished without passion.

—George Hegel

There are many ways to harness board member passion for your organization's great work and channel it into highly productive fundraising activities. We can even make it interesting—and fun. In this section we will discuss activities that will generate new friends for your organization, fuel the fire of board member passion, and generate great fundraising results.

Each board member can—and should—take on a specific task to support the fundraising program. They can find a role in which they are comfortable, whether they are involved in soliciting or not. If they are afraid of asking, then they can pile all their friends on the bandwagon!

Remember, success breeds success. And *friends* are success. New friends bring in more new friends. Friends open the door to even more social networks, all of which get your organization higher on your community's radar screen.

Fundraising becomes a natural outgrowth of all the energy and enthusiasm generated for your cause. Doors to major donors start to open with ease because of all the buzz in the community, and many new smaller donors start responding to invitations to events and requests for contributions.

This chapter will give you specific, practical methods for setting your fired-up board members to work, opening doors, making connections, reaching out, and helping to bring new supporters into your nonprofit.

First let me say a bit more about why friends of your organization are so important, whether they become donors or not.

FRIENDRAISING BUILDS SOCIAL CAPITAL

A nonprofit needs friends just as much as it needs money. As I mentioned earlier, Hildy Gottlieb, in her book *FriendRaising,* really hits the mark in reminding us that we want everybody working with us and wishing us well, whether they give lots of money or not.

There are so many ways that friends are able to help out. They can volunteer, spread the word, make key introductions to potential donors or government officials, and generally expand community moral support for our important mission. As we all know, friendship is far more enduring than money.

The overall goal with a nonprofit is to serve the community, and that means engaging as many community people as possible in your mission. It also means we want as many people as possible to know about us, to talk about us, and to tell others how important our work is.

The more friends we have in our community, the stronger we will be! I call it being on somebody's radar screen. All of us are so barraged by media that we are too often on information overload. Our lives are so busy, and there are so many images firing at us daily, that we block out most stimuli in order to even function.

So getting a nonprofit's signal to show up on someone's radar screen is a hard job, especially when that person is an important community opinion leader or a philanthropist.

However, once we have our community's awareness, we can end up becoming one of the most important nonprofit groups in the area. Our organization will be noticed. We will be paid attention to. We will also be able to raise lots of money because half the battle is already won: our mission has captured people's hearts and minds and they are talking about our work. Do not underestimate the power of positive attention to our cause.

Social Capital

One of the most valuable assets each board member brings to your group is his or her social capital. Social capital is a term used for a person's connections and social networks. Sociologists study social capital as a phenomenon that helps to build stronger communities and strengthen bonds among people. You can also say that your organization itself has a certain amount of social capital.

The connections we all have to each other form a crucial web of human interaction. This means that we live our lives in webs of interdependence with others.

Our networks are a sort of glue that holds us together. These relationships ground us within a context of friends, professional associates, family and extended family connections, religious and social groups, service people, and political, governmental, educational circles.

For example: Why are some women called "soccer moms?" Because they are part of a particular social network based on their kids' activities: a sphere of connection and influence, which also overlaps with other circles.

Social networks offer a host of benefits to organizations, communities, and individuals as well. Our connections with others help to keep us emotionally and physically healthy. Some sociologists say that joining an organization cuts an individual's chance of dying within the next year in half.

From families to nations, social networks play a critical role in determining the way community problems are solved, organizations are run, and the degree to which individuals succeed in achieving their goals.

There is no doubt that developing social capital for our organization is a highly important task, one that is perfectly designed for board members.

It is important to capitalize on our board members' own social capital to further our organization's urgent work solving community problems. So the job is clear: we have to ask our board members to pull in their networks and *introduce our organization to everybody they know.*

Remember, however, that when you put your board members to work on this issue, we are not simply looking for donors. We are literally—and deliberately—seeking to expand our organization's network and social capital. We are looking for friends, as well as a chance to shine brightly on the community's radar screen.

These efforts generate visibility and attention. They are not about money alone, which should make squeamish board members more comfortable. At the same time, they are vitally important for our cause and the difference we want to make. All good fundraising absolutely requires a setting of positive word-of-mouth PR, constantly humming in the background, supporting everything we do.

The Staff's Role: Know Where to Focus

Here are some words of realism for the staff who are directing your board's friendraising and fundraising efforts. As a nonprofit leader guiding your board, it is up to you to point the board members in the right direction.

Think through where they can help out the most. Bring them names of the key players in your community or region whom you would most like to get in front of. Don't expect your board members to have as complete a view of the philanthropic environment as you do. Help them prioritize their own efforts and the people they want to focus on.

Like any smart fundraiser, you are managing the prospect list behind the scenes. You already know the VIPs you want to have at your socials, tours and events. You know who the social mavens are in your community. It is up to you to set the priorities, based on your analysis of your prospects and your potential.

Some of the activities I am going to describe in this chapter are quite labor-intensive. They will require lots of personal time and attention—from you or a board member following up folks who attend Small Socials, Tours, or other events.

To stay sane, here's what you have to do: prioritize. You only have but so much time and energy to spend on your fundraising and friendraising activities. You have financial goals to reach, and you need to generate visibility in the community.

We all know you can't go after every wonderful person who may be interested in your cause.

> *So, focus your time and attention down to the people who matter.*

Choose the people with the deepest pockets, with the best connections, with the most extensive social networks—because they will spread the word for you. They have the influence to bring people with them; and they have the capability to become major donors.

> *To be successful, narrow, narrow, narrow down your focus.*

The activities I describe in this section can serve as an underpinning to a major gift program, an annual fund or community engagement effort, depending where you focus. Clearly the major gift prospects are fewer in number and will receive the most personal attention and face time. You will be plotting long term strategies to develop these relationships and you'll find important ways for board members to support you.

Following here are ways to get your board members to work opening doors and bringing folks into your organization's circle. These methods will require staff support and guidance. Don't turn over any of these projects to be managed by volunteer board members and hope they will be effective.

It will be important for you to firmly direct behind the scenes. And remember since the board members are well-meaning volunteers with little time, again, focus them where their energies can pay off the most.

Getting the Door Open

We all know that within our board members' social networks there is a gold mine of potential friends and donors. The board members understand this as well, aware that their networks are full of folks who might be interested in supporting our cause.

How do we open the door to these contacts? Most board members think they cannot just call up their friends and acquaintances and demand "we need you to be involved!" This is often a huge hurdle. I have encountered this feeling myself when I serve on a committee or a board. How do I make the connection between my friends and my favorite cause of the moment?

All board members need help in figuring out a "nice" way to introduce their friends to their organization. They want their friends to know that they are passionate supporters of your organization, but they just do not know a genuine way to go about it.

First, let us look at the word "nice," and then explore five suggestions on how to open doors.

The Soft Sell   I come from the soft sell school of fundraising and friendraising. I apply "being nice" to the entire process, start to finish. Since I am a Southerner, I call this the more genteel "white gloves and pearls" approach.

My manner is softer than that of some other fundraisers. But that does not mean I am less serious. You better believe that I am working as hard as I can to change the world. I am passionate and enthusiastic. At the same time, I am polite about it, and I never want to be abrasive, offensive, or intrusive.

It's amazing, though—you can say many things you never thought you would if you have that smile on your face and in your voice.

Being gracious and polite does pay off because we draw people to us (remember energy is contagious?) instead of pushing them away. As representatives of nonprofits, we need to be folks that other people want to be around.

We should never come across as aggressive; instead, be enthusiastic, kind, and welcoming. Cheerfully aggressive is fine, but plain aggressive is a turn-off.

Do remember: nice does not mean vague or unmotivated. I am very, very intentional about the result I mean to create, and I am usually successful. I know that the method I espouse—both passion driven and polite—works. Let your board members know that they can be "nice" and still be passionate advocates for your mission.

TIPS AND TECHNIQUES

Here are five easy ways your board members can open the door, connect their friends to your organization, expand its social capital, and help find a new group of potential donors.

1. Be personal advocates wherever they go.
2. Spread the word by mail.
3. Have Advice Visits with important prospects.
4. Host Small Socials of potential supporters.
5. Host Mission-Focused Tours of your organization.

BOARD MEMBERS AS "SNEEZERS," ADVOCATES WHO SPREAD THE WORD WHEREVER THEY GO

> *You can really tell if somebody cares about doing something by their tone of voice.*
>
> —Lewis Cullman, Philanthropist

Your board members need to be *advocates* for the mission of your organization; they need to talk about it wherever they go. If they are burning with passion for the cause, then they should be all over their friends, and everybody they run into, telling them to get involved and help with this important cause.

I want board members who can be what Seth Godin termed "sneezers" in his book, *Unleashing the Ideavirus*: advocates whose news and excitement about our cause are simply contagious. Godin says that we want to refine our message into something "so smooth that once someone is exposed to it, they are instantly hooked."[1]

Wherever they go, our trustees can be spreading the good word about the difference we want to make in the world. When they sneeze, or express their opinion, news about our cause spreads like a virus. It's just an "idea virus." And the idea they are spreading multiplies as it goes from person to person.

One board member tells 5 people who all tell five more people that your upcoming event is going to be the coolest thing in town this year. All of a sudden, your event has the buzz and it is almost sold out two months in advance.

When board members are passionate advocates, they increase awareness in the community through word-of-mouth news and conversation. The marketing pundits talk more and more these days about the power of person-to-person communication; your board members can create epidemics of news themselves simply by transmitting information.

> The Tipping Point *reminds us that we can be like social glue to spread the message of our cause. We can be evangelists for our organization.*[2]
>
> —Malcolm Gladwell

Just imagine how wonderful it would be if you had all your board members unleashed, pouring out their excitement for your cause all over the community. Just think what you could accomplish if your organization was top on the community's radar screen. Raising money would be so very much easier. Attendance at events would skyrocket. The newspaper would be calling you to do profiles on your good work. People would want to serve on your board! Board meetings would be "happening" events.

This is the kind of energy that can change the world and solve every problem we have on planet earth.

You can turn your board members into roaring advocates for your organization wherever they go. Board members who are well connected to the organization should naturally *want* everyone they know to be familiar with this important community organization and to understand why it matters.

If I were a board member of a conservation fund, for example, I would simply assume that everyone in the community would want to be sure that we were preserving enough green space for the future.

I would not be hesitant or apologetic! I would naturally expect that all my friends and acquaintances would want to help in any way they could. I would automatically assume that they would not want our community to lose its water and air quality.

And I would be all over them! Remember, this is the "glass is half full" *abundance* perspective on winning friends and donors for your organization. Here is a great example:

IN THE REAL WORLD

My friend Peggy Link Weil was on the board of the Women's Center in Chapel Hill for years. Every year, she would host a table for the annual luncheon.

I could always expect her call each year to come to the luncheon, which I attended. The annual art show came in January. First she asked me to attend the art show with her, which I did. Then she asked me to be a sponsor for the opening, which I did. The next year she asked me to send notes out in Raleigh to enlist other sponsors for the art show, which again I did.

Now was Peggy shy? Not at all! Or aggressive? No way. Was she "trying to take advantage of our friendship?" Of course not.

She was passionate about the cause. She naturally expected I would gladly support her cause and help her out. Of course I helped her! Did I understand her commitment to the Women's Center? You bet! Did her work help generate more visibility, connections, and financial support for the Women's Center? Yes!

> *I am personally convinced that one person can be a change catalyst,*
> *a "transformer" in any situation, any organization. Such an individual*
> *is yeast that can leaven an entire loaf. It requires vision, initiative,*
> *patience, respect, persistence, courage, and faith to be a transforming leader.*
>
> —Steven Covey

SPREADING THE WORD BY MAIL

As we know, one of the fundamental fundraising tools of every nonprofit group is its mailing program. Your organization's mailing list is used for event invitations, newsletters, and public announcements, as well as for asking folks for their financial support. It is the basic tool for managing your social capital—and your donors.

Your board members need to adopt the mailing list as their own. Who in the community needs to be hearing news from your organization? Who should be asked to important events or to help contribute urgently needed funds?

How many of their friends and acquaintances can they get on the master mailing list for events, news and solicitations? Board members should use the mailing program as their personal tool to connect their own social network with the organization and its mission.

Personal Notes to Friends

Personal notes are a powerful communications tool. Remember, in this age when people are oversaturated with impersonal messages from the mass media, the rare personal note stands out. People are far more willing to trust a personal reference or recommendation from someone they know.

It's a great idea for trustees to send personal notes to their friends along with newsletters or clippings of laudatory articles about your nonprofit. The newspaper article serves, in effect, as an outside endorsement of your organization.

Your board members might be surprised at the kind of response they will receive from this type of communication; their friends will undoubtedly mention it to them, creating a perfect opening to launch into their elevator speech!

Their personal note could say a number of things: *"I thought you would be interested in this,"* or, *"I would love to tell you more about this cause,"* or best of all, *"I would love to pick your brain about this project because I am a board member,"* leading in to the Advice Visit, which we will discuss shortly.

Even squeamish board members who are concerned about being "nice" can send communications to their friends gently introducing the organization.

Expanding the Mailing List

I like the idea of setting up board members to "own" an important part of the mailing list. It can serve as their personal tool for communicating to their social networks about your cause.

Consider creating a small board Task Force to oversee a project for adding all the board members' personal contacts into your system, with notes on who knows whom.

Let the board members themselves set their own goals and ask each other for names to add to the list. If your board members "own" the project, then it will be far more successful than if the staff drives the effort.

Firm goals are a must; for example, every board member can be asked to provide a certain number of new names, or they can decide they want a total of x new contacts from board members this year.

New names can come from many aspects of board members' lives: school contacts (either from them or from their children); family members; clergy and church friends; people who are active in the community and serve on other nonprofit boards; folks who may have a personal tie to the mission; their friends and social contacts; elected officials, government officials, and community leaders; people who provide personal services such as their hairdressers or CPAs; business owners and managers; and, of course, any known donors or philanthropists in their circles.

When you add these new names, be sure to note which board member has the original relationship. Consider a field on your mailing data base: "Known by." Then you can segment your mailings by board member, pulling out each board member's contacts for a personal handwritten note. This is useful for personal invitations to events as well as for solicitations.

I recommend that board members focus on two types of names for the mailing list:

- *VIPs (Very Important Prospects)* are civic, political, philanthropic, religious, corporate, or social leaders in your community. These key decision makers and major donors should of course be your top priority, because not only do they give, but they are also important opinion leaders who can influence many other people.

  The VIPs may also be the "sneezers" in your community, easily spreading the news about your organization. It is easy to find out who these people are in your community. Start here when building friends, connections, and donor prospects.

  VIP prospects should of course get special treatment in your mailing program, with personalized invitations to important meetings and events. When you are sending out solicitation appeals, always break this group out so you can tailor special requests to them for larger gift amounts.

- *Friends.* This is the place for all the other names within your board members' social networks. You will want many, many people in your community on your Friends list.

  While they may receive more generic, less personalized mailings, they are no less important. You never know who may be deeply passionate about your cause. Here is where board members can add their neighbors, book clubs, social groups, church friends, and all the many people they know in the community.

Remember, however, that the purpose of this activity is not just to create a list for solicitations; it is to expand your social capital and create a list of potential supporters, friends, and volunteers. If you introduce the project as a solicitation list, some board members will be *reluctant to respond if they think it is for solicitation only.*

The real purpose is to expand your organization's social networks in the community and introduce more and more people to your important mission. It is a target list of all the folks you want to support your organization's work.

ADVICE VISITS: SEARCHING FOR HIDDEN GOLD

> *Only those who will risk going too far can possibly find out how far one can go.*
>
> —T. S. Eliot

A personal one-on-one meeting is my favorite way to introduce a person to my organization or favorite cause. I call this meeting the Advice Visit, because that is truly what I am after—advice.

My only goal for visiting this person is to ask them what they think of my project and ask for some serious guidance. I always appreciate other people's thoughts about my causes, especially if the thinking comes from important potential donors with deep pockets! This visit is emphatically *not* about money.

I don't have a hold on all the best ideas, and I don't know everyone who might be interested in my project or cause, or the people my volunteers might steer me to. It takes lots of people, all thinking together, offering lots of advice, to figure out how to put an organization smack in the middle of the entire community's radar screen.

There are several interesting metaphors for this valuable friendmaking and fundraising technique. In a way, Advice Visits are like treasure hunts, because when you get together personally with someone for an exploratory conversation, you are looking for treasure. As with all treasure hunts, you are not certain where and how to look, or whether there is any treasure to find. But if you are meeting with a community leader, chances are good that your visit will be highly productive.[3]

You could also look at the Advice Visit as if you were opening a box of chocolates, remembering Forrest Gump's comment that "you never know what you are gonna get!" I have certainly had some surprises, but I do not think I have ever been disappointed in any Advice Visit I have undertaken.

> *I wish each Board member would schedule meetings with leaders of business/industry. I need them to go with me to make introductions and help me at least establish contact.*
>
> —Development Director

"Can I Pick Your Brain?"; Advice Visits Can Open Important Doors

My favorite way to open a door is a one-on-one private Advice Visit with someone who can help my nonprofit. This is a perfect opportunity to promote my cause and cultivate a potential donor in a direct, personal way.

Advice Visits are easy and even fun. In fact, I can't think of a better door opener and cultivation tool around. You can do more in a half an hour with one important prospect than you can do in an entire evening of small talk at an event.

If you have ever read *What Color Is Your Parachute?*—in my view, the best job hunting guide ever published—then you will appreciate this strategy. *Parachute* describes a meeting called the Informational Interview. It asserts that *anybody* will be willing to talk to you if you are seeking their advice and counsel.[4]

When you go to the interview, you are, in fact, genuinely seeking that advice—about careers in the case of job hunters, or about your very important cause if you are promoting a nonprofit.

People are usually complimented when someone approaches just to ask for advice. *You would be surprised at the number of doors that will open if you just ask for advice.*

If you have never tried an Advice Visit, then a world of possibility and connection awaits you. People *want* to help nonprofit causes, because they care about their communities, their regions, their country, and their world. You *will* find help where you seek it, and you will be particularly successful because you are not asking directly.

You are merely setting up a situation in which the help can be offered if the person is so moved. In fact, you will probably be amazed at the person's willingness to help you.

Here is another reason I love the Advice Visit: The person I am talking/listening to invariably gives me an important lead or suggestion that will help me further my cause. Best of all, the person almost always *offers to do something to help me.*

Aha! This offer to help is a great step forward.

If the person offers to take any action on behalf of my cause, even if it is just a phone call, then guess what! They are *involved!* When someone acts to help your cause, then that person is becoming invested in your success! They become part of your team. They are putting themselves on the bandwagon. It is just so easy!

Ask them to meet with you to give their advice, and the next thing you know, they get excited and decide to become aligned with your cause and on your bandwagon. They will have done all this themselves, with very little nudging from you.

If the person you are visiting is a potential major donor, note carefully her questions about your project. The questions she asks contain valuable information. Why? Because they indicate the direction of her inner thinking about your cause.

I always pay careful attention to questions I receive during my Advice Visits. They may point to important opportunities I am missing, connections I need to make, or gaps in my case for support. They are also a window to my potential donor's thinking about my project.

I like to have my Advice Visits in a coffee shop or restaurant. It is always good to get out of the office environment into a more casual place. Morning coffees are easy to arrange now that they are part of many people's schedules.

Using the Elevator Speech to Get the Appointment

I manage to get Advice Visits by employing my very best elevator speech. I give just a teaser and then ask to take them out for coffee. Here is an example:

I am friends with a well-known philanthropist in Raleigh. He is an attractive older gentleman, and we always have a good time when we get together. He likes to visit with me and is usually interested in what I am up to. I protect this relationship carefully, and do not go to him too often. When I do, it is important.

For example, I might call him and say "Hi Frank! I am working on an interesting project to help transform a group of struggling high schools with high drop-out rates. We are just getting started and it is a big effort. Can I come pick your brain about this?"

Frank will always say, come on! In fact, he usually makes a real effort to visit with me, even if he has to change his schedule. He knows from experience that the visit with me will be interesting and probably entertaining.

Note the elevator speech above: a quick statement about the issue (What You Say); spoken enthusiastically (How to Say It), followed up with a Request to Meet in Person. Once I am in his office and get started, I carefully follow my Advice Visit Rules listed below.

If you want money, then ask for advice. If you want only advice, then ask for money.

Rules for the Advice Visit

When I make an Advice Visit, I have some inviolate rules to recommend. I developed these rules when I used to visit with very busy Wall Street types as Director of Development for the Kenan Flagler Business School.

Rule One: Make Sure You Are Interesting, Not Boring   As you tell your person about your cause and seek his advice, you should be watching carefully for his reaction. Your internal radar, so to speak, should be going round and round constantly.

If your prospect seems to be not very interested in your cause, then you should not drag on. If you start to lose his attention, then change the subject or be out of there in a flash. You do not want the person to remember you as overstaying your welcome. If you are perceived as boring or droning on and on, you will never be welcomed back!

Rule Two: Ask for a Short Appointment and Leave at the End of That Time
Always practice good manners and get up to leave when you said you would. If your prospect is on a roll, talking and talking, and asks you to stay, then do so. But never overstay your welcome. When you are visiting an important and extremely busy person, nothing is worse than a well-meaning visitor who stays forever and will not shut up. The person gets labeled "tiresome" and that may be the kiss of death!

If you are interesting and depart promptly, then your prospect will be much more likely to see you again when you come to call on him or her. I even like to leave deliberately when the person is not quite finished talking to me, even if he has warmed to the topic and has plenty more to say. Then, when I call for a follow-up visit, he will be happy, even eager to visit again, because he has more to say and knows I will not stay too long.

Rule Three: Make Sure the Person You Visit Does as Much of the Talking as Possible   You are after his advice and thinking. Only tell him enough about your project to keep him interested. The important points are to share your personal passion and excitement for the cause and why you are personally involved. Then just ask questions, such as:

- What do you think about the project?
- What about the organization?
- What about the need; is it real?
- What interests you personally about the problem we are addressing?
- What do you think our best strategy is for lining up support?
- Who else would be interested in hearing about this?

- Who else can help us?
- How can we get them on board?

Then listen, listen, listen. Ask just enough questions to keep the conversation going.

I once heard a remark at a cocktail party about a woman who was considered an excellent conversationalist. After she left a conversation, the person she was talking to said, "What an interesting person!" Do you know what this lady did? She only asked questions and got the other person to do the talking.

You can go far by just asking great questions and then keeping your mouth shut. You will be amazed at what you will find out in the Advice Visit. But you won't find it out if you are doing all the talking. Many nonprofit supporters think they need to do a "pitch" when they have this visit. A pitch is the last thing they should do. Instead, they should be quiet and listen.

People will offer to do so many things for you! If they suggest a prominent person in the community whom you should approach, then always ask them if they will help open the door to that person. That way you will not be making a cold call; this influential person will be helping to make the introduction, in effect, blessing you and your cause. I guarantee you will find treasure in everyone you meet!

Board Members Find These Rules for One-on-One Advice Visits to Be a Relief

Board members are usually quite happy to find out that they do not need to be prepared for an endless, detailed presentation. They are comfortable with the idea of seeking advice and input. After all, they are the community representatives on the board.

It is totally appropriate for them to be asking other community leaders for their best thinking on how to achieve the organization's goals. They do not have to present a detailed case for support in order to be effective personal advocates for the cause.

If you equip board members with these guidelines for Advice Visits, you will be surprised at the energy and gusto with which they will tackle meeting with their friends, associates, and community leaders. They had been thinking that if they made any personal calls, they were supposed to be asking for money. Not at all!

You will find that they actually *like* these visits. Just be sure they file a call report of some type after the visit, even if it is only a quick e-mail back to the staff letting them know the key issues that were covered and, most importantly, what follow-up actions are needed.

Good follow-up is vital! Otherwise the interest and energy developed during the visit may go to waste. It will fade from the person's radar screen. As social capital experts note, a person's social network disintegrates if it is not refreshed and kept up to date.

If your board members take on Advice Visits with vigor, they will become actively engaged in bringing their own friends into the fold as well as VIP community leaders whom they know.

As they take on their appropriate role as personal advocates for your mission, they will help expand your organization's social capital, making valuable friends and contacts who will be willing to help you out in many different ways.

GATHERING FRIENDS WITH SMALL SOCIALS

In addition to private one-on-one Advice Visits, your board members can help organize and host group meetings to spread the word about your cause.

Socials and group events do not involve the prospective friends and donors as directly as Advice Visits, but they do offer the chance to connect with larger numbers of interested potential supporters. You can expand your community relationships and make friends faster—although not as in depth—through group socials.

A Small Social can take several formats. It can be a coffee, a tea, dinner, or cocktails. It can be breakfast meetings or luncheons with several people. It can include from three or four people to over one hundred.

The Small Social can take place just about anywhere: in a restaurant, a coffee shop, a board member's office or home, on a front porch, or at your organization's offices. The point of the Small Social is that it is a group event and requires a special format in order to be successful.

There Are Four Rules to a Successful Small Social

> *It's easy to get intimidated if you are asking someone from help. But inviting somebody to be part of something that you are proud of is easier.*
>
> —Diane Paces-Wiles, Former Board Member

The first rule is that a board member or volunteer should do the inviting and hosting. That person is reaching into his or her social capital networks to bring new friends into the organization.

The second rule is that these events are free for those invited. Someone else is picking up the tab. The host or group of hosts should chip in to cover the expenses of the event and/or get what they need donated.

A third rule is that this is a *cultivation* event designed to introduce people to your organization or, if they already know you, to fire them up and involve them in your mission. Your goal is to bring them closer to your group and its work.

Should you ask for financial support at a small social, especially if your main goal is to raise friends, not necessarily money? A soft appeal for financial support is okay, but it is *not* the focus of the event—and the request can throw the event's entire tone off kilter if it is not done carefully. I prefer to take the slow road and keep the solicitation out of the picture, if you are trying to develop long-term relationships with people who can be potential major donors.

I remind eager board members who want to solicit, that it's just like trying to move too quickly on the first date. You don't want to go too fast when you are courting someone. Taking things more slowly works out better long term. To rush right into soliciting makes people feel like all you want out of them is their money, and they are right!

Experienced fundraisers know that fundraising success today depends on what you did 6 to 12 months ago. There is a long lead time that cannot be ignored. And the faster you ask for money, the less you will raise.

If you feel it is appropriate to ask for financial help at a Small Social, be sure you are passionate about addressing the need. Be sure the conversation is about correcting social ills in your community, not about money.

The last rule for small socials is that you must plan your follow-up before the event. What will you do to continue to connect these new friends to your organization?

Please do not even think about having an event like this unless you know exactly how you will follow it up and are sure that you have the staff or board members ready to make follow-up calls.

I have heard too many sad tales of brilliant cultivation events staged by worthy causes, full of powerful and influential people who could help the organizations fly high; regrettably, no follow-up ever occurred.

Board and staff members may go all out to get the right folks to their big social event. Then when it is over, they find themselves too exhausted or unorganized to tackle the hard work of the next step—face to face conversations or Advice Visits with the VIPs who attended.

Terry Axelrod, in *Raise More Money,* calls this type of Small Social gathering a Free Feel-Good Event (but only if it does *not* include a solicitation). Although I will not use this "feel-good" term in front of my guests, I will use it with my board members so they can understand exactly what we are after.

Another matter of word choice: I don't like to call these socials "events." What would you rather attend: a porch party at someone's home, or an event? Even calling it a "wine and cheese reception," stale and overused as that phrase is, sounds more interesting than the word "event."

Be careful with your wording: what you say helps to "brand" your events as fun or not. And do remember that most people would rather spend their free time doing something enjoyable, rather than something that sounds a bit too earnest and hard-hitting. I would prefer to attend a "social," than an "event." How about you?

The goal of throwing the party is to be interesting and provocative about your cause, while at the same time helping people to enjoy themselves. We all take fundraising too seriously sometimes, but our prospects do not. If you can manage to make your events enjoyable and fun, I promise you will have more people on your bandwagon! And you will raise more money!

What Type of Small Social Gathering?

If you want to approach a society crowd, you might best consider drinks or cocktails at someone's home. If you are connecting with corporate leaders, then coffees or lunches would be more appropriate.

Being a Southerner, I understand that many Southern social networks are based on two things: story telling and having a little drink. I often invite friends over to have a glass of wine on my front porch and hear about my latest project, favorite community issue, or political cause.

When I combine what Southerners like the most—the drink and the story (not to mention the porch)—we can have a good time and still get serious about how to make a real difference to our community.

IN THE REAL WORLD

A Small-Social Example

When I served on the board of Raleigh's now world-class Carolina Ballet, we hired an outstanding new artistic director, Robert Weiss. As a board member, I hosted a casual cocktail "porch party" to introduce him to some of the movers and shakers in Raleigh.

My guests were pleased to come; they wanted the chance to meet someone the whole community was talking about, before many others in the community had met him. People like to be in the know, and my friends enjoyed being among the first to meet a major new artistic leader in town.

From the Ballet's perspective, the Small Social porch party gave us an opportunity to build relationships with a key group of important potential supporters. Some of the people who came to that porch party eventually became board members and donors to the Ballet. However, money was not what I was after that afternoon. I wanted to open doors, by making introductions and creating new friends.

My role as a board member in hosting the event was merely to identify important people I wanted to involve with the Ballet and introduce them to the Artistic Director. His smart staff did the rest. I was not involved in soliciting, only in organizing a little gathering. My role was to do some friendraising and get more folks interested in and excited about the Ballet.

About 30 people attended, and 30 more could not come but looked forward to meeting Robert Weiss another time. We added everyone there to our bandwagon that evening and identified just as many more people who would be getting involved in the future.

Remember, just the act of inviting people helps put your organization on their personal radar screen. Even if they do not attend the party, they did receive the invitation, which is clearly a bit of personal marketing for your organization. When you are sending out personal invitations to socials, it helps to remember that the invitation alone is an important tool to connect new people to your organization.

Don't think that the energy you put into the invitation and the list is wasted because fewer people actually attended than you expected. Everyone who received the invitation got a bit of snazzy marketing in their mailbox promoting your organization on their personal radar screen.

How to Stage a Small Social

The program for a Small Social involves three steps: the Volunteer's Welcome, the CEO's Message, and the Follow-Up. This entire sequence should only last about 15 minutes, especially if people are standing up while they listen. Any longer and you will lose people as they drift away to the corners or into another room.

Staging a Small Social Step One: The Volunteer's Welcome Here is a chance for your volunteer host to speak from her heart and tell her friends why she is involved with your organization. The Volunteer's Welcome is very powerful. It should be easy for the volunteer/host to give this speech because he or she does not have to do a presentation about the organization; instead, the volunteer gets to tell his or her personal story.

We all, as smart fundraisers, know the personal story is more powerful than any facts, figures, or formal presentation about the organization. The volunteer's story is more important than the staff's, because a volunteer is involved only out of the goodness of his heart, only because he cares. As we discussed earlier, volunteers come from the high moral ground of caring about their community and are "cleaner" than the staff.

When I am attending such an event, I am frankly more interested in why a volunteer thinks this project is important and meaningful to the community than I am in hearing from the staff. The volunteer's story is usually more compelling and interesting to listen to and tends to grab me emotionally.

Staging a Small Social Step Two: The CEO's Message Here is the chance for your CEO to shine. Your CEO is your organization's leader and gets to show up as visionary and inspirational. His talk needs to be short and sweet, ten minutes max. It needs to be big picture or nothing at all.

Too often, the CEO's presentation is too dry and factual. I can understand this because the staff deals head-on every day with the powerful emotional experience of their real work in the community.

I find that because of the constant emotional demands on them, CEOs typically need to distance themselves a bit from their heartstrings. As a result, sometimes their presentations come across a bit more businesslike and less from the heart than those of the volunteers.

Staff leaders may be passionate people, yet when speaking about their organization, they can shift into a more professional, clinical tone that emphasizes programs instead of the results their organization achieves through its good work in the community.

The CEO has the limelight for a few minutes to deliver a high-impact message about your organization that conveys passion and urgency. Think Martin Luther King's "I have a dream" speech. Think of any of the most rousing speeches you ever heard; that is the spirit needed in the CEO's message. "It is well worth taking the time to craft it well," says Terry Axelrod, "and to coach the (CEO) to deliver the talk powerfully. . . . It needs to clearly convey 'the gap' between where your organization is now and where you need to go to fulfill the next phase of your mission."[5]

IN THE REAL WORLD

I was working with a community health clinic that serves the homeless, disadvantaged, and needy populations of the region. To see the people coming to the clinic could break your heart, wonderful folks with dignity and pride, driving rusted cars, but old-fashioned enough to be wearing their Sunday best to go to see the doctor.

The PowerPoint presentation the staff gave about their work was full of pictures of buildings with square footage, photos of doctors and nurses, and more buildings. There was little about the people the clinic treated.

We redid the presentation to simply tell stories. Stories from the doctors,' the patients,' and the staff's perspectives. Stories that could bring you to tears and touch you deeply. My client was now ready to go out into the community and show, effectively and passionately, the great work her group does.

Here are key points about the CEO's Message:

- *Tell them about the IMPACT the organization is having on the community.* How are people benefiting from your work? Show the difference your organization is making in the city, in the region, and in the world.

- *Use stories.* Paint a picture of your nonprofit with stories that can graphically and emotionally illustrate the need your organization addresses. Stories are easier for people to remember than facts.

- *Use emotion.* Be willing to wear your heart on your sleeve. Above all, be passionate! Explain the urgency of the situation. Be willing to use colorful language. Remember that people give money out of emotion.

- *Talk about the need.* This is why your organization exists: to help fill an urgent community need. Tell about the people who are suffering, until you can see your audience react with emotion. The bad situation you describe is why you so much want their help.

    You can feel confident that, once you have gotten the need across to them, your audience and your community are going to want to help you. And they will.

- *Build credibility.* These days Americans have less trust in nonprofit institutions than they once did. A 2006 poll by the United Way found that only 51% of Americans trust nonprofits to do what they say they are doing to do with donations they receive.

    The Brookings Institution found that only 11% of Americans believe that nonprofits do a very good job of spending money wisely. If your organization has been around for a decade or more with an unblemished track record of service to the community, then you have enormous credibility. People will feel you have earned their trust.

- *Share your dream for the future.* Where is your organization going? Where do you see yourself heading? What are the needs you are not able to fill? What are your dreams? Don't use jargon like "unmet needs"; that kind of language is too far removed from the urgency of what is happening out there on the street.

Approach the talk as if you are certain your audience is going to be as concerned as you are and as interested in a better future. You know they want to see their community whole and healthy. Expect that they are already sold and just need a bit of cheerleading. Tell them how they can help.

- *Present a clear request for assistance.* The call to action is the most important part of your talk. You will need to tell them exactly how they can help. Why are they there? What specifically do you want them to do? Get them to take some action to support you.

Wanting to take action to help each other is a fundamental part of being human. In fact, even Charles Darwin (the author of a major theory based on scarcity, not abundance) concluded that human beings are biologically inclined to help each other.

So call your audience to action: "We need friends out there in the community to help spread the word about this situation. This problem is not going to be solved with our current group of supporters, board members, and volunteers alone. It is too important to be left to just us. We need the whole community up in arms to help out!"

Then offer a short list of how your organization needs help, and be as specific as possible. Do not suggest more than three things they can do.

You might say, "We need you to do three things: First, write a letter to the editor of the newspaper. Second, come volunteer this month. Third, host a small social like this one to help us reach more people. Our goal is to have a small social event every month this year. Please help us reach this goal. We need hosts for July and September; can you be a host?" In a context like this one, you could also seamlessly add the optional request for a contribution, as just one more example of your need for help.

IN THE REAL WORLD

Sample Requests for Help at a Small Social

- Spread the word! Tell others about this work, and help us get our mission on the community's radar screen.

- Come volunteer and make a difference.

- Bring your friends in for a tour.

- Introduce us to a local philanthropist, government official, or corporate leader who would want to know about this problem and who can help.

- Host a Small Social of your friends to hear about our organization and bring more folks onto our bandwagon.

Staging a Small Social Step Three: Follow-Up, the Most Important Action of All
Why have an event at all if there is no plan or staff to follow up with the people who attend? But this happens all the time; nonprofits work hard to bring major community leaders to their events. These dignitaries start to get excited about the cause, but then nothing happens for months to remind them about the organization. The excitement and momentum that was generated gradually fades away.

Sometimes clients will say to me, "Why should we have a cultivation event? We had a great one last year but nothing ever came of it." When I ask why, I find out that the follow-up for the event was weak, or got pushed aside because of more pressing organizational priorities.

Two years ago, a client held a remarkably successful gala, led by board members, featuring the president of a country as keynote speaker. The event raised $100,000. To this day group leaders are unsure whether there were any tangible long-term fundraising results from the gala. The Deputy Director mused recently about the event:

> One could certainly argue that our positioning with donors was improved (getting a major country president to speak at your event is no small task); our image as an organization was enhanced, but other than raising $100,000, which was great, did it bring in anything major subsequently? I would argue no. And that is a whole lot of work for $100,000. Maybe energies could have been better spent cultivating a major gift in the $1 million range, or more. These are the kinds of trade-offs and decisions that need to be made when deciding where to put our board and staff energy and resources. Was the event lovely? Yes. Will some people remember it? Yes. But I am not sure that translated into any real long-term strategic fundraising benefit.

My client is considering a common problem we all face with enthusiastic boards that tend to think in terms of events: is it all really worth it? Can't we raise the money more efficiently by focusing on major gifts?

Of course the answer is yes! With better follow-up, perhaps staff or board members could have used the event as a springboard to cultivate an important group of prospects for major gifts. But the organization did not have staff assigned to focus on individuals for major gifts, so the follow-up never happened.

What is appropriate follow-up? Here is where staff and board can work together and share responsibility for follow-up calls.

The first thing to do is to prioritize the list of calls to be made. There should be a "must call" list and a "would like to call" list—broken down along the lines of the VIP and Friends mailing lists we described earlier.

Any donors who are currently considering funding requests from your organization should be among the first called. For example, if you have a proposal in to a foundation or corporation, be sure to call their representatives who attended first.

Or, if you are trying to obtain an appropriation from the state legislature and several elected officials attend your event, follow up and thank them first.

Follow-up can be done in three ways: phone calls, personal visits, or an invitation to a second event. All these help to keep your organization and the recent event's excitement fresh in the mind of your guest/prospect.

The magic open-ended question: "What were your impressions of . . . ?

A simple phone call is easy. A board or staff member can call and ask the magic, open-ended question: "What were your impressions of the event?" This question is the *golden key* to finding out what is going on inside your prospective donors' hearts and minds. It is open-ended enough to offer a safe platform for whatever comment your prospect wants to make.

I love this question. It has helped me many a time with prospects. When I was not sure about the next step or where the person's real interest was, I could always rely on this simple question. It has saved my day when I did not know what to say, or was having trouble getting the prospect to talk to me. Ask the question and presto, you are off and running with the prospect in the lead.

You can make a follow-up personal visit if needed. Say an important philanthropist has attended your gala and appeared to be impressed by the event and your cause. Now the door is open for an Advice Visit with this person, which will move you into a closer relationship.

If you miss the opportunity to make follow-up phone calls or personal visits, be sure the person is touched in some way by your organization within the first few months after the event. You can send out a newsletter with a personal note signed by a board member, or a personalized invitation to another event.

Follow-up is like spinning plates on sticks. One of my early mentors at Duke University had a great metaphor for following up. He described the process of cultivating major donors as much like the performance of the guy on the old Ed Sullivan show who would spin lots of plates up in the air on sticks.

He would run back and forth putting a little spin on plates that were getting wobbly. When all the plates were spinning around fast, he would take a breather to add yet another plate spinning in the air. When he was ready, he would stop one and take it off the stick.

Cultivating major donors is like this. You have to give enough personalized attention to each individual donor: keep each one's plate spinning on a stick. Note that you can only handle a certain number before the quality of your attention drops and a plate falls. Face time is a vital element of cultivating major donors – and it takes time to make personal

TIPS AND TECHNIQUES

Follow-Up Cards Are Important!

Remember to hand out Follow-up Cards for every gathering you hold. This lets the attendees self-select whether they want any follow-up communication. Follow-up cards are important because they help you get the prospect's permission to communicate with him or her personally.

(continues)

TIPS AND TECHNIQUES

Follow-Up Cards should:

- Capture the person's contact information, including phone and e-mail address.
- Ask what most interested him personally about your organization and its mission.
- Ask who else he knows who would be interested in your organization, and would he be willing to help make an introduction to this person?
- Give him some boxes to check off. Would you like to:
  - ❑ Join our mailing list?
  - ❑ Hold a Small Social of your own?
  - ❑ Make a contribution for $_____ to help us accomplish X, Y, or Z (you fill it in)?
  - ❑ Volunteer?
  - ❑ Host a tour?
  - ❑ Other _____?

visit and calls. When a donor is involved, excited, and ready to give, then you can stop spinning and catch a plate.

MISSION-FOCUSED TOURS ILLUSTRATE YOUR GOOD WORK

Carefully scripted tours of your organization are a powerful way to tell everyone you can about your organization's good work and to illustrate urgent needs in the community graphically. The tour lets your work speak for itself.

Your guests will hear staff members or even clients/students/stakeholders express in their own words their personal first-hand experience of your organization's mission—and the good it does—in the community.

My recommendations for Mission-Focused Tours borrow heavily from Terry Axelrod's Point of Entry concept in her *Raise More Money* fundraising model. With a bow to Axelrod, here is my own twist on her legendary work.

The tour I am recommending has highly specific steps: you will plan ahead to identify each person who will be speaking and script them on what they will be saying.

This tour should move quickly, with each person who presents not talking for more than a few minutes each. Once you get the format for the tour set, don't vary it—and offer it repeatedly to every member of your community that you can get in the door, particularly prospective donors and community leaders.

If you decide to launch a tour, make it into an entire project. Stage it over and over. Create goals for the number of people you want to have coming through each month.

Identify the staff member(s) who will take responsibility for arranging the tours and for the follow-up. Running these tours can be a big staff commitment, particularly because you should do excellent follow-up or no tours at all! If they are done effectively, however, they will provide enormous benefits to your nonprofit.

The tour should only last for exactly one hour. People are busy, and they are more willing to attend if you promise just this short amount of time.

If you want to have as many major community leaders come through as possible, then you should get the word out that your tour/presentation is short, sweet, and powerful. The time limits will force you to be both cogent and compelling—quite an exercise, but certainly worth it in the long run!

As for scheduling, I suggest that you select a particular day or days of the week, at a certain time of the day, and run the tour weekly if possible. For example, each Wednesday afternoon at 2 P.M., your staff could be prepared to expect a tour, and hopefully you will have guests coming through. Or you could run the tour on several afternoons, again at a certain time and following a certain format, if your staff can handle this.

For example, at a local rescue mission, we set up a tour to run every Wednesday at 11 A.M. The staff was prepared every Wednesday to host a tour, so board members could easily find a time to bring over their friends and acquaintances.

We knew that 11:30 was the time when the homeless children in the child care center were saying grace over their lunch. Now that would break your heart to see!

A few days before the tour, the person who issued the invitation should *always* follow up with guests who are planning to come. That call on the day before the tour will help keep it on their priority list, and it is an absolute must. The inviter may also offer to pick up his guests and bring them over.

Your tour should follow this format:

- *Greeting the Guests.* Gather guests in a conference room and offer them refreshments while they sign in and chat with each other. Welcome them with coffee or refreshments. Have someone sign people in, and make name tags for them. Ask them to come 10 minutes early so you can start the tour exactly on time.

- *The Volunteer's Welcome.* A volunteer host should welcome everyone, speaking for two or three minutes. That person should share why she is here today and why she is personally involved in your organization. I like for the volunteer hosts to be board members when possible.

  I have described in detail the Volunteer's Welcome in my previous outline for Small Socials. You can follow the exact same guidelines: the volunteer speaks from the heart and tells guests simply why she cares enough about this organization to be there today.

  Her story is more powerful than any facts and presentation you can make, because she is saying not what you do but why it is important. Remember that the major reason the volunteer is more powerful than the staff is because she is involved *only* out of the goodness of her heart.

  You should at all times have a volunteer with you for these tours. It strengthens the presentation immeasurably, because you have someone along who simply cares a lot and is not paid.

Here is a moving story about a Volunteer's Welcome for a tour.

IN THE REAL WORLD

I was helping a client, a small college, launch its first major capital campaign. The college was in rural North Carolina and tended to educate local kids, right off the farm, who did not have the resources to go far away to college. But these great kids really wanted an education so they could better themselves in life.

To create a successful Campaign Cabinet, we worked for almost a year to enlist the best, most powerful leaders in that part of the state. We were successful: we had the largest landowners in the area, all the important political leaders, the owner of the third largest bank in the state—a top-notch group of influential leaders who wanted to help the college raise money.

To introduce our case for support, we created a carefully scripted tour of the college, complete with student testimonials and all the right mission moments. For the first tour, we decided to take the entire Campaign Cabinet around the campus.

I needed a Volunteer's Welcome, so I asked a college trustee who was on the Executive Committee of the Campaign to open and welcome the group. I asked him to share why he cared enough to serve on the board and on the Campaign Cabinet.

The trustee stood up for his welcome. This wonderful gentleman, now a wealthy real estate developer and donor, suddenly remembered how he had felt back when he graduated from high school and didn't have enough money to go to college. He remembered how badly he wanted to get off the farm and make something of himself and what that college education could mean to him.

The dear gentleman broke up with emotion as he remembered his own longing to go to college. He could barely talk. Here was the perfect illustration, in flesh and blood, of this little college's wonderful mission in the world: to help kids help themselves. No story could have been more powerful.

Of course, I was in the back of the room saying, thank you God, for providing such a personal, evocative and moving mission moment for this little college.

- *The CEO's Message.* This is the chance for your CEO to be inspirational and engaging. Follow the format for the CEO's message that I described earlier for Small Socials. The CEO can give the same talk as in a Small Social; however, this presentation will be more dramatic and easier to deliver because the guests will be right in the middle of your organization's activities. They will be able to see for themselves the powerful work your nonprofit does in addressing important community needs.

- *The Tour Itself.* Decide which areas to visit and which staff members, volunteers, or clients/students/participants might be the most powerful for visitors to see and hear. Be sure to have staff from different lines of work tell their own story in their own words. Also make certain that you carefully rehearse everyone who attends the tour. Your staff members must be willing to be coached repeatedly so they emphasize the right points. Remember: it is more difficult to speak cogently for three minutes than it is for twenty minutes! Be sure to end the tour on time.

- *Follow-Up.* There are two types of follow-up to a tour, and both are important. First, you should have all guests fill out a Follow-Up Card, as we described above, and then you must personally contact each person within a week of their visit.

  ○ *The Follow-Up Card.* Ask guests to sign a Follow-Up Card that captures their address and other contact information and lets them check off possible subsequent activities. Offer on the card a short list of ways your organization needs help; be as specific as possible. Ask the same information as I suggested on the follow-up card for Small Socials:

  ○ *Personal Follow-Up.* It is imperative to have a personal phone call or conversation with each tour guest within a week to get their feedback and to continue the communication that was begun with the tour.

  Your guests will be moved and interested after the tour. You will need to tell them exactly how they can help your organization. Just knowing about your organization's great work is one thing, but you should also ask them to take some specific action on your behalf.

  As I have described earlier, you can say, "We need friends out there in the community to help spread the word about this situation. We really need your help! This problem is not going to be solved with our current group of supporters, board members, and volunteers alone. It is too important. We need the whole community up in arms to help out! We need people to do the following things:" and give them no more than three options.

  When you make the personal phone call to follow up, it is as easy as saying "what were your impressions of the tour?" as we discussed before for Small Socials. The person who makes this call can be staff or volunteer. Whoever calls must be ready to implement specific follow-up activities with the guest.

  When you make the follow-up phone call, you are looking for a good read on the prospective donor. How did he react? What intrigued him the most? You are looking for his interests and for the parts of the tour that spoke to him most personally. Your goal, of course, is to try to match his interests with your organization's needs.

  When a guest offers a contact or makes a suggestion, follow through impeccably. Ask for more people who should come on a tour. Perhaps ask them to host a group of their own friends on a tour. Find lots of reasons to have more contact with that person. This is the beginning of a long-term relationship with your tour guests to turn them into donors and supporters.

  Remember that follow-up is the most important part of a tour. If you cannot handle superlative follow-up, do not have the tours. You will just be opening doors that may close again in a couple of months. At the minimum, tour guests should go on your mailing list for future solicitations. They will probably be expecting that type of follow-up!

Here's a great story illustrating the follow-up from a tour.

IN THE REAL WORLD

I was working with a Rescue Mission on a capital campaign to build a new wing for homeless women and children.

It happened that one of the original founders of the Rescue Mission was on his deathbed. He was a wonderful man, very successful and respected in the community. His family had a foundation which made grants to community causes but the Rescue Mission had lost touch with the family over the years. We were hoping that through the tours, we could reestablish contact with the family. Our hope was actually to ask the family to name the new wing in honor of their patriarch, the founder of the Mission.

We established a tour of the Rescue Mission to tell the story of our great work helping the homeless in the community. We invited this gentleman's sons to come on a tour. Happily one of the sons came and was very impressed with our presentation.

Of all things, after the tour, I found myself walking out of the door with the son. All right, I said to myself! So I asked my trusty all-purpose question: "what were your impressions of the tour?"

"Oh, my" he went on and on about how impressed he was with the organization and its plans. We had a nice conversation there on the steps of the Mission. In the course of our talk, I was eventually able to ask him about the possibility of the family considering the naming of the new wing. He asked me to bring a proposal to him the next week and told me the family would certainly want to consider it.

Other Ways a Board Member Can Introduce Someone to Your Organization

In addition to talking up the organization, adding friends to the mailing list, going on Advice Visits, hosting Small Socials or Tours, there will always be additional ways a board member can open the door, introduce someone new to your organization, and help cultivate a relationship with that prospect.

Resourceful fundraisers and trustees can come up with additional creative ways to forge connections with potential donors and make connections with new friends. A board member can, for example:

- Send a note or a letter to their friend introducing the organization.
- Call their friend on the phone to ask their advice or to introduce your organization.
- Set up a meeting or lunch for your CEO to get to know their friend.

- Sign a letter to the person introducing the CEO or Development Director and asking for a meeting.
- Invite the friend to an event, and be sure to *bring* the person with them to the event.
- If it is a fundraising event, encourage them to be generous with buying raffle tickets and/or auction items!
- If the person is on the board of a foundation, the board member can send a letter in support of a current proposal or set up a visit for you to meet them.
- For board members who are unsure, perhaps they can wait until they "run into" the prospect; then they can deliver their elevator speech and ask for an Advice Visit.

BOARD MEMBERS IN ACTION: SUCCESS STORIES

From the Children's Theatre of Charlotte, here is a story about a board member who was too nervous to be involved in any corporate solicitations and how she connected with her friend who was a local corporate CEO—with great results:

IN THE REAL WORLD

We had a dedicated board member who was a stay-at-home mom. She made it very clear that she could *never* take on a corporate relationship; her comfort level and focus was to be an enthusiastic solicitor of individual donors.

A few days after a board meeting in which I presented a list of corporate prospects, she mustered up the courage to call me and let me know she knew the CEO of one of these companies quite well. I thanked her and asked, "How are you willing to utilize this relationship?"

She said, 'well . . . maybe I *could* sign a letter . . . .' I said, 'That's great!' and promptly had one prepared for the prospect, along with a package of information about the Theatre.

The CEO e-mailed her a few days later to let her know he had received it, that he thought very highly of our organization, and wanted to know how he could help. She forwarded the e-mail to me with the message: "What do I do *now*!?" We again talked through her relationship with him and came up with a plan that was on the edge of her comfort level, but she moved forward with a request for financial support (and lived to tell about it)!

He made a commitment that the company would support our organization—not specifying an amount—and she thanked him. Within 48 hours we received a check for $10,000 from the company, making the gift in honor of our (brave!) board member. She was flabbergasted!

This was a particularly rewarding story to tell at our next board meeting for a number of reasons: great affirmation for our board member . . . a fabulous gift to our campaign . . . and a clear signal that development really is all about relationships.

—Linda Reynolds, Director of Development

Here is a success story from author Linda Lysakowski of involving board members in identifying capital campaign prospects.

IN THE REAL WORLD

A lesson I learned early in my fundraising career is to never judge a book by its cover. I know, we all learned that in elementary school, right? But how quickly we forget those lessons of our childhood when we get caught up in the world of major donors, high rollers, and movers and shakers. In my consulting practice, I have never ceased to be amazed at the number of contacts that have been made through the most unlikely sources.

One of the most dramatic of these was a quiet young woman, chair of the board of a small human service agency, who was a factory worker and not someone that would be likely to have connections with the community's movers and shakers.

Her organization, however, was getting ready to launch a capital campaign; during the screening process, several names of people in the community were being considered for the lead gift to the campaign.

As we went through the list, asking who might have a connection to these people, the board chair was, as usual, pretty quiet until we got to the name of one of the community's leading philanthropists. I had secretly been hoping that someone, anyone, on the board, might have a distant connection to this person. Imagine my surprise when the board chair spoke up, 'Oh, I guess I could contact him, he is my brother-in-law.'

From that time on, I was careful to include *all* the board members in the major donor screening process, knowing that sometimes the least likely person may be sitting there not realizing they have these fabulous connections until the list is reviewed.

—Linda Lysakowski

Here is a story of a Small Social from the North Carolina Writers Network. Like many fundraising events, it was wonderfully successful, even if it was exhausting for staff:

IN THE REAL WORLD

At the North Carolina Writers' Network, we had tremendous success in the last year with a new fundraising event that our board members conceived and implemented. Because this event took place in someone's home and had themes and/or elements outside our usual area, it had big-time appeal.

We had a Southern supper at twilight held at a beautiful, historic home. Besides the cachet of a large and famous place, there was the lovely dinner and grounds with 12 famous featured writers. There were book sales, signings, and readings from our authors. It was a perfect September evening.

At $100 per person, we sold out , and folks could not sign up fast enough! (Sponsors had already covered our costs.) The only negative was that it was so huge and exhausting that our staff was stretched almost to the breaking point, which they were not prepared for. So we will do things differently next time, and get more help.

Lessons learned: there are lots of folks out there who will support us if we give them a fun event on *their* terms, not just our terms.

—Cynthia Barnett, Executive Director

Here is a success story of board members actively raising $130,000 for an annual campaign for a Communities in Schools organization.

1. First we researched bigger gift donors.

2. At a board meeting, lists of those donors were put on the walls with space for board members to sign up.

3. Because of the success of our Hockey Team, the Hurricanes, we called the campaign the "Power Play."

4. We named team captains, and during that spring board meeting, board members signed their name to a team of their choice. The competition began to see which team "won," with the most dollars raised.

5. We held a kick-off major event with a local radio personality, radio voice of the 'Canes, as the MC.

6. Our Development Director prepared scripts and follow-up suggestions, and we made sure that every donor was promptly thanked and that the board was continuously apprised of donations and which team was "in the lead."

7. It was a four-week campaign. With the Board actively pursuing their contacts, we raised $130,000 in four weeks!

What we learned:

1. Every board member is a "member" of the Resource Development Committee, as each board member is asked to give a "personally significant gift" as well as assist in fundraising.

2. The competitive nature of the campaign made it fun for the board.

3. Members not only contacted former donors but sought out funds from their suppliers, customers, and others, so as to enlarge our donor list and pool.

—Susan Hansell, Executive Director

Engage Your Board Members in the Fundraising Plan

- Friendraising builds social capital for your organization.

- Help your board members get the door open with a soft sell.

- Board members can be "sneezers," personal advocates who spread the word.

    - Spread the word by mail through personal notes.

    - Expand the mailing list with VIP and friends' names.

- Advice visits help search for hidden gold.

- If you want money, ask for advice; if you want advice, ask for money.

- Can I pick your brain? Advice Visits open important doors.

- Use the elevator speech to get the appointment.

- Rules for Advice Visits:

    - Make sure you are interesting, not boring.

    - Ask for a short appointment and leave at the end of that time.

    - Have your prospect do most of the talking.

- Gather friends with Small Socials.

- Rules for Small Socials:

    - Always have a volunteer to host.

    - The event is free to the guests.

    - It is a cultivation event only, solicitations are optional and must be handled carefully.

    - Plan your follow-up before the event.

    - The CEO's message needs to be visionary.

    - Ask for specific help.

    - Do not have the social unless you can handle the follow-up.

- Mission-Focused Tours illustrate your good work.

    - Have a volunteer to host.

    - The CEO shares the organization's vision. Various staff members present short vignettes about your cause and their work.

    - Follow-up: what were your impressions of the tour?

▨ NOTES

1. Seth Godin, *Unleashing the Idea Virus* (Dobbs Ferry, NY: Do You Zoom, Inc., 2001).

2. Malcolm Gladwell, *The Tipping Point: How Little Things Can Make a Big Difference* (New York: Little, Brown and Company, 2000).

3. Terry Axelrod, *Raise More Money* (Seattle, WA: Raise More Money Publications, 2002).

4. Richard Nelson Bolles, *What Color Is Your Parachute?* (Berkeley, CA: Ten Speed Press, 2006).

5. Terry Axelrod, *Raise More Money.*

CHAPTER 6

Create a Dream Team Board and Set Your Board Up to Win!

Never doubt that a small group of committed individuals can change the world. Indeed it is the only thing that ever has.

—Margaret Mead

How we enlist and manage our boards has everything to do with their ultimate success, not only in fundraising but in the leadership they offer our organization as well. We all agree that there are many factors that play into creating an effective board of trustees for a nonprofit organization.

We all know it is not an easy job. Who is on the board matters of course, as well as how all the members work together. How they are recruited can set up high expectations or lead to failure. How they are oriented, led, and assessed all impact their ultimate performance.

And, as fundraising expert Kim Klein said in her essay, "When Board Members Wriggle Out of Fundraising," "building a fundraising board takes more time than it should."[1]

Managing an unwieldy group of volunteers is, in itself, a great challenge. When those same volunteers are relied upon to provide visionary leadership, financial resources and careful oversight—there's a lot of pressure to perform. No wonder there is so much disappointment with nonprofit boards, considering what we expect from them

Creating a great board may seem like an impossible dream. But it's not. If you decide that you want to have a high performing board, one that has talented, effective, and passionate members who work smoothly together, guess what—it is entirely possible.

WHAT DO WE REALLY WANT FOR OUR ORGANIZATIONS?

The first task is to look at what we really want for our organizations. In the best possible world, what would your organization—and your board—look like if it were wildly successful? What would be happening? How would everyone be working together? And here's a good one: what impact would you be able to have on the world if everyone were performing at a high level?

Visioning what success looks like is an important step in making it happen. Then there are a lot more steps we must take to realize this dream board. Remember our earlier discussion of how we sometimes get the boards we deserve. Our board's performance can be traced directly back to the time, attention, vision, and creativity that we bring to them.

Here's a little pep talk about working with your board. I have seen too many nonprofit managers complain that their boards are not functioning anywhere their potential. We can accept this lack of performance, or we can do something about it. We can assume responsibility and apply some fresh approaches to this familiar, well-worn problem, and get good results—no matter where we are today.

This chapter outlines a number of best practices and ideas for creating a lively and passionate team out of what may be a group of smart, but underperforming, board members. We're all aware that it's one thing to have the right people on your board; it's another to have them working well together as a seamless team.

Board management and development is talked about quite a lot, but in practice it is neglected too often. A lot is riding on your trustees' leadership capabilities. We all know too well that so much of our organizations' success starts at the very beginning with a high performing board of trustees. As I have said all along, if you want your board to help in fundraising, you have to have an engaged, passionate, and organized board.

We will treat a variety of topics in this chapter to help you create and mould a high performing board that is anchored in its vision, and prepared to tackle its fundraising responsibilities.

How to Set Up Your Board to Win

These pages will show how to:

- Enlist the right people with the right outlook and skills, and recruit them—and their excitement; draw them in through their sense of possibility and vision.
- Set expectations early in the game, including clearly defining the board's specific fundraising responsibilities.
- Orient new members appropriately so they can hit the ground running.
- Clearly define what you need your board to do and give your board substantive, meaningful work.
- Set up a Governance Committee—a management structure for the board itself.
- Establish appropriate self-assessments to monitor—and encourage—board performance.
- Get to know your board members personally so you can understand each person's unique talents and passions—and then put them to work happily.
- Solicit your board members properly and thoroughly, ensuring that they all make proud personal gifts to your cause each year.

- Keep fundraising up front on their agenda so they can stay involved and take action where they are needed.

Let's start by envisioning a Dream Team Board for your organization. Wouldn't it be wonderful to have the most passionate, committed, and effective people from your community, those who can make your organization wildly successful? Can you picture your board as an abundant source of leadership and energy available for you to tap?

You simply have to decide that a Dream Team Board is what your organization needs, deserves, and will attain. If you drive a stake into the ground and make a firm commitment or declaration that this is your goal, then I will venture that you will be successful. You are only limited by your attitude. Remember that the scarcity versus abundance outlook works everywhere in life with boards as well as fundraising.

As Dr. Wayne Dwyer says in his best seller *The Power of Intention,* if you want to create something new in your business or personal life, then you must "continuously contemplate yourself as being (already) surrounded by the conditions you wish to produce." This is the essence of the power of creative visualization.[2]

Contemporary philosophers tell us to "act as if " what you want has already happened. It's our attitude, how we are "being"—i.e., how we are showing up to people—that has everything to do with the success we will create. This is true of the work that goes into creating the board leadership we want for our organization, and it is also true of fundraising success.

So we can decide to "be" innovative, bold nonprofit leaders who *deserve* the most talented people in our community on our team—and the board members who can help us accomplish our mission.

Enlisting New Dream Team Board Members

So much of our board members' ultimate performance is based on what is expected of them from the very beginning. Obviously, board engagement, commitment, and action all start in the selection and recruitment process.

The approach you use to enlist new board members can set up your board to be a dynamic team that tackles its charge with energy, responsibility, and heart—or not.

A high-quality, formal, organized enlistment and orientation process will set you apart from other organizations and will ready you and your organization to win. Handling this entry moment well with each new member is a key foundation of high-performing boards.

> *I think organizations should absolutely go after their Dream Team boards; they should seek out the right mix of people who share a common passion for the organization. You want the right blend of skills and people who will put energy and time into the board's work.*
>
> —Tom Ross, Executive Director,
> Z. Smith Reynolds Foundation

The most important time to create board members who are active and engaged in fundraising is their moment of recruitment. This is when the initial expectation is established. People, especially volunteers, want to know exactly what is expected of them. It is also important to clarify continually what the organization needs them to be doing, now, this month, this year.

Board members are happier if they know what it will take to be a successful board member. People are typically willing to step up to the plate; they just need clear expectations.

Enlistment versus Recruitment

I like to use the word enlistment rather than recruitment. Enlistment implies that I am talking about what is possible for our community, and I am asking the new board member or candidate to share my vision. When I enlist someone, I am evoking their own vision and passion for my cause.

The word recruitment, on the other hand, speaks to me about persuading, selling, and even arm-twisting. When board members are enlisted, they can become our partners and teammates, working together to support a mutual vision for change. When they are recruited, they may be making a more superficial commitment.

Setting Expectations Early

What is the expectation that you lay out at the beginning? What kind of enlistment strategies are you employing? How do you approach this task so that you start out in a winning situation?

If you take a professional, deliberate approach with potential board members, they will react in a similar fashion and take you much more seriously. This is the first step to creating committed, engaged board members.

Remember that you are enlisting volunteers to do an inherently foggy job. The role of a board member can be defined in many ways. No one really knows precisely how to be a good board member, and every organization needs and expects different things from its board.

Again, you have to be clear about expectations and the work at hand: "This year our board is focusing on . . ." Or, "in the next three years we have these challenges and this is how the board can be involved." You have to be clear and you have to be enthusiastic. Board members want to do a good job, but they cannot unless you tell them what that good job looks like.

Be sure, at this time of enlistment, that you do not understate the responsibilities of the job in hopes that the new member will gradually want to take on more. Say from the start what you want. The more you ask, and the more clearly you specify, the more people are likely to perform. So spell it out: "We need our board to . . ."

Here is a secret for helping to enlist the "right" people for your board who will do the work that you describe—evoke their vision. What do they care deeply about? What brings them meaning and even joy? How do they want to contribute to the common good or to their community?

Inspire them with your own vision that fits into theirs. Then make a powerful "Big Request" for their help in achieving something ambitious, something visionary, and something powerful for their community or the world.

People, including the busy, important people you really want on your board, tend to respond more to an exciting idea than to any other approach. They are more apt to join your board if you float out a vision and an opportunity that inspires them to want to be part of the action. If you are really going to make a serious difference in your community, then inspire them with the possibility of achieving something important.

In fact, one of the country's top performance coaches, Howard Goldman, in his book *Choose What Works,* talks about the power of the Big Request. "Your power is directly correlated to your ability to make big requests. The bigger the requests you make, the more dramatic the results you will initiate. . . ."

"Your ability to make powerful requests is based on your confidence that what you are doing is important and worthy of the support of others. . . . Your efficacy is directly linked to the strength of your conviction." Although Goldman is referring to business situations, his thoughts are directly applicable to the work of nonprofit organizations, whose aims are "important and worthy."[3]

Board Members Want Clearly Defined Jobs

In fact, board members welcome explicit expectations. As I said earlier, the job of non-profit trusteeship is inherently unclear. They deserve specific jobs in which they can see clearly that they can actually make a difference. Otherwise all they will do is come to meetings and just offer their opinion. I don't know about you, but I could use some work out of them in addition to all the talking.

Why exactly are you bringing them together? Consider that some boards only meet unless there is work to be done or some important issue to be discussed. These boards have eliminated routine meetings and come together on an "as needed" basis. Too much of nonprofit board governance has drifted to the routine. No wonder so many of our smart, talented and capable board members are disengaged.

While you may not want to go this far, it is helpful to "drill down" into the work at hand and discover what the organization needs that board members can take on themselves. Can they "own" a fundraising event? Can they adopt a Mission-Based Tour program or decide to become Ambassadors for their organization. Where can they focus their efforts to offer the most aid to their organization this month, this year?

Knowing what important work is needed and doing it is what gives them a sense of satisfaction that their participation makes a difference. Too many board members wonder if they have been effective as members, because the measure of effectiveness is vague.

Of course, they want to do a good job and come through for their organizations. (I hear a bit about board member guilt these days.) However, human nature being what it is, they forget their good intentions, especially if the tasks are not assigned clearly. Being very busy with their lives and work, board members do not think about our organizations in the way we do, those of us who live and breathe the mission and operation every day.

IN THE REAL WORLD

"When you set proper expectations from the start, there is little need to enforce. When we do need to enforce, it usually comes with gentle reminders (telephone conversations) from me, the board chair, or the development committee chair.

This past year, we had two board members who missed several meetings. I called them and suggested that maybe they could help in another way other than as board members. I did this by saying something like 'I know how much you care about our organization and you've been so helpful in your own way, but . . . , etc.'

In both cases, the thing that was keeping board members from resigning when work and family pressures got to be too much, was not an unwillingness to help, but guilt that they were not doing more. So, I offered them other, less time-consuming ways to help. They are still friends to the agency and do not feel guilty. I actually hear from them more often now."

—Adam Hartzell, CEO, Interact

So, if we set expectations explicitly, our board members will be grateful, because we have saved them time. Then they do not have to spend their own energy trying to figure out what to do; instead, they can be in action, which is where we need them the most.

All too frequently staff members make generalized, nonspecific appeals for help that do not grab the attention of board members. For example, "we need help raising money" or "we need help getting sponsors for the gala."

Generalized requests for help usually do not work, and the staff members become disheartened as a result. Instead, staff should be more specific and say, "We need to identify ten corporations that can give us $25,000 each. Who do you know?"

Or, in the case of the gala, "We are looking for ten sponsors at $10,000 each. We are having a brainstorming session immediately after the board meeting; please join us for 20 extra minutes." Or another board member can say, "We need each board member to sell three tables for the gala."

> *Boards that work best are those that demand the most from their members, not the least!*

—Michael Davidson[4]

Board Members Do Not Want Unrealistic Expectations and Confusion about Their Purpose

A major problem with nonprofits is the dual leadership structure of board and staff together, which we have discussed earlier; this structure creates overlapping areas of responsibilities.

Often the job descriptions of the board's appropriate roles and responsibilities are clear on some issues and unclear on others. And that is the nature of the game. In fact, there are as many definitions of exact board/staff roles as there are organizations. Precise, one-size-fits-all delineations of roles do not work across the board.

The answer to this problem is simple: Every organization should create its own definition of what a good board member is. Organizations that present a clear set of job duties for board members will be rewarded with happier, more satisfied members, and they will find that it is easier to bring in new board members as well.

For example, you could say: "Our board focuses on our connections to the greater community. We have identified exactly who we want to establish relationships with and have assigned board members to specific roles fostering these connections. We want to make sure that our organization is well known among the power players in our region."

> *Big results require big ambitions.*
>
> —James Champy

Many board job descriptions, which we will review in detail, may be specific on the small details, but do not outline the board's overall governance responsibilities. Perhaps more important than a general definition for the role of a board is defining a specific role for each board member; this valuable process can go a long way to build up the energies and interests of individuals involved.

When board members are not clear about their job and purpose, and when they are not able to use their skills to help advance the organization's mission, they may start heading in the wrong direction.

In his essay, "Boards that Work, Work," Michael Davidson cautions that without meaningful work, the board members will withdraw, or engage in "activities that are not productive or which are driven by their own agendas, e.g., second guessing the Executive Director, 'helping' staff to do their jobs better, using their board position to advance personal goals . . . ." We certainly do not want this to happen![5]

TIPS AND TECHNIQUES

Consider this as an occasional rule: "Ask not what your board members can do for you but what you can do to enhance your board members' experience."

> *Life is largely a matter of expectation.*
>
> —Horace

Clearly, when we are convinced of the urgency and importance of our organization's work, we are able to ask a lot more of our friends, teammates, donors, and board members. And they will respond! We all wonder why our talented, accomplished board members are such a disappointment. Maybe they are not inspired with the idea of the real difference they want to make in their community. Somehow the monkey gets put on your back, not on the trustees' back.

However, if board members are in on the powerful, generative discussions we talked about earlier in the book, if they are integrally part of determining your organization's future—and if they "own" that future—then they will show up differently for you and for the organization.

Get their help in determining where your nonprofit needs to be heading, and then let them help figure out how to get there. (This does not mean traditional rote strategic planning, either, as we discussed earlier. It means strategic *thinking*, not planning.)

The enlistment process can become an exciting, creative proposition, one that engages board members in the excitement of a new project that will create something out of nothing. A "something" that will solve urgent problems in their community.

SET UP A GOVERNANCE COMMITTEE TO KEEP YOUR BOARD ON TRACK

The Governance/Nominating Committee is the most important committee on your board. The job of enlisting new board members who have the skills, talent, networks, and passion to help advance your organization is a vitally important task.

Too often the job of recruiting board members is neglected until the last minute, and then relegated to a temporary nominating committee, which may or may not take its work seriously. Poorly organized nominating committees tend to rush through their work. I have seen nominating committee members take the easy way out by recruiting friends and relatives. Obviously, individuals selected this way may not be the right people to advance your organization.

Change the Nominating Committee to a Governance Committee

To be at its most effective, you should eliminate the nominating committee completely and instead form a Governance Committee with broader responsibilities. Instead of being in action for only a few months each year, the Governance Committee is a standing year-round committee. Its job is to look after the processes and functioning of the overall board as well as the enlistment process of new board members.

The Governance Committee is the recruiting, assessing, and social committee of the board. Here are its jobs:

- Maintain an inventory of the skills, capabilities, and other desirable characteristics of present members as well as members you are seeking to add.
- Conduct an annual Board Self-Assessment on how well the board is functioning, both as a whole and as individuals.
- Monitor meetings to ensure their effectiveness and efficiency.
- Oversee the involvement and engagement of all board members; check in with those who miss meetings and those who have many absences.

- Monitor board vacancies and enlist new board members who fit the Dream Team profile.
- Meet quarterly to identify and review the cultivation status of potential board members.
- Manage board social events so that all board members can get to know each other.
- Manage appropriate board orientations, and invite the rest of the board to attend them.
- Manage appropriate board diversity.
- Manage the overall board's continuing education.

One of the Governance Committee's major jobs is to look after board vacancies on an ongoing basis, covering the functions of a nominating committee.

A smart Governance Committee that takes its work seriously will constantly be looking for great potential board members. It should always keep a pipeline of several prospective board members who are identified and under cultivation. The committee should be regularly engaged in selecting and interviewing potential board members, slowly cultivating them until they seem ready to be asked to serve, and you need them to serve.

Why the additional functions of a Governance Committee? Because it is important to have an internal group of peers who look out for the care and feeding of the board itself. Only peers can ask "How are we doing?" or "What do we need to do to be more effective?"

Organizations that have active Governance Committees typically have a happier, more engaged board, one that is clearer about its expectations, its work, and the results it is creating. The Governance Committee is like a watchdog over all the board's activities and operations. Among its duties are:

- *Monitoring the board's overall functioning.* This process gives you a way to identify problems or breakdowns. (And we all know that they will occur!) They will be the cheerleading group that can help inspire everyone on the board to tackle vigorously any tough issues and the work at hand. Every board needs an enthusiastic cheerleader or two.
- *Monitoring social time.* Additionally, I am a firm believer in having enough social time for the board members to get to know each other. As I mentioned earlier, how can a group of people work collegially together as a board or committee if they don't even know each other?

  No group can function effectively unless the members have a friendly relationship. As I've mentioned before, the coffee social before each board meeting can be most valuable. This is when casual, friendly, personal conversation happens, which generates trust and cohesion within the group. The Governance Committee makes sure that these important social times happen.
- *Acclimating new members.* New board members have a particularly hard time fitting in and feeling comfortable making their contributions, when they are not well acquainted

with other board members. Think about how you feel when you enter a new group of people who all know each other and who are already working together. We all too often neglect our new board members, leaving them to fend for themselves and meet other board members haphazardly.

The Governance Committee makes certain that the new members are properly oriented and acclimated and that they get to know the other board members. The Governance Committee makes sure those often forgotten and overlooked name tags are ready for *each* board meeting. Someone on the Governance Committee needs to take special responsibility for making introductions for the new board members so that they will feel comfortable.

- *Monitoring board member engagement and satisfaction.* Another major function of the Governance Committee is monitoring board member happiness, engagement, and satisfaction. Remember, as we discussed previously, that board members who are dissatisfied with their role and their experience are more likely to catch that dreaded and contagious disease, board member malaise.

- *Guarding your board's informal culture.* We have explored earlier the difficulties of changing the culture of a group of people, including its ways of operating, communicating, and making decisions. The Governance Committee can be the guardian of your board's informal culture, working to keep these attitudes positive, engaged, and focused on the big picture. If a negative or disengaged energy sets in, it can be difficult to cure.

  The Governance Committee can help safeguard the good energy and positive outlook of new board members. The last thing you want is for your new, enthusiastic board members who are energetically embracing their new roles to confront tired "same old, same old" attitudes. They are likely to lapse into inaction very quickly, as the old board culture takes over and kills their enthusiasm.

It is up to the Governance Committee to be sure that no energy-sapping malaise ever sets in. To keep this unhappy condition at bay, this group should use its full range of inspirational and management tools: exciting, visionary retreats; honest self-examinations and self-assessments; a professional, deliberate recruiting process; ample social time for board members to create friendship and collegiality; and ensuring that meetings are dynamic, engaging, and dealing with important issues that affect the organization's future.

The Governance Committee members are also the ones who ask: "How did we do?" Their job is to look at how the board operates, how it conducts meetings, and how effective the time is that the entire board spends together.

Consider the Power of Asking: "How Did We Do as a Board in Our Meeting Today?"

After the full board meeting is formally adjourned, the Governance Committee can convene informally and ask themselves: "How did we do as a group today?" What an interesting conversation: a chance to open up informally, and share opinions and issues that the formal

Robert's Rules of Order meetings don't allow. This type of discussion draws out a new type of conversation. It is an out-of-the-box approach to group process.

What is "group process" anyway? The term refers to the informal modes and ways a group functions together. How the "culture" of the group operates. How it treats its members. What it values. Who dominates. Who hides. What alliances there are within the group. How it communicates among the members and the tone of those communications.

Does the group respect differences or ignore them? Is there collegiality or division? I have a friend who is a shrink and who sits with me on a foundation board. After one particularly long and somewhat tiresome conversation about a planning issue, she remarked to me, "I just love to sit back and watch the group process of this board!"

Being a nonprofit fundraising consultant and having gone to business school, it had been a long time since I had taken a psychology course or even heard the term "group process" —but board meetings are a showcase of group process, for better or worse.

In her book, *Exposing the Elephants: Creating Exceptional Nonprofits,* Pamela Wilcox suggests asking the following questions to reflect on board performance. These questions have come from her experience, with comments that have come from mine. And these are the things the Governance Committee should consider in evaluating how the board performed:

- Does the President (Board Chair) chair the meetings effectively? Why or why not?
- Do the agenda items relate to and support good governance? Are we addressing the important issues in our meetings?
- Are all board members contributing, or are a few dominating our discussions?
- Are we seeking feedback from our key stakeholders?
- Are we scanning the horizon for trends and outside influences and taking action?

IN THE REAL WORLD

I tried out the how-did-we-do question once with startlingly valuable results. I was the newly appointed chair of the newly formed foundation for a retirement community.

We were having our first meeting, and it was my first experience running a meeting with these particular people, some of whom, I did not know. It was quite a formal session, in which we carefully followed our preplanned agenda. Like a good chair, I pretty much knew ahead of time who would be saying what and what the outcomes and decisions would be.

After our formal meeting, we adjourned. I decided to take a bit of a risk, since I didn't know all the players. I sat back and asked everyone if they would stay a few minutes to talk about the meeting and how we felt it went.

All of a sudden, people seemed to relax. They looked so much more engaged in this question than they had earlier in our business meeting! Someone revealed that she

(continues)

did not know why she was asked to serve and wanted to be sure she could do a good job. Others made personal remarks about their interest in our work.

Then the little old lady on my left spoke up in a soft voice. I knew she was the largest donor ever to this organization; we were thrilled to have her voice as a leader on this Foundation board, particularly to be able to thank her and honor her relationship with the community.

What she said floored me: "I don't think I want to come to these meetings because I can't hear a thing that people are saying. I think I had better resign because I am hard of hearing."

What an important piece of information! We really wanted and needed this wonderful generous donor to remain involved and active in our fundraising program, and on our foundation. It could have been a disaster if she had resigned because she felt a bit alienated and had not told us why.

We were able to change the meeting venue to another room with better acoustics, thus keeping her happy and engaged and allowing her to feel part of the foundation's business. I have never been so glad that I asked a simple question for feedback!

Wilcox also suggests a lighthearted way to manage the business of monitoring board meeting behavior: "Create a checklist for good board conduct; assign someone at each meeting to check off the list and report in the last hour. Make it okay to goof up by awarding funny gifts for bad behavior. The idea is that everyone makes mistakes; doing it wrong is how everyone learns to go it right the next time."[6]

I love the idea of clearly identifying "good board conduct." It is something that is not discussed. We all know what is *not* "good board conduct." Just think of the meetings we have sat through in survival mode, exasperatedly listening as someone goes off endlessly on an irrelevant tangent, or indulges in unproductive hand-wringing, or brings up old decisions that had been laid to bed months ago.

A Dream Team Board: Who Do You Want?

Board Member Profile

Another important function of the Governance Committee is the monitoring of the overall board profile of skill sets, making sure that you have the right people to round out your Dream Team's capabilities. Many organizations analyze their board membership through various criteria, such as demographic profile, skill sets, diversity, stakeholder representation, and geographic representation.

Being the dedicated fundraiser that I am, I focus particularly on social capital: what networks might a new board members bring into our organization? What fundraising doors can they open? Who do they know? What is their giving potential?

At the same time, we need to be careful of enlisting board members or contacts solely for their professional expertise. We need to be sure they also have the passion and care for our mission. If they do not, they may bring a clinical and businesslike approach to the work of our board, thus missing the boat. They may also weight the board's conversations too far to the dispassionate. We certainly don't want that!

Chait, Ryan, and Taylor especially caution against pushing too hard for an ideal board based on "a mix of technical expertise, wealth, diversity and political connections."[7]

They worry that "trustees expressedly recruited for technical expertise are likely, either as a matter of preference or at management's direction, to concentrate on technical aspects of the organization . . . . This type of board-as-Swiss-army-knife has been recruited to do everything *but* govern."[8]

It is just as important to understand how your potential board members *think* in addition to what they *know* in terms of expertise. Chait, Ryan, Taylor recommend that qualities we look for in future board members might include "quality of mind, a tolerance for ambiguity, an appetite for organizational puzzles, a fondness for robust discourse, and a commitment to team play."[9] I'll vote for the team players myself as a vital attribute!

Desired Skill Sets for Dream Team Boards

Notwithstanding the reservations voiced above, I like to see some specific skill sets on my boards. Since this is a book about fundraising, I'll be up front and ask for my favorite skill sets first:

- *Fundraising experience.* I look for experience in fundraising whenever possible, either as volunteers or as professional fundraisers. People who already know and understand fundraising are invaluable. Their knowledge and expertise helps to back up your own recommendations to the board about smart fundraising strategies.

    Having these valuable members will save you time and energy and even heartache, because they will help set the overall pace of your fundraising. They help motivate the rest of the board, set an example for everyone, and keep everyone in line supporting a well-thought-out fundraising plan.

    I have worked at both Duke University and the University of North Carolina-Chapel Hill, where there were hundreds of fundraisers on staff. I was always surprised at how few of my colleagues were serving as volunteers on boards. I wondered if any organizations had asked them. What a wonderful resource for your nonprofit, if you can nab a professional fundraising executive.

    Experienced fundraisers are always helpful to reign in less-than-productive fundraising strategies. Boards without prior fundraising experience sometimes drift to easy answers such as "Let's find 100 people to give us $1,000 each; then it will be easy to reach our goal," or "Let's have another event to raise money to fill our deficit."

We all know that these types of strategies will not raise the money you need; they will distract your board into high-effort, low-outcome activities. Having board members experienced in successful nonprofit fundraising will keep you from having to be the "naysayer" when a well-meaning but ignorant board member comes up with these ideas.

- *Marketing, sales, and advertising.* So much of what we do is based on old-fashioned marketing and sales. I have those skills in my back pocket myself, because of an MBA in Marketing and also Professional Selling Skills training by Xerox in their heyday back in the 1980s. I'm careful not to be obvious about these skill sets here in the non-profit sector, but I sure use them every day!

  Just look at the marketing and sales work you do as a nonprofit leader: you are developing and promoting a "brand" for your organization through its reputation in the community. Your annual fund and, if you are lucky, your major events also develop their own "brand" image that helps to make them successful or not.

  In a way, marketing and sales are the lifeblood of nonprofits. We are, in fact, in the persuasion business. When you are writing solicitation letters, designing your case for support and brochures, you are using standard sales and marketing skills—tailoring your product to meet the needs and interests of your audience. You use public relations skills to "sell" your message to the media and to draw audiences to your performances or create clients for your programs.

  Board members who offer valuable marketing and sales skills are not that hard to find. Look for successful real estate agents, bank marketing officers, advertising agency people, salespersons in any field. These folks know how to frame a "pitch" and close a sale!

- *News media.* I love to have someone who works in the media on my boards. They can offer expert advice on how to define our messages and how to get visibility for special projects and programs. Not to mention that they can help get the story of our organization in the local newspaper and/or aired on local television.

  As nonprofit leaders, we are too often focused on the importance of our work in the community. We neglect our public image and telling our story to the community. I say that letting the world know about the issues we are tackling and our good work is *just as important* as the work itself.

  Raising visibility of the issues helps generate community support overall for the homeless, for ending hunger, for better education, healthcare, environmental protection, or for support for the arts.

  In addition to opening doors within the media world, reporters can help you shape your story for maximum impact. They can tell you how to frame your issue and what angle will be most appealing to the public. They help you get your organization high on the community's radar screen—and create that all-important background buzz that supports fundraising.

- *Politicians.* I like to pepper my boards with current or retired dignitaries from political life from both sides of the political spectrum. Retired politicians in particular often play an important role as community leaders. They lend credibility and weight to your board and add their influence in the community to your cause.

Just think about all the supporters who voted for them. These supporters tend to respect the elected official's judgment and will probably pay careful attention to the issues they choose to support.

Being a well-worn realist, I am fine with having an influential politician on your board who may not attend many board meetings or appear as engaged as others. These individuals can still help you in many ways. Nonprofits need to remember that the government sector can be just as important a funder as the traditional sources of individuals, foundations, and corporations.

Having an elected official on your board is a wonderful way to cultivate that most important funding stream from city, county, state, or national government resources. However, such people can offer invaluable service to your cause *if and only if* they are active and supportive behind the scenes where it can really count.

- *Business people.* I like every board I work with to have some members with specialized business skills, including a banker, an investment manager, and an attorney, not for extended *pro bono* services, but to offer a professional opinion to unknowing board members whenever the conversation drifts to matters of finance, accounting, legal issues, and investments.

  Of course these categories of board members are typically well connected to people with money—potential donors to our organization! Once again, we do need to be careful that our board does not become just a menu of skill sets but is instead a group of skilled people who can think broadly and creatively when we need them.

- *Social and community leaders* are, of course, always very important. Having major philanthropists on your board is even better! If not these individuals, how about a family member or spouse who is just as capable as they are and who also has the same contacts? How about a younger family member who wants to groom him or herself to assume a future role in the community?

USE A BIG REQUEST TO ENLIST BOARD MEMBERS

You cannot put too much emphasis on the actual *process* of properly selecting board members. It is vital to your nonprofit's ultimate success. The people you are bringing in must have the talent and passion to be able to run your organization in the future.

Governance Committee members should take the slow approach when cultivating potential board members (just as we all should do with potential donors). One or more committee members should meet a prospect early in the process and tell him that he has been identified by someone already on the board or staff as someone who might possibly be a potential board member.

- A member of the committee should ask to take him to coffee or lunch, to tell him more about the organization.

- Tell him you understand he will not make a decision immediately, but you want to take the opportunity to introduce the organization to him and explain the role of the board.

- Tell him you all would like to get to know him as well, and particularly want to see where his interests are.[10]

It is important to take your time in the enlistment process: If you work slowly and well, you will find that this more deliberate approach to board member enlistment is much more comfortable for everybody. The people being recruited have time to consider their decision. You have time to get to know them a bit and see if they would fit. When the decision is made for them to join the board, they are familiar with your work and ready to go to work.

Be sure to coach your Governance Committee so that they approach the enlistment effort in a manner both deliberate and enthusiastic. You might even want to hold a special meeting to psyche them up. I call this "getting them grounded in their vision and their plan."

Always encourage their thinking again about their vision for your organization, and ignite their passion and excitement for its future. Help them remember the big picture of why they want people to help, so these trustees will be engaging and inspirational as they put Big Requests out there in front of talented board prospects.

Approaching New Board Members: The Wrong Way

Let us assume for the sake of discussion that you or the CEO are approaching a board prospect. You may be shy and nervous about enlisting new board members. Do not let yourself start out by apologizing: "It won't take up too much of your time" or "We don't ask a lot of board members," or, worst of all, "Just your name and contacts would be so very helpful."

Are you recruiting out of desperation? Do you secretly think that people do not want to serve on your board? Is that a proud, powerful stand to take?

I would not be particularly complimented if I were approached like that. If I sensed a drop of desperation in my recruiter, I would be wary. I do not want to be in the position of doing the organization a favor. As Kay Sprinkel Grace puts it in *Beyond Fundraising*:

> Board members recruited in this way seldom develop a level of respect for the organization that leads to commitment. The urgency posed to them in the recruitment process is an urgency to expand the board, rather than the urgency of the community needs their board service helps meet. The damage compounds when these same individuals are assured, "there is nothing much to serving on the board, don't worry, it won't take much of your time."[11]

She is correct. The new board members' commitment and motivation will go downhill from there. They will never be fully invested in your cause. They will never fully commit to taking action to help your organization. They know they are there merely to fill a seat, and so they are likely to be disinterested and disengaged, almost from the start.

Will people recruited in this fashion tackle fundraising with vigor and courage? Probably not, unless you can find a way to awaken their passion and vision by linking them personally with your organization's work.

Are you holding your potential board members "small," so to speak? Are you expecting the least possible from them? Why not approach them from the abundance point of view, expecting that they are likely to be interested, passionate, and committed to your cause?

Approaching New Board Members: the Right Way

If you are the person to approach the conversation with the prospective board member, do so as if you are recruiting a teammate —or approaching a major donor. You are looking for someone to join your cause who cares as much as you do. It is vital that you share with this person your vision for the organization and your sense of urgency about the work to be done. Be proud! Be enthusiastic! Be passionate! Just as you are when you are fundraising!

Chances are, the person you are approaching will feel complimented and will be engaged right along with you. Remember, energy is catching!

Your excitement—passionate and committed—will inspire the same feeling in your new board member, and you will have enlisted a new companion for your organization's journey, someone who embraces your organization's cause as you do. This is the kind of person you need *to be* when you enlist board members, and this is the kind of person you want to enlist.

I will let you in on a secret. People really want to help each other. As performance coach Howard Goldman says, people want to be a part of something exciting. People want to contribute. All you have to do is invite them to help and to contribute.[12]

Be sure to tell a potential member *why* she of all people is the person you want for the board. As with a major donor, when you say why only he can make the gift, you should tell your potential board member why you want exactly her, what she brings to the plate, and why only she can be the right board member at the right time for your organization. It's a wonderful compliment to the person you are approaching, and it encourages her to respond positively.

Throughout this process, your stance as a nonprofit leader is crucial. Are you standing in a place of powerful, urgent vision? Or are you standing in a powerless place where you hold yourself to be less than the people around you?

Board Member Job Description

The formal written job description for board members is an integral tool for helping you get the most out of your board. It should outline specific duties and expectations, including participating in fundraising.

The job description should spell out clearly your expectation for their time commitment, the policy on board attendance, and the expectation for service on committees and participation in fundraising. What is the particular job that you might want this individual board member to tackle? Be able to say "this is where we need you!"

Be sure to present your organization's financial position and its current and long-range plans. Be able to answer that age-old question for any group of people gathered together at any point in time: "What are we trying to accomplish?"

Whatever the expectations are, they must be clear. An effective board needs standards for member participation in all areas of the organization. Everyone must be clear what needs to be done and when, in order to advance the organization and its work.

Information Form

Ask your new board member to fill out an information form with all her contact info. In addition, ask for her other affiliations and interests, so you can get an idea of her social networks. Ask her on this form why she joined the board and what it is about your mission that interests and inspires her the most.

Ask about her skills and experience in: fundraising, events management, letter writing, public speaking, volunteering, sales and marketing, public relations, mailings, strategic planning, corporate board membership, and so on. This will give you a deeper idea of the range of abilities she can offer your organization.

LET'S AGREE ON FUNDRAISING ACTIVITIES FOR EVERY BOARD MEMBER

In the Board Member Job Description, you must outline exactly what board members are expected to do regarding fundraising. There must be some activities that *all* board members are expected to do regardless of their inclination and means.

Have a specific discussion with potential board members about these expectations. It can take a lot of nerve, when you are asking someone to join your team or for a favor, to make a Big Request of them.

> *Too often staff members don't explain during enlistment that fundraising is an important role for board members. There is almost a fear that if they ask the potential board member to commit to fundraising then he will back off and refuse to join the board.*
>
> —Tom Ross, Executive Director,
> Z. Smith Reynolds Foundation

Again, fight against your tendency to understate your expectations. Remember that if your organization is to accomplish what it really needs to this year, it will take an important Big Effort. When you tell the new member why you need him in particular, be sure to also let him know that you will respect his commitment of time and will be well organized.

Wouldn't you rather have a few really committed and passionate people on your board than a lot of disengaged folks? You want people who will demonstrate a level of leadership and ownership of this organization, and no others.

This is the kind of board that can change the world.

Be Specific When It Comes to Their Participation in Fundraising

Explain that all board members support fundraising in different ways. Remind the candidate that he does not have to solicit in order to help. Don't leave it up to your Governance Committee to outline the fundraising responsibilities, they may dodge this at the last minute.

Throw out several types of activities that board members typically undertake to support fundraising at your organization and note where he stands on these. Discuss these activities and see how he reacts. Do not wait and be surprised or disappointed. It is imperative that you look the candidate in the eye and address the responsibilities of the job up front. Remember, the Big Request is what inspires people to get excited about what they can make happen.

TIPS AND TECHNIQUES

Checklist of Basic Fundraising Requirements of All Board Members

You can adapt this list based on your specific fundraising program:

❑ We require all board members to make a proud annual gift to the best of his or her ability.

❑ We expect 100% board participation in our public events. (Name the events board members are expected to attend.)

❑ Bring your friends and contacts to our events.

❑ Help thank donors to the organization.

❑ Help make new friends and contacts for the organization.

❑ When appropriate, ask for contributions.

❑ Know and support the fundraising plan.

❑ Be sure the fundraising program has adequate internal and external support.

Proud Annual Gift

The most fundamental expectation of a board member is that she make her own gift to the organization to help underwrite its programs and its mission. Board members should be the providers of both time and money. If they do not "own" your cause, then who will?

We all know that, when you go out to create friends and donors for your organization, board gifts are essential to the whole organization's credibility. Board donors are setting the example for everyone else in the community to support your group's good work. They need to be inspiring others to follow their good example. Their leadership in this area sets the stage for all other fundraising. There is no excuse for board members not coming through with an annual gift.

We all know of funders who expect full participation of all board members in supporting their organization financially. Use the words "We require 100% participation in the annual fund." And make it clear that this means giving! Never accept the old excuse: "I am giving my time; so I am not giving my money."

I particularly like Kay Sprinkel Grace's suggestion of the rule of one-thirds with your board. One-third of your members should consider your organization their top philanthropic priority. Another third should consider the organization among their top three giving priorities. The final third should be people who may not be large donors, but who can contribute skills, networks, and specific skills that the organization needs to carry out its mission.

However, I also know of a prominent national board that has a more exacting set of standards. This organization expects its board members to place it among their top three philanthropic beneficiaries, with no exceptions. They actually asked someone who was a billionaire to step off their board because he could not place the organization in his "top three." I certainly support this kind of aggressive standard!

Soliciting your board correctly so that everyone gives will be taken up later in this chapter.

Attending Events

Attending important events is a must with board members. I hear too many laments from Board Chairs and Executive Directors that the board members do not even attend events. It is disappointing to staff when board members do not show up to support your public and fundraising events—and bring their friends.

Where are they when you are filling up your organizational bandwagon? Where are they when you are leading your charge up the hill? Make it crystal clear that board members are expected to attend events *and* to bring friends, acquaintances, and potential donors.

Let them know that you expect 100% participation in major public events, especially those oriented toward fundraising. It is a good idea to spell out what those events are.

Set Priorities with Events

In defense of board members, some have said to me, "They have so many events. I just don't know which ones are the most important. I wish they would tell me which events they need me to attend."

Do not confuse your board members by presenting a long list of events and saying, "We want all board members to come!" Instead, respect their time commitment and tell them about the important ones.

Participating in fundraising events is clearly a priority for using board member time. The board members are setting a leadership example by being out in front of the community, showing up as leaders in front of your donors. In addition, you want them to be meeting and thanking donors at all times.

Jobs for Board Members at Fundraising Events

I particularly like to give each board member a personal assignment at fundraising events. They usually like a formal role as host, as well, in addition to being a happy party attendee.

I may tell them their particular assignment is to meet Donor Bill Smith, for example. Seek him out in the crowd and tell him, as a board member, how much you appreciate his support. Mr. Smith will be pleased and complimented that a board member thought enough of his support to thank him personally.

Also, the board member is usually pleased to have a particular role to play that will directly support the event's success.

Thank Donors

All board members need to be responsible for helping to thank donors. Here is a non-threatening, happy way to involve the entire group in fundraising. We have seen earlier how speedy thank-yous phoned to donors by board members can actually increase contributions by 34%.

There are many ways to set up systems for board members to thank donors. Penelope Burk, in *Donor Centered Fundraising,* and Hildy Gottlieb, in *FriendRaising,* both outline in detail excellent procedures for board member thank-yous.

Be sure your board members actually know who the donors are, so they can thank them both formally—in letters and phone calls—and informally, when they run into them socially and professionally.

Board members appreciate getting lists of your newest donors at board meetings. I am surprised to hear from many board members that they were embarrassed because they did not know that a friend or associate had made a gift. Help them out by letting them know who is giving to your organization.

Help Make New Friends and Contacts for Your Organization

Clearly one of the major expectations for board members is to offer their social capital and networks to help the organization. They need to be creating a bandwagon of people they can bring in to help out. We have discussed many ways board members can expand your organization's reach in the community. It's a vital role for each trustee.

When Appropriate, Ask for Contributions

We have already established that board members do not all have to be solicitors and that board members can play many roles to support fundraising without soliciting.

However, when it is appropriate, yes, they get to be the ones soliciting. "Appropriate" means that a particular member is the right one to make the approach and has agreed to be the solicitor. No one is asked to make solicitations they do not want to make.

Know and Support the Fundraising Plan

This should be a requirement for every board member. Exactly what *is* the fundraising plan for this year? What *are* our goals? What *do* we need to make happen in order to raise the resources we need to carry out our important community work?

I am always surprised when I am on a board and the fundraising report is so very short and sweet. Rarely is the full plan presented to the board for them to discuss and "own." Time and time again, I have seen the staff present the fundraising program—and then no one on the board says a word, in effect, leaving the monkey on the staff's back.

Once, when I was a brand new board member of a university-based art gallery, I listened carefully to the young development officer's presentation of the fundraising program. It did not sound too extensive, and the young officer made it sound like it was her responsibility, not anyone else's.

Being the bold board member that I typically am, I raised my hand during the question period after her report and simply asked, "Is there anything we can do to help you?"

You should have seen the look on the young woman's face. She was stunned. She almost fell out of her chair. Then a look of gratefulness and relief came over her face. I could see immediately that this was so unusual, so out of the box, that she just could not believe it. (Actually the other board members looked at me as if I were a bit crazy.) Clearly, this was not business as usual for a board member to ask if she could help.

I tell this story with all due affection and sympathy for staff. I served many years as a staff fundraiser, slugging it out, fundraising on my own, wishing I had more help from my powerful board members who could have made it so much easier.

Carry Out Specific Fundraising Tasks That You Commit to Do

A friend who is the president of a major nonprofit in Asheville recently complained to me: "My board members just won't make their campaign calls! They say they will but then they don't!"

Obtaining their agreement to make calls, and then getting them to do it, are frequently two different enterprises. Later in this chapter, a section titled "Set Your Board Members Up to Win" will discuss ways to prepare board members to assume more responsibility and to support each other in completing their assignments.

Be Sure That the Fundraising Effort Has Enough Resources, Both Internal and External

We all know that one of the major duties of board members is to be sure that the organization has sufficient financial resources. But here is an expectation that is seldom mentioned.

That said, it does not necessarily mean that they need to go out and raise the money themselves. It does mean they need to ensure that the fundraising programs are successful.

They have got to pay enough attention to know what is going on. No board member likes nasty surprises, especially those of a financial nature! Board members must make sure that the fundraising programs are adequately staffed and that the staff is supported and happy.

For-profit companies view their human resources as a great treasure. They develop their employees, and train and coach and groom them, knowing that the company would run aground if they lost their knowledgeable work force.

Somewhere in the nonprofit sector we all got the idea that staff is supposed to make huge sacrifices in order to serve the mission of the organization. What will you get if you have an overworked, underpaid, demoralized staff? You will get costly turnover and disruption of programs. I am all for treasuring your staff, rewarding them however possible, and investing in their development!

When fundraising staff departs, taking with them cordial relationships with many donors, the organization never understands the devastation to its fundraising program until months later.

TIPS AND TECHNIQUES

A well-run organization has a stable, happy staff.

I was doing a feasibility study for a client that had a long tradition of low investment in administrative overhead—and was proud of it. However, because of low salaries, the agency had experienced a great deal of turnover in positions that dealt with its own and its clients' programs.

When doing the interviews for the study, I asked community representatives about the organization's public image. I had several surprising replies. The responders said that the organization was known for poor customer service and that there seemed to be chaos in the front offices.

This disorder in customer service was because of frequent staff turnover. When staff members left, they took with them the knowledge of how to do the job. Thus the people doing the work were frequently so new that they did not know how to do their jobs. This turnover ultimately affected the organization's public image and community reputation.

Support the Fundraising Staff

Too often I have seen staff changes and turnover at nonprofits actually *wipe out* fundraising programs! The person managing the annual fund departs, and, with her, out goes most of the annual fund program.

I have been amazed to find organizations with fundraising programs in a shambles because of repeated staff turnover. Board members have no idea how much their fundraising staff are worth and what would happen if they left.

If you walked out the door and left your job right now, what would you be taking with you? If you are a good fundraiser, you will walk out with something that is invaluable to your organization, something that money cannot buy, something that your employer can't replace, because it is intangible and impossible to define or value.

You will take with you the personal relationships you have with the organization's key donors—the most valuable asset your fundraising program has. You will take with you your knowledge of one donor's golf game, another donor's pride in her family, when particular donors like to meet, what they like to eat, their quirks, preferences, likes, dislikes, interests —and most of all, your understanding of why they believe so deeply in your organization.

We all know that fundraising is based on relationships between people. When a fundraiser leaves his or her job, taking personal relationships with them, then your organization loses a part of its ability to maintain connections with its donors. It has trouble nurturing the people whose investments and gifts keep the lights on and the office running.

Too often when a top fundraiser leaves, the nonprofit's leaders do not understand what has happened to the fundraising program. They do not realize how vital it is to keep up the contact with their important donors. The fundraiser has been spinning those plates on the sticks and no one is there to keep up the communication that keeps them spinning. The sad thing is that they do not realize how vulnerable the fundraising program is at that moment.

Too often the ball—or the plates—get dropped. The donors are left without a contact from your organization for months, perhaps years. If they are forgotten, they drift away, and your organization loses a vital stream of funding that may never be picked up again. The disruption in the fundraising program is not recognized until months later.

We all know that donors deserve better treatment. They deserve to have someone at the organization who remembers who they are, who knows them personally, and who maintains contact with them, offering news about the excellent work the organization is doing in the community.

If top managers really understood this fact, they would do everything in their power to keep fundraisers from leaving their jobs. Does your boss know how much you are really worth? Does the board? Do they know what would happen to the fundraising program's momentum and consistency if you left?

I had as a client a small college that thought it had adequate investment in staff. The college had purchased a large, complex fundraising software system. However, the school scrimped on the training program, with the result that the staff never learned to use the system effectively.

In addition, the person who was originally trained left her job, and the expensive software system just sat there, not updated and not used. Updates to the system arrived periodically, and they just sat on the shelf, uninstalled. When I came in as a consultant to help them prepare for a capital campaign, I saw that the huge investment in the new system had been for naught.

Welcome New Board Members into the "Club"

Board Orientation

Just as board members should be carefully enlisted, so should they be carefully oriented. A board that is not properly oriented to the organization and its work will be an ineffective board. It is rude to ask someone to attend board meetings dutifully when you have not properly filled them in on what they should be doing, or what the organization is up to.

Sometimes new board members find themselves simply sitting in on the meetings, not understanding what is going on. It can take as long as a year to become oriented to some complex nonprofits.

I am willing to bet that many nonprofits only give lip service to orientation. What does it really take to bring someone up to date, to give them enough of an overview that they can begin to be effective immediately?

Some organizations conduct board orientation over time, setting up hour-long sessions before each board meeting. Then orientation becomes a way of life for these groups, and board members who are not new may choose to attend to learn more about some portion of the organization's activities and mission.

> *Our board members need to feel truly welcome and socially integrated into our board. Rather than leaving this to chance, we worked hard to develop a program to welcome and connect new board members with those with whom they will be working.*
>
> —Nonprofit CEO

My client, Twin Lakes Lutheran Retirement Community, a continuing care retirement community, was running a very complex health care system. Many board members, particularly those without a financial background, did not understand the various ins and outs of Medicare and Medicaid reimbursements and how these affected the organization's strategic planning and policies.

The leadership of Twin Lakes decided to have a series of board education sessions— at the board members' request—once a month, before each board meeting on topics chosen by the board members. These sessions were well received and well attended by the board members, who now felt more included, more up to date, and therefore more engaged, in the organization's leadership and management.

How you bring in new board members is so very important. This is their welcome ceremony! Make it engaging and enjoyable if at all possible. Your overall purpose in the orientation is to connect your new board members with your work in a meaningful way to deepen their interest and commitment to your cause.

Orient Your Board with Care

Here are the topics you should include in an orientation.

- Your nonprofit's mission and vision: why are you in business and what are you trying to accomplish?

- Challenges and opportunities in carrying out your mission: this perspective is particularly important for board members to understand clearly.

- Your financials: review them thoroughly and create opportunities for new board members to ask detailed questions. Look at the projected budget for the coming year and your most recent audited financial statements. Discuss the implications of financial trends or certain financial items.

- Your programs and services: how do you do what you do? What is your impact on the community?

- Direct presentations from staff: be careful about information overload from staff presentations. You may want to spread this out over time. However, it is important for the board members to know and respect each staff member and their work.

- Direct presentations from people who use your services.

- What the board members are expected to do.

It is important to make introduction and orientation fun and interesting for the new board members. Let them know how much you appreciate their service! This is their Welcome Party. Make it special.

In looking at the list just given, consider how interesting and useful it would be to introduce this material directly to *all* board members. This type of deeper background information is the guts of your organization and your board's work. How can the board function at its highest if it is not deeply familiar with your organization?

Consider making the orientation sessions on these deeper topics open to the whole board. This material is not necessarily treated in a Robert's Rules of Order board meeting. It is the stuff of planning and retreats. It is the "generative" stuff that inspires creativity and a wider range of possibilities for your organization.

Orientation Materials for New Board Members

Be sure they have the following materials:

- A full board list with contact information, including job titles and work and home contact information.

- A calendar of all board meetings and key events for the coming year.

- Your most recent audited financial statement.

- Your long-range/strategic plan.

- Your budget for the current year.

- Lists of committee assignments and each committee's duties.
- The board member job description.
- A list of staff members with their contact info and job titles, as well as home contact information if appropriate.
- Your bylaws and articles of incorporation.
- Any board policies or organizational policies important to the organization.
- Fundraising plan and duties of all board members regarding fundraising.

TIPS AND TECHNIQUES

Questions a New Board Member Might Want to Ask

- Financial: How solid are our finances? How independent or dependent are we on fundraising?
  - Cash controls: are we safeguarded from embezzlement? How careful is the process of safeguarding and reporting on checks and cash that come into our organization?
  - Audit: how clean was our last audit?
  - Endowment: how much endowment do we have and how is it invested? What is its annual return? What is our payout rate from the principal?
  - Cash flow: what are our operating reserves?
- Disclosure:
  - Is there an enforceable code of ethics for board and staff?
  - Is there an enforceable conflict of interest policy?
- Strategic:
  - What is our strategic plan?
  - Is an operational plan created each year?
  - Are there any opportunities for a merger in our future?
  - What are the trends in the overall market that we serve?
  - Are there changing government policies or laws that will impact our service area?
  - What opportunities does the changing environment offer us?
  - Is our organization stale or in danger of becoming irrelevant?
- Marketing:
  - How visible are we in our community? If we are not as visible as we would like, are we taking steps to increase our public profile?
  - What are the key messages we tell the community about our organization?
  - Have there been recent articles about our organization in the newspaper and/ or profiles on TV?

(continues)

Questions a New Board Member Might Want to Ask

- Fundraising:
    - Is there a fundraising plan each year for our organization?
    - How much do we need to generate each year in raised funds in order to meet our budget?
    - What are our fundraising challenges and opportunities?
    - What is the breakdown of our raised funds: corporate, foundation, individual, and government sources?
    - Who are our major donors and how tight are our relationships with these donors?
    - Are we making the most of web fundraising opportunities?
    - How clean (error free and updated) is our fundraising address and donor database? How many donors do we have on our list?
    - What is our renewal rate on donors?
    - How much time does the organization and fundraising staff spend on events versus other types of fundraising activities?
    - Does a small group of board members "own" fundraising or does the whole board take it on as a major responsibility?
- Staff:
    - Is our fundraising staff stable and happy, or is there a lot of turnover?
    - What is our fundraising staff's level of experience?
    - How are the relations between the executive director and the fundraising staff?
    - Does the executive director take an appropriate role in fundraising?
    - Are there professional development funds in the budget to send fundraising staff to meetings and conferences to further their skills?
- Is our board involved in:
    - Thanking donors by letter or by phone?
    - Helping to secure sponsors for events?
    - Going on cultivation and thank-you visits to key donors?
    - Selling tables for events?
    - Securing auction items for events?
    - Selling memberships to our organization?
    - Asking for contributions?
    - Opening doors and making important contacts with potential donors and funding sources for our organization?
    - Providing the names of potential donors?
    - Writing personal notes for solicitation and thank-you letters?
    - Hosting tours of our organization?
    - Hosting small socials, coffees, luncheons, and other events to expand community awareness of our organization and build friends?

The Board Member Notebook: What to Emphasize

Many organizations provide bulky notebooks to their board members with too much information. I have seen board members roll their eyes when the "Board Manual" is mentioned.

Although these repositories of information are helpful, be careful of overkill. New board members' eyes can start to glaze over when such a vast amount of material is presented. Give the board members only what they need to know to be successful. I would not expect them to read so much! Busy people want good staff support; brief them only on what they need to know, and eliminate the rest.

I would much rather they be well versed in the emotional impact of our work in the community, rather than be experts on facts and figures or our organization's history. Let them have personal experiences of our work in the field, so they can talk about it to their friends and contacts with passion and urgency!

Board Member Mentors

Assign each new board member to an experienced "buddy" board member. This is a wonderful way of helping new members feel acclimated to the "club." The Mentor board member can take the new person under his or her wing and make personal introductions to the other board members. The primary job is to help the new person get to know the other board members and to answer the new person's questions.

The Mentor can also give the new person the lowdown on what is expected and needed. He or she can smooth the entry for the new member in many helpful ways. Think how much you would appreciate this type of help when entering another culture or group. New board members appreciate this more than you can realize. The person-to-person collegiality that this can foster is an invaluable teambuilding asset.

HOW TO GET TO KNOW YOUR BOARD MEMBERS

The best way to get the most out of your board members in fundraising is to meet individually with each one. As you might expect, they will share more information with you privately than they will in the large meeting. It is also vitally important for you to establish a close, supportive, one-on-one relationship with each individual board member. Get to know your board members personally. As with major donors, face time is vital!

We all know that every board member has *something* to offer in fundraising. However, we do not know what that is until we sit down with them and find out where they want to fit in; what their interests are; what their experience is in fundraising; what they want do to; and what they *might* do if coaxed and supported. Most importantly, find out who they know!

What to Find Out about Your Board Members

The meeting with each board member is just like the Advice Visit discussed in the previous chapter. You do not know what you will find until you visit with them and find out. When

I meet with board members, I like to find out a lot of information about them: What interests them most about our mission and our good work in the community? What are they passionate about? What keeps them involved with our organization?

Know What Motivates Your Board Members   The most important thing for you to know about your board members is *why* each one is involved in the first place. Be sure to know their hot buttons, their interests, and above all their own motivations for serving.

Remember, they chose to join your board because it met some interest or need inside them. They joined because the mission was important to them personally and they wanted to use their skills to help advance that cause.

Your job is to provide opportunities for them to fulfill these wishes. When they are satisfied, they are more engaged in all aspects of your organization, including fundraising. If they are not satisfied, then they tend to withdraw or become disengaged. Or worse, they can take on activities that are not productive.

If you can remember what your board members want from their service, and help them realize these intentions, you will have a happier board.

Know of Previous Board Experience   Has your board member served on nonprofit boards before? Is he serving on other boards right now? You want to know whether you will need to educate this person in the basics, or whether he can hit the ground running.

Most board members who are experienced understand the environment of nonprofits. They know the difference they want to make by serving on your board. They tend to be more focused than inexperienced board members. They know what questions to ask, like the ones listed previously. You will not need to spend a lot of time educating them about the basics.

What Is the Depth of Commitment?   How committed are they to our organization? What kind of impact do they want to make? What special area or committee do they want to focus on? What are their special skill sets that our organization can make use of? Why do they think they were recruited for our board? What were they told about our organization when they were recruited? (You may need to clear up some misconceptions!)

Is the Board Member a Good Speaker?   Could he be trained to speak about your organization to community groups? Could he make a presentation about your organization?

What Are the Board Member's Fundraising Interests and Experience?   Does she have any fundraising experience? Does she like to be involved in events? If so, where could she plug in? What are her attitudes about fundraising? Is it the "F-word" or is it a benign, or even engrossing activity?

If she is afraid of fundraising, try to introduce some new concepts into her thinking. Show her how board members can make a huge impact without having to solicit. Give her concrete examples of how board members are all helping your fundraising program.

Where Can He Operate as a Fundraiser?   What are his social networks? Where does he go to church, shop, vacation, play? Is he involved with his school, college, or university? Or his children's schools? What is his professional network? Where within all these networks are contacts and information streams that might support your organization's connections?

Who Does She Know?   It is important to review your prospect list with each board member. See who on that list your board member may know and who he or she might be willing to help cultivate. If one member is a business executive, you can also bring a list of the corporate relationships you are trying to develop. Seek the board member's help in building closer relationships with these companies.

You will invariably find, after reviewing a list of prospects, that your board members have more connections than they realized. The next question is: how do we create a cultivation strategy that makes the most of this relationship?

The Board Commitment Letter: Get It in Writing!

What commitments are you actually asking your board members to make? As we have discussed, it is vital for you to outline clearly what you are asking your board members to do and ask them to agree to their responsibilities in writing.

If you do not set standards and expect that they be kept, then you cannot expect high performance. Remember that people respond to formality and clarity. If you have to make exceptions to the standards for board members; be very careful about it or you will dampen other members' energy.

Those board members who work hard to fulfill their commitments will know when other board members forsake theirs. You must hold all board members to the same standards. Otherwise, you will quickly lose the morale of those that "do."

TIPS AND TECHNIQUES

Your Board Commitment Letter Should Include These Expectations:

- Personal annual gift commitment: state the expectation of personal donations explicitly; you can also make a certain dollar figure optional. That amount can then come from the board member personally or be gathered by her from other sources.

- Meeting attendance: set the requirement for the number of meetings a year that can be missed without a special dispensation.

- Committee participation: lay out your expectations regarding committees.

- Due diligence: explain their duties to oversee the organization's financial, accountability, and legal responsibilities.

- Participation in fundraising activities: spell it out.

SELF-ASSESSMENTS KEEP EVERYONE FOCUSED

Accountability and feedback will sharpen a focus on good board conduct and measurable outcomes. Clearly, if you establish a standard of performance, then you are able to measure progress toward this goal.

Assessing the board is a delicate matter. Pamela Wilcox, in *Exposing the Elephants: Creating Exceptional Nonprofits,* suggests that a board self-assessment is "fraught with danger" because the board members will be "understandably defensive." "Done poorly," she notes, "the result is hurt and angry board members, which does little to improve the board's overall purpose."[13]

Carefully done, an annual self-assessment of the board can be a powerful management tool. Knowledge is power. Shining the light on an issue will help define it as a problem, which can then be addressed.

If it is properly managed, the board self-assessment can pinpoint simmering problems beneath the surface as well as obvious issues (such as the obnoxious board member) that board members are just too polite to discuss. It can be a cure to the unrelenting "niceness" of boards and their tendency to force conformity through the lowest common denominator of consensus and quiet down any disturbing issue.

I recommend that you go for it: conduct a board self-assessment. There are various surveys available; I post one on my Web site that I particularly like. In addition, BoardSource offers a very thorough, if pricey, self-assessment tool.

There is an essential key to a successful board self-assessment that will ensure that your result is not hurt and angry board members: a neutral consultant. This person can be invaluable in managing the feedback process. Have the consultant administer the survey, interpret the results, safely and impartially facilitate the board's discussion of the results, and —here is the key—guide the board through recommendations to improve its performance.

TIPS AND TECHNIQUES

Here is my recommended list of board self-assessment questions. I have borrowed heavily from the list presented by *Best of the Board Café,* edited by Jan Masaoka:[14]

Please rate your assessment of the Board of Directors' performance on a scale of 1 to 5, with 1 = Not At All Confident, and 5 = Very Confident.

How confident are you that as an effective governing body, the board:

1. Has a strategic vision for the organization?   _____
2. Ensures legal compliance with federal, state, and local regulations?   _____
3. Monitors financial performance and projections on a regular basis?   _____
4. Monitors and evaluates the performance of the executive director on a regular basis?   _____
5. Has adopted an income strategy (that combines contributions, earned income, and other revenue) to ensure adequate resources?   _____

6. Has a clear policy on the responsibilities of board members in fundraising? _____

7. Has adopted a conflict of interest policy that is discussed regularly? _____

8. Currently contains an appropriate range of expertise and diversity to make it an effective governing body? _____

9. Regularly assesses its own work? _____

10. Orients new members properly so they can hit the ground running? _____

11. Creates opportunities for social time so the board members can to get to know each other? _____

How confident are you that most or all board members:

12. Are adequately knowledgeable about our programs? _____

13. Act as ambassadors to the community on behalf of our organization? _____

14. Follow through on commitments they have made as board members? _____

15. Are appropriately involved in board activities? _____

16. Are clear on what their specific jobs are to serve our mission? _____

17. Know what results and outcomes each board member needs to create this year? _____

Can you rate our board meetings:

18. Are they interesting and engaging? _____

19. Do they focus on results and outcomes rather than process and reporting? _____

Open-ended questions:

What information would you like to have in order to be a better board member?

_____

_____

What questions do you have about our board, your role, or our CEO's role?

_____

_____

What suggestions do you have for:

Improving our board performance? _____

_____

Improving our organization's performance? _____

_____

How would you like to be involved in helping our organization this year?

_____

_____

A well-done board self-assessment can be an important teambuilding exercise, resulting in happier board members, pleased because their voices were heard and actions were initiated to address their concerns. Your result will be more engaged board members who were glad they were listened to.

I suggest that a brief questionnaire, perhaps online, be administered annually. It should be answered anonymously in order to generate honest feedback.

Another technique for following up on the commitments of individual board members is to review the original Board Commitment Letter that each one signed and to ask board members to assess their own performance.

MAKE SURE ALL THE BOARD MEMBERS GIVE

> *If our true believers don't help us, who else in the world can help us do this?*
> —Albert Camus

Where do the board members stand when it comes to their own giving? How can you as staff make sure they all give to the best of their abilities?

The Proud Annual Gift

The most fundamental expectation of a board member is that each must make his own gift to the organization to help underwrite its programs and its mission. This was item #1 on the list of "Fundraising Requirements of All Board Members" earlier in this chapter. The board's first responsibility in supporting fundraising begins with its own giving.

Board members should contribute early and often, providing both time and money. They need to hear this idea over and over and hear it clearly.

- "We expect 100% participation in giving."
- "We expect all board members to make a proud annual gift to the best of their ability to support our organization's mission."
- "We need 100% board participation before we go out and ask our community for support."
- Or the quite blunt directive: "Give, Get, or Get Off!"
- Or a kinder approach: "We want the Three Ws: Wisdom, Work, and Wealth."

As Linda Lysakowski aptly puts it in *Recruiting and Training Fundraising Volunteers*, "the board members should be ready to put their money where their heart is."[15] I would add: if they will not do so, then you are dealing with a problem! This chapter will help you to resolve it.

Board members cannot possibly ask others for funds if they have not given themselves.

> *I think it's a funny odor; you can just smell somebody who is a board member but hasn't given.*
> —Nonprofit Consultant

Why Should Anybody Else Give If Board Members Do Not?

Without your board's full, hearty financial support, your fundraising program is likely to limp along, risking your programs and hurting morale. The best way to demonstrate deep support for your organization's fundraising efforts is with 100% board participation in giving. It is expected; it is required. It is not a *"would like to have"*; it is a *"must have."*

As Jerry Panas says in *Finders Keepers,* "Good trustees give sacrificially . . . . Trustees are expected to give to the very best of their abilities. . . . If trustees don't give devotedly —why should anyone else?"[16]

All of us have heard the recalcitrant board member's protest: "I give my time, that's enough! I should not be expected to give money too." These board members are trying to avoid a fundamental fact: it takes effort *and* money to take organizations where they need to go.

Letting Down the Staff

I hear the same sad tale over and over from executive directors and development staff: not all of their board members are donors. They whisper this to me, their consultant and friend, as a dirty little secret. They are a bit ashamed to admit this terrible situation. There is a sense of helplessness about it all. They feel so let down by their board members—in a matter that really counts!

These directors would not feel so bad about it if they shifted their point of view. Instead of feeling and acting powerless about this bad situation, they should assume responsibility for it.

> *I just wish my board members would give more in line with their financial capacity. Some do; most could do more: for example, we have perhaps ten $5,000 donors who could easily give $25,000; and we have three or four $100 donors who could double their gift, which is not a lot financially but would make a statement of their commitment to and understanding of the organization and the role Board leadership in giving plays.*
>
> —Executive Director, Major Regional Nonprofit

It Is Our Fault That Board Members Do Not Give 100%!

In fact, we could make full board participation a reality if we handled it correctly. The real issue is that we frequently do not set up solicitation of the members in the right way.

We, the nonprofit directors and fundraisers, are in charge of the fundraising program and the kinds of information and impressions board members receive about it. We help set the board agendas. For all our skill and prowess as fundraising professionals, unfortunately we sometimes botch the solicitation of our own boards.

If we have been cultivating our board members properly and continuously—just as we would any major donors—the board solicitation should be a piece of cake. If we have done our homework and know what each one is interested in, what he or she wants to accomplish on the board, how he wants to contribute to our organization's work, and where she wants to fit into the fundraising program, it will be easy.

If you devote care and personal attention to board members, you will be surprised by what they will do for you. If you instead expect them to be excited and involved by just attending boring meetings that focus on small details, you can be sure they will drift into inaction—and nongiving.

Here is how we sometimes go wrong:

- We are not clear enough about the expectation of giving.
- We do not set up the ask in the right way.
- We do not put the issue in front of them often and clearly enough.
- We are shy about all of it.

Why the Difficulties?

First, look at your own position/status vis-à-vis your board. You work for them. It is difficult to have sway over them when you are their employee. Will they treat you with respect if you are not a peer? Doubtful, especially when you are asking for a contribution. You are asking them for too many favors as it is.

In situations like these, it actually does get a bit like "begging." The conversation turns to being one about "money," rather than about vision. It is hard for you as a staff member to have a conversation with your board members about their giving, without it lapsing into the wrong tone. Instead of being high-minded and full of clear noble purpose, the exchange becomes more like nagging, complaining.

The Solution

Other board members can talk to *each other* about their gifts and put the transaction on the proper higher plane. They get to discuss among themselves such ideas as:

- Our group commitment;
- Our vision for the organization;
- The obligation of us all to support the work with our time and our money;
- The fact that we are the highest powers at the organization and need to set the example for everyone, including the rest of the community.

You as a staff member can never say something like "give, get, or get off." But other board members can! Arrange for other board members to handle the issue of board gifts. You can put all the words in the asker's mouth; just do not let those words come out of your own!

SEVEN RULES FOR SUCCESSFULLY SOLICITING YOUR BOARD

- Rule One: Make the philosophy clear; show why board members need to give generously.
- Rule Two: Say what you expect, in *both* written and spoken form.
- Rule Three: Get board members to solicit other board members.
- Rule Four: Give the subject of board donations lots of visibility.
- Rule Five: Take charge of the process yourself.
- Rule Six: Give the members lots of credit and acknowledgment.
- Rule Seven: Tie the board's gifts directly to your program results.

Rule One: Make the Philosophy Clear; Show Why Board Members Need to Give Generously

The importance of their participation in giving is rarely explained properly to trustees. Instead, the issue of their giving is apologized for, snuck up on, swept under the rug. When the reasoning for their giving is established in an open and straightforward way, the director and staff can cheerfully and enthusiastically expect board members to step up to the plate and give.

Raising the Credibility of the Fundraising Program　As I've mentioned, board gifts are the essential foundation for building credibility for your fundraising efforts. That is a sufficiently important idea that it deserves to be brought up again and again.

We all know that you cannot, with any credibility, go out into the community and ask others for contributions if your inner circle is not right there with you. But do your board members really understand this?

We all know of many funders who require giving from 100% of an agency's board. They will not make gifts to organizations that do not have that support.

There is a well-known story in my circles in North Carolina of a foundation that was poised to make a significant gift to a nonprofit. In the final stages of consideration for the grant, the foundation asked for information on giving by the board of the organization. When the foundation leadership found out about lackluster cash contributions from this particular board—which was far short of 100% participation—they backed off from the gift!

Getting the financial support of your board need not be the biggest challenge of your year. After all, board members are not ignorant. They know that their cash contribution lends vital credibility to your fundraising efforts. They know they are supposed to give. They know that they signed a commitment letter when they agreed to serve, and they promised they would make a gift. The problem may sometimes be that they are extremely busy people and need to be reminded of their duty to give.

Rule Two: Say What You Expect, in *Both* Written and Spoken Form

It is important to spell this expectation out in your board enlistment materials and in the commitment letter that members sign when they join.

You must make sure that the commitment to give is written in plain English, in black and white, for everyone to see. Do not stop there, however: you must also talk out loud about it often.

This is a bigger challenge than you might think! Too many board chairs apologize when they bring up the subject of board giving. They are not definitive about what is expected or encouraging about giving. They instead show their embarrassment at having to mention it at all. They need to recognize the power of asking. "The moment you ask for money. . . ," writes Lynn Twist in her essay, "Fundraising from the Heart," you will be taken seriously."[17]

The most important person to speak to the other board members about their gifts is the leader of the board, its chair. He or she must have the guts to be direct about the obligation. For example: "This is a clear expectation of all members of this board, and I am going to be following up to encourage you!" with the board leader making eye contact as she speaks.

Here is a story about a dynamic leader at work—asking. A friend of mine attended a breakfast meeting at which Jim Hunt, the dynamic former governor of North Carolina, spoke about an important project to strengthen the state's education system.

Jim Hunt is one of the great leaders of the South and has fearlessly tackled many important projects since he retired as governor a few years ago. Like an impassioned Southern preacher, Governor Hunt can spin a tale of urgency about important community needs. His track record, including being elected to an unprecedented four terms, shows that he can gather important people to help his causes.

At the breakfast, he stood and looked at all the community and business leaders around the table and bluntly said, "I am asking you all to support his project. It needs your help or it won't succeed. I expect each of you to make a substantial gift." He did not beat around the bush, and he made direct eye contact with each person.

When Governor Jim Hunt looks at you with a specific request and direct eye contact, you can't run and you can't hide! The way he framed his request gave it importance and emphasis. There was no question about what each person at the table was being asked to do. It was, as mentioned earlier, a Big Request, a powerful one that inspired people to immediate attention—and action. The ability to ask in this way has contributed much to Hunt's success.

Too many board chairs are so nervous about this issue that they soften up their manner. They speak about giving in a tentative tone of voice. They look down and around instead of making eye contact with other board members.

If you doubt that your board chair can make a clear, emphatic, and direct oral request to the board about the importance and necessity of full financial participation, then find another board member to make this speech. It is up to you to make this happen.

Rule Three: Get Board Members to Solicit Other Board Members

Never, never, never put yourself in the position of soliciting your board members. Do not forget the fundamental fundraising rule of peer-to-peer solicitation: when it comes time to solicit the board, get out of the way and have someone else do it!

How can you have any credibility soliciting your board when you actually work for them? Doesn't work! Forget it and don't even try. It puts you in the awful position of supplicant, powerless and subservient. And when you ask and they do not give, I will bet you will feel pretty bad about it, which is not good for you or your organization.

You *must* have board members solicit other board members. Even if you write (but don't sign) all the letters, design the pledge card, and set up and manage the whole affair, you still are not the person out front doing the asking. I recommend that you manage the campaign and never let yourself be the one out front.

TIPS AND TECHNIQUES

Ways to ask your board members: face-to-face solicitations versus asking by letter.

- **Mail solicitation:** Many boards do just fine with a solicitation by letter. The problem with this approach is that the letter may get misplaced; it may not be properly followed up; and the emphasis on the board member's individual gift is certainly softer on paper than it is eye-to-eye.

  I, for one, have had good results with solicitations by mail, as I describe later. However, I was successful because I made sure my board members had close relationships with our organization and were up to date and involved in our initiatives. They already knew the importance of their giving. Soliciting by mail will only work if your board members are engaged and active.

- **In-person solicitation:** A formal face-to-face solicitation by another board member can be a powerful experience. It clearly gives more importance to the request.

  The personal visit is a good opportunity to educate the board member about your organization's fundraising effort. It gives that individual a chance to experience directly what it is like to be called on for a contribution to the organization.

  The member who is visited gets to hear some important information: how the case for support is articulated, what giving opportunities are available, and where he or she can focus their particular gift. This equips the person being called on with techniques to use in the future with other potential donors or board members.

I would base my choice of using mail or in-person strategy on the giving potential of the board and on the amount of the requests. My personal rule is that I will be willing to solicit gifts under $1,000 by mail, while an ask of $1,000 or more deserves a personal visit.

You may have several board members who can make significant annual gifts. If so, have them approached in person and ask for the substantial amount that the organization needs and that you know they can afford. Sometimes a board member is willing to match or challenge the other members' gifts. This is a wonderful way to inspire and motivate the rest of the board members to make a stretch gift.

Soliciting for Different Amounts from Board Members   It is important to know each board member's capability and ask at that level. There are various ways to screen your board for their giving potential.

If you are on top of relationships with your board and know them well, you probably already have a clear idea of how much each person can or should be giving. If not, you could create a screening committee to determine this delicate but important information. This would be an appropriate function of your Executive Committee or your Development Committee.

Giving as a Transforming Act   Many fundraising pundits say that both soliciting and making financial gifts are powerful, transforming experiences. Lynne Twist describes the act of soliciting as raising the bar of participation: it asks the donor/board member to become an active partner in an organization's work to address a critical community need. When an individual gives, that donor creates a different relationship with the organization; he or she becomes "an investor" with a substantial stake in the agency—and its results.

Board members, especially, must be "moved," Twist writes, "to give their money and moved to allocate their financial resources consistent with their deepest commitments."[18]

Giving by those on the board can be a clear indicator of board commitment, and that is why the issue of nongiving by board members takes such a toll on staff morale. When employees, who live and breathe the mission daily, see that their board members are not aligning themselves with the work at hand, they can become deeply discouraged. The board's lack of donations is seen as a signal that the board members are not fully committed to the organization and its work.

On the other hand, this signal may not be true. Give the board members the benefit of a doubt. Keep your expectations of them set to their highest potential, continue to expect the best from them rather than the worst, and then follow these seven rules. You will be surprised at your success.

Rule Four: Give the Subject of Board Donations Lots of Visibility

Put reports on the status of fundraising front and center at board meetings; in presenting that information, be sure to focus on board gifts. Talk about these donations as if they are important, which they are. If you are giving board members constant feedback on fundraising results—and keeping the figures in front of them always—then board gifts will be easier to discuss openly.

If you are not putting fundraising in general at the top of your agenda, then you will make it far too easy for your board leaders to sidestep politely the whole issue of their own giving, and you will be leaving money on the table that should go into the agency's work.

Some organizations create a separate line item in your revenue/fundraising budget for board contributions to add emphasis. This gets the board members' attention for sure!

- *Report regularly on the status of board gifts.* Make this item part of your regular fundraising reports. For example, have the board chair say, "I'm pleased that we have 82% of our board member gifts in so far this year. Thanks to all! And those of you who have not yet given, I know who you are!" He/she can say this with a smile and everyone will be just fine with it. Those who have not given will quickly look for the pledge card in their meeting packet.
- *Put pledge cards and return envelopes in every board member's packet.* The member should never have the excuse of not being reminded enough or of not having the right envelope/material easily at hand.

IN THE REAL WORLD

I have a story to tell on myself about board donations. I was a board member of the Gallery of Art and Design at North Carolina State University, and I was helping add some new ideas to their fundraising programs. Board members were enjoying a new task of adding personal notes to solicitation letters. They were really starting to get involved in fundraising and having a good time doing it.

The Gallery did its solicitation mailizng once in the fall and then followed up in the spring, near the end of the fiscal year, with a clean-up mailing focusing on lapsed donors. I have to admit that paperwork is not one of my strong suits, particularly snail mail, and I misplaced the annual solicitation letter and pledge card that came in the fall. I forgot that I had not made my annual contribution!

Was I ever embarrassed when I got the follow-up mailing in May, with a personal note signed by a fellow board member who also worked in fundraising professionally! Dreadful! Here I was, playing a lead role in fundraising, and I had neglected to send my own gift! I still remember how awful I felt when I opened the letter and read her note: "I didn't think I would need to be writing you this . . ." Ouch!

In my defense, however, if the Gallery staff had simply let me know of the situation, I would have sent my check immediately. If the issue had been front and center at every board meeting, if the running tally had been fed back to me every time I sat down at that table, I would have known and taken care of my board gift sooner.

So please take a lesson from this story. Do not automatically be disheartened by non-giving board members. Do not think the worst about them; instead, think the best, and give them a clear reminder. Like me, they may have simply forgotten about it.

- **Set a deadline for all board gifts to be completed.** Some organizations have had great success by telling all board members that they want their contributions in by a certain date, early in the year. That way the agency gets the money sooner, and the members are put on alert that they have an obligation.

The Problem of the Disengaged, Absent Board Member   These are difficult cases. Board members who are not around a lot will miss all this attention to the issue at hand. They will not be receiving regular reminders because they are barely on your bandwagon.

These absent board members are usually the ones who are not giving. These people usually need special treatment: a specific call or letter from another board member explicitly asking for their active involvement. They must be approached about their gift personally and directly, or they will drift away into their fog without any thought of sending money.

Again, staff can track the situation, identify who needs additional prodding, and then—behind the scenes—make sure it happens.

Deliberately Choosing Not to Solicit a Board Member   In some rare cases you might decide to skip a board member in the annual solicitation. This might be advisable when someone has just made a large capital gift. Since requests are tailored to each individual's interests and situation, a smart fundraiser will know whether soliciting someone for a small annual gift will impede or help the overall relationship with that person.

Annual Solicitations during a Capital Campaign   It is important to give the annual campaign a clear identity separate from the capital campaign. You must make it distinct—and a separate ask. I have seen too many capital campaigns in which major donors were pulled out of the annual solicitation.

Donors themselves have come to me and said, "Why isn't XYZ organization asking me for money? I haven't been asked to contribute for a couple of years and I don't understand why." I would tell them that we had pulled all the campaign prospects out of the annual solicitation effort in order to be sure they were treated personally.

Taking campaign prospects off the list for the annual solicitation can backfire on you. These potential donors may want to be asked for support. By leaving them out, you run the risk of decimating your annual fund during the campaign; with rare exceptions, make solicitation of *all* donors an essential part of the process.

Of course, there may be good reasons for removing some people from the annual campaign. For very high-potential prospects, the annual solicitations cannot be simply your routine phone/mail effort. These people expect and deserve personal treatment. If you cannot give their annual solicitation the customized, personalized attention it deserves, you risk alienating them with a "dear friend" or some other impersonal letter.

It is important to think carefully about your prime prospects, whether to include them on the annual list and how to give them appropriate personal attention.

Double Solicitations for an Annual Gift as Well as a Capital Campaign   When I was working in fundraising at Duke University, the staff made sure that all prospects for the capital campaign understood they were being asked to make a gift to the Duke Annual Fund as well as the capital campaign. We called it the "double ask" and were proud of it.

In some cases, if a capital campaign prospect took place in a reunion year, the donor received a "triple ask" of three solicitations: the special reunion gift, a regular gift to the annual fund, and a capital campaign contribution.

Duke clearly operated its fundraising program from a perspective of abundance! Talk about knowing that your organization is doing important work, and expecting that people will join right in with you. This is the way to do it! If more nonprofits embraced this point of view, there would be much more successful fundraising, and more powerful and effective organizations.

Deliberately Skipping a Board Member's Annual Gift Solicitation   When I was development director at the Kenan-Flagler Business School at the University of North Carolina-Chapel Hill, we deliberately broke some rules. There were two particular board members whom we regularly did not ask for annual financial support.

One was our largest benefactor, who was in the process of endowing the business school to name it for his family. The other was a well-known and loved leader in the state, so esteemed that he seemed to be the grandfather of all good works in North Carolina.

In the first case, the benefactor was already giving liberally to our school; there was no need to ask for an additional gift in the annual board appeal. I gave him ample credit for his generosity in my reports on board gifts.

In the latter case, we did not want the other gentleman to feel obligated to support us financially. What we wanted from him was his endorsement, because that gave us more credibility than any monetary contribution could ever do.

The decision to forgo a solicitation appeal to these two gentlemen was my boss's. I concurred, however, and I understood the bigger picture in our overall relationship with these very prominent and gracious men.

Rule Five: Take Charge of the Process Yourself

You will not get 100% board participation unless you arrange for it to happen. As I have said before, staff has to direct the entire effort like a quarterback behind the scenes.

You must take charge. Do not—repeat—do not leave it to chance. If you do, you will end up with a lackluster performance by your board, less than full participation, and a demoralized staff. If you practice these seven rules, you are likely to reach full participation easily.

Rule Six: Give the Board Members Lots of Credit and Acknowledgment

Remember the rule of positive reinforcement? I am sure that if you have kids, students, or a spouse, you've used it. It's very simple: reward the behaviors you want to develop, and those behaviors will show up more often. We have to realize that board members typically do not get much thanks or acknowledgment at all.

Give Credit for All the Resources Board Members Bring In   I am in favor of giving multiple credits whenever possible. If a board member makes a gift from his or her business and asks that it count as their annual gift, accept it happily. You still have the option of coming back later—at the right time, of course—and asking for a personal gift in addition to the corporate gift.

Every gift of resources of any type from a board member should be an occasion of joy and celebration! Recognize everything; give credit again and again for gifts that board members bring in from foundations and corporations and in-kind resources.

Giving ample thanks makes them all feel great and successful. Remember that success breeds success. Create an environment of abundance, rather than scarcity, in your handling of board contributions. Make the members feel they are creating abundance, even if you are not so sure. Creating the feeling will help make the reality happen.

People want to be part of success. They do not want to be part of failure. Hand wringing in any form should be banned from the boardroom! Thanking for contributions should be part of every board meeting.

Rule Seven: Tie the Board's Gifts Directly to Your Program Results

Let the board members know what they are accomplishing through their gifts, just as we do with all donors. (Don't we?) Give them meaningful information on the results they have created.

If you are implementing the visibility techniques we discussed in the last chapter by showing the cause-and-effect link between better fundraising results and better daily operations, your board members will not only be more active in fundraising, they will be more active donors personally.

If you can get them enthusiastic about what they are actively accomplishing through their work and their personal gifts, you will have lots more money coming from them. Like all donors, they experience joy when they see the results of their gifts.

- "With your leadership, support, and financial contributions, we were able to accomplish X."
- "The generous gifts from board members allowed us to go even farther to do Y."
- "The board's gifts made all the difference in our ability to reach Z."

These are the magic words that board members (and donors) love to hear.

Implementing the Seven Rules: A Model for Success

During my tenure at the Kenan-Flagler School of Business, I had a Dream Board made up of more than 60 high-powered, wealthy executives. I made sure that soliciting them was a major item on our fundraising calendar each fall.

The board solicitation occupied a prominent part of my attention at that time of year, for two reasons. The project was quite complex; we created detailed personalized letters for everyone, and this effort brought in a substantial amount of important unrestricted funds.

Here is the model I found effective and followed for my annual board solicitation. This plan kept me fully behind the scenes, carefully directing the entire effort. I never was in front asking, but I was the quarterback making sure it happened!

- *Draft the letter.* I drafted a snappy, compelling one-page solicitation letter, emphasizing our great results and our opportunities to come.

- *Set an appropriate ask amount for each board member.* You can do this yourself or with a screening committee. I knew my board members well enough to do it myself. If I had a question, I consulted my dean or other board members on a case-by-case basis. We did not need a formal screening committee.

- *Personalize each letter with a different ask amount for each person.* Each letter was tailored to the recipient, and each board member was asked for a different amount, ranging from $1,000 to $10,000 depending on their circumstances.

- *Get the board chair, or the most prominent person on your board, to sign the letter.* I often asked Hugh McColl, chair of NationsBank, to sign the letters. He was a business colleague of the other board members and was held in high esteem. One year I even sent the letters to him in Charlotte so he could personally sign his name and write personal notes on some. Clearly that type of personal touch by an important figure adds weight and power to the appeal.

- *Always give your board members a personalized return envelope with their pledge card.* I included, of course, a return envelope in the mailings. I had special small envelopes hand-typed that would send the contribution directly back to the dean. This very personal touch had a significant impact on the recipient: it made the mailing much less anonymous. They had no doubt that the dean himself would open and see the return pledge cards and checks.

- *Send out the letters.* The letters went out in early November each year, on a set schedule.

- *Follow-up.* A letter went out in December to those who had not given in response to the first appeal. Sometimes this follow-up letter was signed by our dean and referred to the earlier letter from Mr. McColl. This note was softer than the first solicitation letter.

- *Results follow-up.* I gave my dean monthly reports on who had given at that point in the year, so he could gently nudge the others when needed.

- *Acknowledge gifts both at board meetings and in private.* The dean acknowledged board gifts at each board meeting, so the donor knew that he considered the contribution an important matter. I made sure I thanked each individual profusely, and other board officers did as well.

- *Follow up toward the end of the fiscal year to create one last chance.* In May, we sent a final letter as reminder to those who had not yet given, again asking for a specific amount.

I encourage you to take a good look at your board solicitation efforts. Do you use a system that is deliberate, carefully designed, and customized? Or are you leaving the outcome to chance? Take charge and you will be pleased with your results!

Set Your Board Members Up to Win

Empower your board members to succeed. The best way to organize your board members for fundraising success is to set things up so that they take direct ownership of the fundraising plan of action. In addition, each person makes their own commitment to be involved in the fundraising activities they care most about.

Put Fundraising Up Front on Your Agenda!

We can direct the level of care and attention our board focuses on fundraising. If you think about it, all the board's information about our fundraising program comes from the staff. The quality and presentation of the information we give them directly impacts their ability—and their willingness—to participate in fundraising

We can set up new conversations about fundraising. Just because our organization has never really tackled fundraising issues in board meetings does not mean that it needs to continue that way. Just because board members were led in the past to think "the staff will do it" does not mean we cannot change.

The ultimate power is in drawing up the agenda for what the board will address. It is up to the board chair and the staff leadership to set up these discussions for maximum engagement, interest, and impact.

The Fundraising Agenda at Board Meetings

I am always surprised at the lack of attention that boards give their fundraising program. I have seen boards debating half an hour on a trivial issue while missing the more important fact that the annual fundraising event urgently needs all board members' attention or it will be a flop.

The time spent reporting on, discussing, and planning for fundraising is amazingly short. I personally cannot think of anything more important, or more vital, to the board's agenda. Too often the agenda is full of dull reports and misses the urgent matters at hand.

Do we create our boards to just sit passively in meetings listening to reports and daydreaming? Or do we identify issues that really matter, such as what can each board member do to ensure the gala's success?

You should allocate a substantial portion of board meeting time to fundraising. These are the topics of things you should cover, not necessarily at each meeting, but frequently.

- *Fundraising results. How are we doing?* How well have our fundraising programs done so far this year? Especially when compared with previous years?

- *What is our fundraising plan?* The board needs to understand fully the fundraising plan for your organization. In the short time allocated for fundraising on most agendas, there is hardly any time for qualitatively evaluating your performance, much less understanding how those programs really operate.

  Take the time for board members to understand what you do, how you do it, and when you do it. They need to understand all the factors that can impact your fundraising program, both positively and negatively. In particular, they need to understand trends. They need to know what you might like to do if you had more resources.

- *How well are we thanking donors?* Do we know who our donors are? How can the board members help thank? How long does it take after receipt of a gift to get a thank-you letter out?

- *What is keeping the development director up at night?* What does he worry about? How satisfied is he with the performance of various fundraising strategies? What does he need the board's help with next? Emerge from your fundraising discussion with a clear understanding of what board members need to do next in order to support fundraising success.

- *Events.* If you have just staged a fundraising event, it is important to devote enough time for review and *closure*. Too often the event is over and people are rushing off to the next important thing to do.

  But board members need specific feedback on what worked and what did not work. What did everyone learn? What would you do differently? If you don't have this conversation, you may end up repeating things next year that never worked in the first place.

  - Acknowledge the hard work of each board member who participated. Reward good performance in front of the whole group. Positive reinforcement goes a long way!

  - Discuss the percentage of board members who attended.

  - What were the overall financial results from the event?

  - Did it make goal? Did it surpass goal?

  - What did you learn from the event? What best practices did you learn to apply to future events?

  - What can you and the board members do today that will help set up next year's event to be even more successful? Recruit next year's event chairs now, while everyone is still glowing about the success.

Can you engage your board members in a massive thank-a-thon to express gratitude to all the donors and attendees, telling them the financial results of the events? "Because we raised XXX, we will be able to reach YY more kids in the schools, or serve ZZZ more clients." Always close the loop between financial results and your impact on the community.

- *What is down the pike in fundraising that we need to know about?* Are there opportunities we are missing? Are there problems we are ignoring?

I usually ask organizations how much money they are leaving on the table by missing fundraising opportunities. Our board members need to know that it is the quality, consistency, and quantity of paid human fundraising staff resources and efforts that have the greatest impact on fundraising results. Boards need to be informed what opportunities had to be missed because of limited man/womanpower.

Just last week I had an organization tell me they were leaving from one to two hundred thousand a year on the table because they did not have sufficient staff to go after grants that had a high likelihood of success. Another international client told me they were leaving millions on the table because they did not have the staff resources to go after major government and foundation grants.

The reasons these organizations did not have any more fundraising staff was because their leadership felt that investing in fundraising was "overhead," which they were determined to keep low. What shortsightedness!

Spending money on fundraising resources is an investment that will return over and over. It is the organizations which invest in fundraising that raise the most money. (Look at college and university fundraising programs.) Organizations that think they cannot "afford" to invest resources in fundraising are the ones that don't raise money. They stay right where they are because they never changed a thing.

Give the Board Members Constant Feedback on Fundraising Results

When board members are actively involved in fundraising activities, they need constant support and feedback. If a gift comes in from someone they helped to cultivate, by all means, share the information and the joy of success. Let them enjoy the fruits of their labors. Complete the circle by letting them be part of the thank-you process to friends they have made for the organization, people they have cultivated and/or solicited.

Gift totals to date are vital gauges of how well you are doing. Report back to your board members often! Do not forget that they are integral members of your team.

Tie Your Fundraising Results Directly Back to Your Daily Operations

As I have mentioned, it is vitally important to connect fundraising results back into the actual projects being funded. The board members need to understand both "What are we trying to accomplish?" and "How much money will it take?"

If they are fully cognizant of those two objectives, they will take stronger, faster, and more urgent action in the fundraising arena. They will actually make their calls instead of putting them on a back burner!

You will be more successful if your strategic and operational plans are right up in front of the board's attention. The board members (and all staff members) need to know explicitly how fundraising success ties into the operational programs. Everyone needs to have a stake in each step of the fundraising program, activity by activity.

No Surprises!

Many executive directors protect the board from this type of direct information. Sometimes the first time a board member will hear about the impact on programs is when there is a shortfall and the CEO says, hesitantly, if we do not make our fundraising goal we will have to cut this and this.

Board members do not want to hear this at the last minute! No surprises! Instead, focus ahead of time on the great potential that your fundraising programs can offer your organization. Let board members know what they need to do ensure that the funds are raised— and what that will accomplish.

HOW TO ORGANIZE FOR FUNDRAISING RESULTS

Moral and Administrative Support

Above all else, we have to remember that our board members are volunteers. They are busy people. With the time they do have to offer our organization, they want to be effective and accomplish something worthwhile.

So it is incumbent on us, as staff, to make sure we are putting our board members to work at their "highest and best use." This means we do not want to ask them to do trivial activities, but to engage in actions that leverage their available time and energy.

In working for our nonprofits, trustees need and deserve great staff support.

Staff to board: "How can I support you?"

Many authors have written about how to use volunteers in your organization, particularly for fundraising. I especially like Linda Lysakowski's *Recruiting and Training Fundraising Volunteers*.

However, few have written about what it actually takes to manage and motivate board members to do what they say they will do. Here, we will talk about the psychology of getting what you want out of your board volunteers.

We must be realistic about what our board members will be able to accomplish with their limited time. Instead of complaining that they did not follow through on their commitments, we should carefully and strategically think through what we are asking them to do. Is it the most important, the most urgent item on the agenda or not?

We must support them every step of the way. It is naïve to think they will trot out of the board meeting, having taken good enough notes to know what they need to be doing next, and go right into action. Some wonderful board members will do this, but do not be disappointed when most do not.

It is not enough to give them a list of doors to open and say thank you, and then turn them loose. What will happen? You may find yourself complaining that they did not do their job.

What you must do is keep the project in front of them, remind them of their commitment, and cheerfully say "Do you need any help or support from me on this?"

One of the most wonderful sentences in the English language is "How can I support you?" Try it on your board members. They will appreciate it, and you will find them more responsive to you and productive for you. This is the way to build good board-staff relationships.

Many board members are going to forget their commitments simply because they are busy people. Some board members appreciate your help in setting priorities for their action and focus. I find from my own experience serving on boards that I always appreciate a staffer reminding me of what I need to do for them right now.

Managing Volunteers

As I have mentioned before, only give any volunteers three things to do at once. After they have accomplished those three things, then you can add more. If you give board members a long list, they are more likely to put the jobs off because it seems like a big project. Giving them small bites of tasks makes the assignment seem doable, and they will hopefully tackle it quickly.

You should feel free to phone and e-mail your board members to check cheerfully and nicely on their progress with whatever they are supposed to be doing. They will probably be grateful for the reminder. If you do not remind them, you may not get the action you want.

I like a cheery e-mail that is sent out to an entire committee letting them know about progress on a project. That is a good way to send a reminder. You have got to keep *your* project up in front on their radar screen, or it will drop down to the middle or the bottom of their to-do list. Do not be afraid of checking in on your board members; do not treat them as if they are too far out of reach to deal with you.

Structure

After the proper setup, what next? Along with a specific time frame and clearly identified actions/moves on prospects, board members need handholding, moral support, coaching, encouragement, and help in order to plot their future moves on a prospect. Without adequate staff support, any well-intentioned board activity will founder. You must remember that your board members look to you to guide the fundraising process.

A tight, well-organized structure is vital to support any group of volunteers. Structure provides a comfortable framework for board members by setting up a specific timeline, with determined commitments of action within a set period.

As anyone who has worked with nonprofit volunteer board members knows, when board members start making commitments to do things for their organization, too often the result is more talk and less action. Getting board members to do what they say they will do is frequently a challenge.

You need to develop a specific time frame and set responsibilities, so board members know exactly what they need to do when. As busy volunteers, they want and appreciate a precise structure that spells out clear expectations.

Here is the right way to set up a workable structure that will empower and support your board members to succeed. This approach is based on fundamental rules of organizational development and teambuilding. It takes the conversation about the project to a much deeper level, one that awakens each board member's leadership potential and personal commitment to action.

TIPS AND TECHNIQUES

The board members themselves have to take responsibility for the results they want to create.

Setting Up a Project for Success—Lessons from the Field

First, the board members themselves get to decide what they want to undertake. You are not deciding for them. It is not your project that you are asking for help on. It is *their* project.

They get to "own the project": what results do they want to create and what deadline have they given themselves for getting those results? If they do not own their goal, then they will not be working toward it. So try to get them to see what is possible if they succeed.

I like to have my boards fully "own" some part of the fundraising program, whether is an annual event, or hosting tours or launching a new speaker series – it becomes a project of the board's rather than a project of the staff's. This is the way to generate personal investment, commitment, and buy-in.

There is a firm rule in management that it is best to have the people who are to do the task actually make the decision to undertake it. Only if they are part of the effort to determine what will be done will they be likely to take personal responsibility for its success.

Whether it is taking ownership of a big event, launching a new major donor gift club, or personally thanking donors, board members should decide what they want to tackle, not the Executive Director, not the staff, and not the Development Committee. Do not make board member projects a "top-down" decision. Make decisions about those efforts as a group, giving all board members an opportunity to consider their own commitment and level of energy for the project. Let each person make his or her own commitment.

A Deeper Conversation

Too often we concentrate on goals, strategies, and objectives and thus neglect the most important question: what will it take from us as a team and as individuals in order to be successful? Will this success be achieved through business as usual, or will it require new ways of working together, new commitments, and new attitudes?

We all know the old adage: if you want to get to a new place and create new results, you will not succeed by doing things the way you have always done them. It will take new ideas, new attitudes and new techniques to achieve different results.

Let your board members think through how they will be working together differently to make the project a success. Suggest this question for them to discuss: what will it take from each person for this to be successful?"

This gives each individual an opportunity to consider what exactly her own personal role will be on the project, and it creates a space for deeper reflection prior to undertaking the task. "What will it require of me in order to make this goal? Are there new ways of acting and thinking that I need to take on in order to make my vision a success?"

You can clarify everyone's desired outcomes and expectations in a thoughtful conversation before starting the project. Do they need to think about new ways of working together to make the project successful? Do they need to change some attitudes of some of the board members in order to succeed? Do they need a new meeting schedule or way to communicate?

Get them in the right mindset for success. Let them have the chance to talk about any underlying issues that can make or break the project. What is really going on with our board, and what do people really think about undertaking this? Take a look at who is standing where on this project. Who is supporting it and who is not? Might someone sabotage it? Where are the minefields? Interesting stuff!

Remember that we talked earlier about letting board members do the talking. When you let them do the talking, then they take ownership; they take leadership, and they make their own commitments for success. They take charge.

They do not have to take charge of the organization, but they can take charge of the annual auction, of a new tour program, of a plan to connect with 20 new friends a year, of a new program to thank all donors personally.

If you can set your projects up correctly, you can awaken new leadership capabilities you never thought existed on your board. People will change from laid back, spoon-fed board members; overnight, they will become hard-charging leaders personally committed to extraordinary success. I will quote General Patton once again: "If you tell people where to go, but not how to get there, you'll be amazed at the results!"

When a project is properly set up, the result will be that your board will really take on—with integrity—the goal they have set. They will come together as a group, creating a greater sense of a team. This can be quite a culture shift for an organization or a board.

Use Task Forces, Not Committees

I like to set up projects, not within a committee structure but within a Task Force, which seems so much more goal oriented than a committee. Committee work may drag on and on without deliverables or results.

Task Forces are formed to tackle specific issues or projects that are well defined within a specific time frame. Board members like the specificity of a Task Force. It allows them to focus intensely and clearly on a specific issue. They can complete a defined project and see solid real results.

I like to end my Fundraising Retreats by setting up Board Task Forces to work on specific issues that came up in our discussions.

For example, I ran a fundraising retreat recently for a client that regularly held a popular and highly successful annual auction. At the end of the retreat, the board members decided to see if they could double the proceeds of their popular annual auction. They formed a Task Force that looked into other auctions held by national level organizations, investigating how they were structured, and what specific techniques were used to create financial success. They then created recommendations for their own auction. The Task Force members ended by making individual commitments to take on specific roles with future auctions.

Task Forces work well for assessing the current situation and creating a plan of action. To carry out the action plan, however, you will need other structures: The Leadership Team and Small Groups.

A Board "Leadership Team" Creates Results

The leadership team is a group of board members responsible for leading and creating the results for a specific project. For example, if your board decides to undertake phone calls to thank donors personally, a Leadership Team will function as the committee running the project (not the staff running the project!).

The Leadership Team creates its own goals and encourages all the other participating board members to achieve success. I work carefully with Leadership Teams on a process designed to set them up to assume leadership and generate their own results.

The Power of Making a Formal Commitment

Until one is committed, there is hesitancy, the chance to draw back,
always ineffectiveness . . . . The moment one definitely commits oneself,
then Providence moves, too.

All sorts of things occur to help one that would never otherwise have occurred.
A whole stream of events issues from the decision raising in one's favor all
manner of unforeseen incidents and meetings and material assistance which no
man could have dreamed would have come his way.

—W. H. Murray, the Scottish Himalayan Expedition

The Conversation: Setting Project Goals

The most important first step is for the Leadership Team to set its own goals—so the members will "own" them and be hold themselves responsible for the project's success. I like to have them define the goals in a declaration or clear statement: We plan to raise $xxxx by yyyyy date in our capital campaign." Or "our goal is to make $zzzz from our annual fundraising event."

The goals must be concrete and stated specifically in a sentence; otherwise the commitment may become vague and unaccountable, and no one will move into action until the last minute.

A formal commitment such as "We will achieve XX number of sponsorships for our annual event" is different from "We hope to achieve," or "We want to achieve," or, worst of all, "We are trying to achieve . . . ."The words "try to" sounds like the team is *not* devoting itself to the project's success.

For example, when John Kennedy announced that in 10 years the United States would have a man on the moon—and NASA had not even been organized—he did not say, "Try to have a man on the moon." He said, "We will have a man on the moon."

Formal commitments in the form of a declaration help board members be clear and straightforward about their goals. These are not halfhearted undertakings. Instead, the commitment declarations provide an accountability mechanism to determine where the board members stand in relation to their goals. I like the idea of "taking a stand" to make the goals. It encourages a deeper commitment, and moves board members to go all out to achieve the success they intend.

Project goals may also include qualitative standards as well as quantitative goals. For example, on the thank-you project described above, one goal may be that all board members have an enjoyable experience during the project. A qualitative goal might be that it is a win-win experience for the staff and the board, with all participants feeling supported and empowered.

A Vision of Success

It is helpful to envision what will be possible for the organization when the new fundraising project is successful. When board members can clearly see a vision of a successful future that includes new opportunities for their organization, they will be much more fired up to take action.

The Leadership Team creates the structure that will give them the kind of results they want. If success on this project requires board members to take on new ways of acting and communicating, then these new behaviors will not come easily to a board that has an ensconced organizational culture.

For example, say your board decides to embrace the role of Ambassadors to key donors. You train your board members, and assign prospects to each trustee for ongoing cultivation. You hold a kickoff, and the board members launch out to connect with their prospects. You organize your Ambassadors into small groups which will meet together by conference call or in person monthly for check in and coaching.

The monthly conference call/check in meeting is a new behavior for your board members. They are not used to this activity. They have an ensconced habit to be independent and not attend meetings. How will you get the new Ambassadors to take this seriously? Who will enforce the structure and the personal commitments for action that your Ambassadors made when they agreed to participate?

That's the Leadership Team's job. It is the role of the Leadership Team to enforce the new behaviors and be the internal support for change. It is always better for board members to police each other than it is for the staff to do it.

When overseeing any project, Leadership Team members take an objective look at what is working and what is not working; they then take action to tweak the plan and/or encourage fellow board members who are not following through. What a nice management tool that releases the staff from a difficult supervisory role.

The Role of Staff with the Leadership Team

The staff needs to check in with the leadership team often to see whether they are on track. The staff ultimately reinforces the new ideas and ways of behaving by touching base with the Leadership Team frequently. Staff manages the rest of the board members by support and coaching the Leadership Team.

Working Teams

It is best to cluster the participating board members into working teams or small groups for mutual reinforcement to support and coach each other. This gives board members a way to create a base of support for themselves without overly taxing the staff.

Clustering people together in Working Teams for training sessions, review meetings, and/or conference calls provides an efficient framework for coaching; the group can be dealt with together rather than on an individual basis. The Working Teams can also help:

- Create a team spirit among board members.
- Create a sense of fun.
- Foster new relationships among board members who do not know each other.
- Provide indispensable moral support and friendship.

The Ultimate Nonprofit Working Team

The goal of the Passion-Driven Fundraising system is to give your nonprofit a highly effective board of devoted volunteers who, working with the staff, bring an abundance of resources into your organization. That is the kind of team the world needs to solve the big problems: healthcare, education, the environment, the homeless boy in the too-small shoes.

Within our boards there is a vast wealth of resources and energy to help accomplish our work in the world. It is up to us to inspire these wonderful folks who care so much about our cause, and organize them so they can create the results they want to see.

We can't leave it up to the board chair, to Robert's Rules or traditional organizational structures designed for nonprofit organizations. We need to apply new approaches designed for the 21st century organization—whether for profit or nonprofit. We need to tap the latest knowledge about organizing teams, creating vision and commitment, idea marketing, organizations as living systems, and inspiring passionate teams.

Our work is too important for us to operate according to rote habit and traditional structures. I say we do whatever it takes to fire up our boards to action. Let's experiment if necessary. There is too much at stake. The world is changing rapidly, New needs and problems to be solved crop up every minute. We've got important work to do and we need all hands on deck!

We have to create nimble, engaged, passionate groups of volunteer board members who can turn on a dime to make things happen quickly. I have shared idea after idea for new approaches to organizing and firing up your board—and getting them to tackle fundraising in a way that will yield real results. I hope some of these work for you.

I invite you to try out all—or parts—of this model to see whether it offers a new perspective and lends power to your board members' fundraising efforts. I would be interested in your experiences with your board, and I welcome your comments at gail@gailperry.com.

Join my blog and become part of a whole new movement to build effective happy fundraising boards that are changing the world faster than we can keep up with them.

HIGHLIGHTS OF CHAPTER 6

Create a Dream Team Board and Set Your Board Up to Win!

- Go after your Dream Team Board.
  - ○ Enlist rather than recruit them.
  - ○ Board members want clearly defined jobs.
- Set up a Governance Committee to keep your board on track.
  - ○ Change the Nominating Committee to the Governance Committee.
  - ○ The Governance Committee asks: "How did we do?"
- Enlisting the Dream Team Board: get the right skills.
- Use a Big Request to recruit board members.
  - ○ Do not enlist out of desperation!
  - ○ Do approach out of vision and passion.
  - ○ Create a specific job description.

- Agree on fundraising activities for every board member.
    - Do not understate your expectations.
    - Give a proud annual gift.
    - Attend events.
    - Thank donors.
    - Help make new friends and contacts for our organization.
    - When appropriate, ask for contributions.
    - Know and support the fundraising plan.
    - Carry out specific fundraising tasks you commit to do.
    - Be sure that fundraising has enough resources.
    - Support the fundraising staff.
- Orienting new board members is a must.
    - Assigning mentors for new members is a great way to create relationships and bring new them up to speed.
    - Get to know your board members by meeting with them one on one.
- Self-assessments keep everyone focused.
- Make sure all the board members give.
    - Make the philosophy clear: show why board members need to give generously.
    - Say what you expect, in both written and spoken form.
    - Get board members to solicit other board members.
    - Give the subject of board donations lots of visibility.
    - Take charge of the process yourself.
    - Give the members lots of credit and acknowledgment.
    - Tie the board's gifts directly to your program results.
- Set up your board members to win and put fundraising up front on your agenda.
    - Give board members constant feedback on fundraising results.
    - Tie fundraising success directly back into your daily operations.
    - Give board member volunteers structure, coaching, and moral support.
    - Let them decide on their goals so they will "own" their fundraising projects.
    - Use Task Forces, not Committees.
    - A board Leadership Team creates results.

▌ NOTES

1. Kim Klein, *Raise More Money, The Best of the Grassroots Fundraising Journal,* ed. by Kim Klein and Stephanie Roth (San Francisco: Charton Press, 2004).

2. Wayne Dwyer, *The Power of Intention* (Carlsbad, CA: Hay House, 2004).

3. Howard Goldman, *Choose What Works* (San Carlos, CA: Wynnefield Business Press, 2004), 103.

4. Michael Davidson, "Boards that Work, Work" (http://www.lp-associates.com/boardsthatwork.-php.).

5. Ibid.

6. Pamela Wilcox, *Exposing the Elephants: Creating Exceptional Nonprofits* (Hoboken, NJ: John Wiley & Sons, 2006).

7. Richard P. Chait, William P. Ryan, and Barbara E. Taylor, *Governance as Leadership, Reframing the Work of Nonprofit Boards* (Hoboken, NJ: John Wiley & Sons, 2005), 177.

8. Ibid.

9. Ibid.

10. Kay Sprinkel Grace, *Beyond Fundraising,* Second edition (Hoboken, NJ: John Wiley & Sons, 2005), 190.

11. Ibid.

12. Howard Goldman, *Choose What Works,* 103.

13. Pamela Wilcox, *Exposing the Elephants: Creating Exceptional Nonprofits.*

14. *Best of the Board Café, Hands-on Solutions for Nonprofit Boards,* ed. by Jan Masaoka (Saint Paul, MN: Compasspoint/Wilder Foundation, 2003).

15. Linda Lysakowski *Recruiting and Training Fundraising Volunteers* (Hoboken, NJ: John Wiley & Sons, 2005).

16. Jerry Panas, *Finders Keepers* (Chicago: Bonus Books, Inc., 1999).

17. Lynne Twist, *Fundraising from the Heart.*

18. Ibid.

References and
Recommended Reading

Axelrod, Terry. *Raise More Money* (Seattle: Raise More Money Publications, 2002).

———. *The Point of Entry Handbook* (Seattle: Raise More Money Publications, 2002).

Baker, Todd. "Death to the Dear Friend Letter," *Fundraising Well* newsletter, November 2003 (www.blackbaud.com/files/Newsletters/FundraisingWell/2003/fundraisingwellnovember 2003.pdf).

Burk, Penelope. *Donor Centered Fundraising* (Chicago: Cygnus Applied Research, Inc., 2003), www.donorcentered.com.

Chait, Richard P., William P. Ryan, and Barbara E. Taylor. *Governance as Leadership: Reframing the Work of Nonprofit Boards* (Hoboken, NJ: John Wiley & Sons, 2005).

Cochran, Alice Collier. *Roberta's Rules of Order: Who Is Robert and Why Do We Still Follow His Rules Anyway?* (San Francisco: Jossey-Bass, 2004).

Davidson, Michael. "Boards that Work, Work" (http://www.lp-associates.com/boardsthatwork.php.).

Gottlieb, Hildy. *Friend Raising: Community Engagement Strategies for Boards Who Hate Fundraising but Love Making Friends* (Tucson, AZ: Renaissance Press, 2006). (Help 4 Nonprofits & Tribes, Community Driven Institute).

Grace, Kay Sprinkel. *Beyond Fundraising,* 2nd ed. (Hoboken, NJ: John Wiley & Sons, 2005).

Greenfield, James M. *Fundraising Responsibilities of Nonprofit Boards* (Washington, DC: BoardSource, 2002).

Klein, Kim and Stephanie Roth, eds. *Raise More Money, The Best of the Grassroots Fundraising Journal* (San Francisco: Charton Press, 2004).

Lysakowski, Linda. *Recruiting and Training Fundraising Volunteers* (Hoboken, NJ: John Wiley & Sons, 2005).

Masaola, Jan, ed. *The Best of the Board Café: Hands-On Solutions for Nonprofit Boards* (St. Paul, MN: CompassPoint Nonprofit Services, Wilder Publishing Center, 2003).

Panas, Jerry. *Mega Gifts: Who Gives Them, Who Gets Them* (Chicago: Bonus Books, Inc., 1984).

———. *Finders Keepers* (Chicago: Bonus Books, 1999).

Robinson, Andy. *Big Gifts for Small Groups: A Board Member's 1-Hour Guide to Securing Gifts of $500 to $5,000* (Medfield, MA: Emerson and Church, 2004).

Ross, Bernard. *Breakthrough Thinking for Nonprofit Organizations* (San Francisco: Jossey-Bass, 2002).

Twist, Lynne. *Fundraising from the Heart Audio-Video Course* (Edison, NJ: Produced by Woman Vision copyright © 2001 Woman Vision and Lynne Twist).

Wilcox, Pamela. *Exposing the Elephants: Creating Exceptional Nonprofits* (Hoboken, NJ: John Wiley & Sons, 2006).

Zimmerman, Robert and Ann W. Lehman. *Boards That Love Fundraising: A How To Guide for Your Board* (San Francisco: Jossey-Bass, 2004).

BOOKS THAT FOCUS ON THE BIGGER PICTURE OF TRANSFORMATION, ORGANIZATIONAL CHANGE, AND....

Bolles, Richard Nelson. *What Color Is Your Parachute?* (Berkeley, CA: Ten Speed Press, 2006).

Dwyer, Wayne. *The Power of Intention* (Carlsbad, California: Hay House, 2004).

Fulghum, Robert L. *It Was on Fire When I Lay Down On It* (New York: Ballentine Books, a division of Random House, 1989).

Gladwell, Malcolm. *The Tipping Point, How Little Things Can Make a Big Difference* (New York: Little, Brown and Company, 2000).

Godin, Seth. *Unleashing the Idea Virus* (Dobbs Ferry, NY: Do You Zoom, Inc., 2001).

Goldman, Howard. *Choose What Works* (Whitfield Business Press, 2004).

Jaworski, Jon. *Synchronicity, the Inner Path of Leadership* (San Francisco: Berrett-Koehler Publishers, 1998).

Luks, Allan and Peggy Payne. *The Healing Power of Doing Good* (New York: iUniverse.com, Inc., 2001).

Moore, Thomas. *Care of the Soul* (New York: Harper Collins, 1992).

Senge, Peter. *The Fifth Discipline: The Art and Practice of the Learning Organization* (New York: Doubleday, 1990).

———. *The Dance of Change: The Challenges to Sustaining Momentum in Learning Organizations* (New York: Doubleday, 1999).

Twist, Lynne. *The Soul of Money* (New York: W. W. Norton & Co., 2003).

Wheatley, Margaret. *Leadership and the New Science* (San Francisco: Berrett-Koehler, 1999).

Donor Commitment Form

Board Member Give and Get Commitment Form

Name of board member _____ Date _____

I am eager to support our organization's mission by pledging $_____ .

I also promise to bring in an additional $_____ from other sources.

I will sell _____ tables for our annual fundraising event.

I will add _____ new names to our mailing list.

I will host _____ people on tours of our organization.

I agree to participate in additional fundraising activities as needed.

This is my commitment as a board member of _____ organization.

AFP Code of Ethical Principles and Standards of Professional Practice

AFP Code of Ethical Principles and Standards of Professional Practice
STATEMENT OF ETHICAL PRINCIPLES
Adopted 1964, Amended October 2004

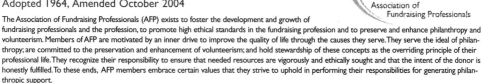

The Association of Fundraising Professionals (AFP) exists to foster the development and growth of fundraising professionals and the profession, to promote high ethical standards in the fundraising profession and to preserve and enhance philanthropy and volunteerism. Members of AFP are motivated by an inner drive to improve the quality of life through the causes they serve. They serve the ideal of philanthropy; are committed to the preservation and enhancement of volunteerism; and hold stewardship of these concepts as the overriding principle of their professional life. They recognize their responsibility to ensure that needed resources are vigorously and ethically sought and that the intent of the donor is honestly fulfilled. To these ends, AFP members embrace certain values that they strive to uphold in performing their responsibilities for generating philanthropic support.

AFP members aspire to:
+ practice their profession with integrity, honesty, truthfulness and adherence to the absolute obligation to safeguard the public trust;
+ act according to the highest standards and visions of their organization, profession and conscience;
+ put philanthropic mission above personal gain;
+ inspire others through their own sense of dedication and high purpose;
+ improve their professional knowledge and skills so that their performance will better serve others;
+ demonstrate concern for the interests and well being of individuals affected by their actions;
+ value the privacy, freedom of choice and interests of all those affected by their actions;
+ foster cultural diversity and pluralistic values, and treat all people with dignity and respect;
+ affirm, through personal giving, a commitment to philanthropy and its role in society;
+ adhere to the spirit as well as the letter of all applicable laws and regulations;
+ advocate within their organizations, adherence to all applicable laws and regulations;
+ avoid even the appearance of any criminal offense or professional misconduct;
+ bring credit to the fundraising profession by their public demeanor;
+ encourage colleagues to embrace and practice these ethical principles and standards of professional practice; and
+ be aware of the codes of ethics promulgated by other professional organizations that serve philanthropy.

STANDARDS OF PROFESSIONAL PRACTICE
Furthermore, while striving to act according to the above values, AFP members agree to abide by the *AFP Standards of Professional Practice*, which are adopted and incorporated into the *AFP Code of Ethical Principles*. Violation of the *Standard* may subject the member to disciplinary sanctions, including expulsion, as provided in the AFP Ethics Enforcement Procedures.

Professional Obligations
1. Members shall not engage in activities that harm the member's organization, clients, or profession.
2. Members shall not engage in activities that conflict with their fiduciary, ethical and legal obligations to their organizations and their clients.
3. Members shall effectively disclose all potential and actual conflicts of interest; such disclosure does not preclude or imply ethical impropriety.
4. Members shall not exploit any relationship with a donor, prospect, volunteer or employee for the benefit of the member or the member's organization.

5. Members shall comply with all applicable local, state, provincial, federal, civil and criminal laws.
6. Members recognize their individual boundaries of competence and are forthcoming and truthful about their professional experience and qualifications.

Solicitation and Use of Philanthropic Funds
7. Members shall take care to ensure that all solicitation materials are accurate and correctly reflect the organization's mission and use of solicited funds.
8. Members shall take care to ensure that donors receive informed, accurate and ethical advice about the value and tax implications of contributions.
9. Members shall take care to ensure that contributions are used in accordance with donors' intentions.
10. Members shall take care to ensure proper stewardship of philanthropic contributions, including timely reports on the use and management of such funds.
11. Members shall obtain explicit consent by the donor before altering the conditions of contributions.

Presentation of Information
12. Members shall not disclose privileged or confidential information to unauthorized parties.
13. Members shall adhere to the principle that all donor and prospect information created by, or on behalf of, an organization is the property of that organization and shall not be transferred or utilized except on behalf of that organization.
14. Members shall give donors the opportunity to have their names removed from lists that are sold to, rented to, or exchanged with other organizations.
15. Members shall, when stating fundraising results, use accurate and consistent accounting methods that conform to the appropriate guidelines adopted by the American Institute of Certified Public Accountants (AICPA)* for the type of organization involved. (* In countries outside of the United States, comparable authority should be utilized.)

Compensation
16. Members shall not accept compensation that is based on a percentage of contributions; nor shall they accept finder's fees.
17. Members may accept performance-based compensation, such as bonuses, provided such bonuses are in accord with prevailing practices within the members' own organizations, and are not based on a percentage of contributions.
18. Members shall not pay finder's fees, or commissions or percentage compensation based on contributions, and shall take care to discourage their organizations from making such payments.

Amended October 2004

AFP Donor Bill of Rights

A Donor Bill of Rights

PHILANTHROPY is based on voluntary action for the common good. It is a tradition of giving and sharing that is primary to the quality of life. To assure that philanthropy merits the respect and trust of the general public, and that donors and prospective donors can have full confidence in the not-for-profit organizations and causes they are asked to support, we declare that all donors have these rights:

I.
To be informed of the organization's mission, of the way the organization intends to use donated resources, and of its capacity to use donations effectively for their intended purposes.

II.
To be informed of the identity of those serving on the organization's governing board, and to expect the board to exercise prudent judgement in its stewardship responsibilities.

III.
To have access to the organization's most recent financial statements.

IV.
To be assured their gifts will be used for the purposes for which they were given.

V.
To receive appropriate acknowledgement and recognition.

VI.
To be assured that information about their donations is handled with respect and with confidentiality to the extent provided by law.

VII.
To expect that all relationships with individuals representing organizations of interest to the donor will be professional in nature.

VIII.
To be informed whether those seeking donations are volunteers, employees of the organization or hired solicitors.

IX.
To have the opportunity for their names to be deleted from mailing lists that an organization may intend to share.

X.
To feel free to ask questions when making a donation and to receive prompt, truthful and forthright answers.

DEVELOPED BY
Association for Healthcare Philanthropy (AHP)
Association of Fundraising Professionals (AFP)
Council for Advancement and Support of Education (CASE)
Giving Institute: Leading Consultants to Non-Profits

ENDORSED BY
(in formation)
Independent Sector
National Catholic Development Conference (NCDC)
National Committee on Planned Giving (NCPG)
Council for Resource Development (CRD)
United Way of America

Index